Constance Bale

# AFRICAN AMERICAN MUSIC

## An Introduction

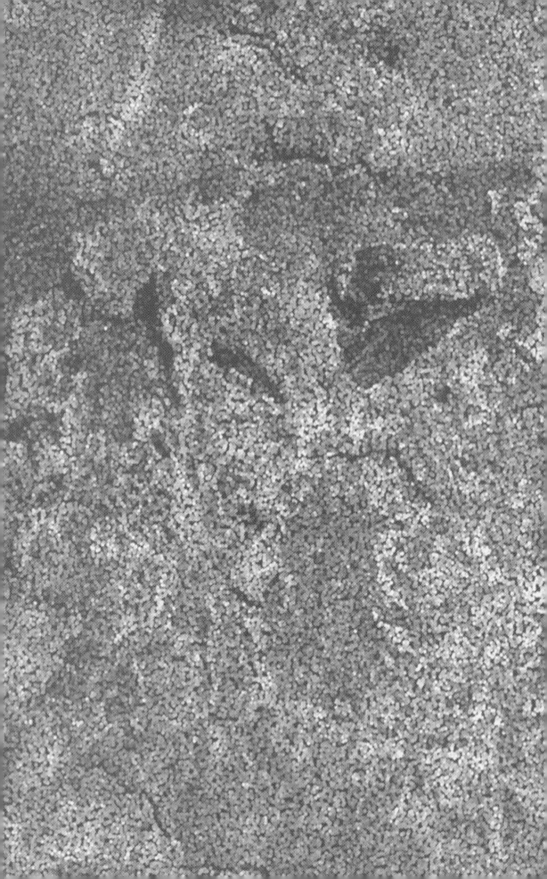

# AFRICAN AMERICAN MUSIC

## An Introduction

EARL L. STEWART

Schirmer Books
An Imprint of Simon & Schuster Macmillan
*New York*

Prentice Hall International
*London   Mexico City   New Delhi   Singapore   Sydney   Toronto*

Copyright © 1998 by Schirmer Books

Schirmer Books
1633 Broadway
New York, New York 10019

Library of Congress Catalog Number: 97–42487

Printed in the United States of America

Printing number

2   3   4   5   6   7   8   9   10

**Library of Congress Cataloging-in-Publication Data**

Stewart, Earl L.
African American music : an introduction / Earl L. Stewart.
       p.  cm.
    Includes bibliographical references (p.  ) and index.
    Discography: p.
    ISBN 0-02-860294-3
    1. Afro-Americans—Music—History and criticism. 2. Music—United
States—History and criticism. I. Title.
ML3556.S87  1998
780'.89'96073—dc21                                             97-42487
                                                                CIP
                                                                MN

This paper meets the requirements of ANSI/NISO Z39.48-1992 (Permanence
of Paper).

Design by Lisa Chovnick/Judy Kahn

*To the memory of Mr. and Mrs. Murphy
and Clarabel G. Matthews,
and to my mother, Gladys Hardesty*

# C O N T E N T S

## PART 1

# Folk Traditions

PART **2**

# The Jazz Aesthetic

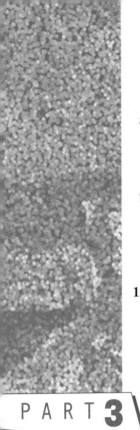

# Popular Styles Since 1940

# PART 4 Theatrical and Classical Traditions

# P R E F A C E

**T**HIS BOOK IS A CRITICAL introduction to most of the important African American popular musical styles that have come into prominence since Reconstruction, including spirituals, the various blues styles, ragtime, the various jazz styles, rhythm and blues, doo wop, soul music, funk, and rap. The styles surveyed are not presented strictly in chronological format—that is, in terms of their chronological evolution. Instead, each style is isolated and treated in terms of its own development. This approach should help students to better understand the distinct characteristics of each style, beginning with its standard form and then delving deeper into its more nuanced manifestations.

A style-focused text has many advantages, perhaps the best of which is that the music takes center stage in the telling of its own story. This approach accommodates the presence of a few biographical profiles. For the most part the author has left in-depth biographical descriptions, even of many eminent artists, to the literature specifically designed to address this area. To assist readers who have such an interest, I have footnoted, at appropriate points in the text, standard biographical references and related works; the bibliography lists many others.

Some of the terminology used in this book is rather specialized, developed by musical theorists to describe specific elements of a performance. It is impossible in a style-based study to avoid some musicological discussion, which some beginners may find off-putting. However, to assist those unfamiliar with such terminology, I have defined all unfamiliar terms on their first appearance.

Music majors are the target of the present study, but general readers with the appropriate musical background may also find the work enjoyable. Within both groups, those who have had some contact with Western classical common practice theory will find the work easily digestible; those with an additional jazz or vernacular theory background, however elementary, will find the work even easier to comprehend. The absence of such backgrounds, however, should not serve as an impediment for those truly enthusiastic about the subject.

The author wishes to extend his gratitude to Professors Gerard Behague, Rebecca Cureau, Alvin Batiste, Walter Craig, and Warrick Carter for the honor and privilege of having studied with them—formally and informally—and for the continuous support they have so generously provided through the years. I also offer gratitude to my former colleagues from the Berklee College of Music, especially Professors Robert Myers and Larry McClelland for the many theoretically and methodologically oriented conversations we have shared; these scholars have greatly stimulated my thoughts concerning the analysis of modern popular music. Gratitude must also be given to Professors Cedric Robinson, Douglas Daniels, Jane Duran, Gerald Horn, Charles Long, Lester Monts, and James Jordan for their prodigious assistance and support; to my research assistants Kendra Shorts, Nirav Shah, Franchelle Hollie, and Wendy Settles; and my colleagues Wayne Sanders, Mary Alyce Harris, and Antonio Gutierrez for the superlative contribution each made to the present effort. Lastly, I extend a special note of thanks to Mr. Jonathan Weiner and Professor Jeff Todd Titon without whom it is doubtful the present work would have come to pass, and to the many superlative musicians who, during the past two years, so graciously allowed me the privilege of interviewing them.

# PART 1

## Folk Traditions

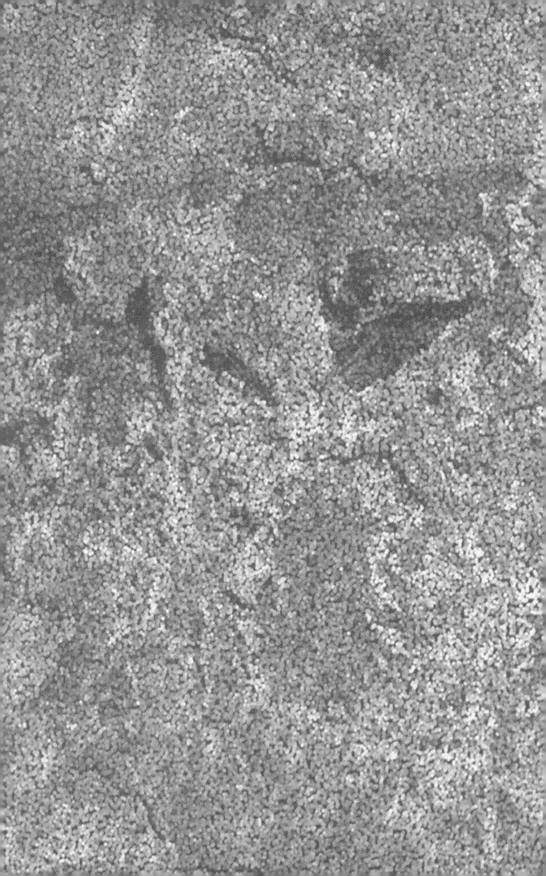

## CHAPTER 1

# GENERAL CHARACTERISTICS OF AFRICAN AMERICAN MUSIC

**T**HE TRADITION of African American music is one of the most exciting and diverse aspects of the North American musical panorama. It is also, arguably, the most important ethnic vernacular tradition in America. This is so, in part, because African American musical styles:

1. have developed in ways independent of the African traditions from which they arise to a greater extent than the vernacular styles of any other immigrant peoples, including Europeans;

2. make up the broadest and most enduring array of vernacular styles in America;

3. historically, have been far more influential—interculturally, geographically, and economically—than all other indigenous American vernacular traditions.

Despite the huge array of vernacular styles that fall under the umbrella of African American music, the tradition as a whole is unified by a rather fixed and definitive set of aesthetic and stylistic features. This chapter will list and explain some of the most important of these features.

## Call and Response

One feature common to most African American vernacular styles is the performance technique *call and response*. In its most elemental form, it consists of a musical statement given by a song leader that is immediately followed by a response from a chorus. As such, call and response always implies a binary, or *two-part*, idea. In practice, both the call phrase and the response phrase are usually performed vocally. It is, however, possible to effect the same type of call and response with instrumental themes.

There are three basic types of call and response. In the first type, the thematic idea introduced by the call (the *antecedent phrase*) is confirmed—often by way of repetition—by the response (the *consequent phrase*). Blues performer Huddie ("Leadbelly") Ledbetter recorded an old field shout, "Go Down Old Hannah," that uses this structure; a leader sings a line of text, and then the other workers repeat it:

Leader:  Go down Old Hannah!

Group:  Go down Old Hannah!

Leader:  And don't you rise no more

Group:  And don't you rise no more.

Leader:  If you rise in the mornin'

Group:  If you rise in the mornin'

Leader:  Bring Judgment Day.

Group:  Bring Judgment Day! Huh!

In the second type of call and response, the thematic statement given by the response *completes* the thematic statement introduced by the call. In James Brown's "Say It Loud," this type of call and response is used most effectively in communicating the central political theme of the song:

Lead Vocalist *(call)*:  Say It Loud

Chorus *(response)*:  I'm black and I'm proud

In the third type of call and response, the response neither corroborates nor completes the thematic idea introduced by the call. Instead, it simply answers the opening melody in a way that provides a musical conclusion to the call-and-response structure. This type of call and response is often used when the musical medium (vocalist, musical instrument) performing the call and the response are different. An example of this type of call and response is illustrated in "Pratt City Blues"; the opening phrase is given by the blues vocalist (Bertha Chippie Hill) but answered by the solo trumpeter (Louis Armstrong).

Call and response is frequently expressed in more sophisticated ways. The blues, for example, shows the influence of call and response on several levels. An even more subtle occurrence of call and response is sometimes found in rag music and jazz. In Scott Joplin's "The Entertainer," for example, the spirit of call and response characterizes the opening theme. Each of the first three phrases of the opening theme is composed of two distinct motives. The opening motive is identical in all three phrases. The second motive, however, has a different rhythmic character, is played in a different register, and is written in chords rather than as a single line (as if sung by a chorus rather than a soloist/leader). These contrasting features give the second motive the character of a response. (Although the first motive is repeated here, the *response* usually constitutes the unchangeable element in the call-and-response style, not the *call*.)

## Attributes of African Vocality

In most African American musical styles—particularly vocal styles—composers use a repertory of vocal, or vocally inspired, devices to emotionalize their music. These devices are called *attributes of African vocality* (or *special vocal effects*). They include (1) *guttural effects* and related utterances, (2) *interpolated vocality*, (3) *falsetto*, (4) *blue notes*, (5) *Afro-melismas*, (6) *lyric improvisation*, and (7) *vocal rhythmization*. Although these devices are associated with the voice, their use is not limited to vocal performance. They are frequently used for the same purpose in instrumental music.

*Guttural effects* include *screams, shouts, moans,* and *groans.* They are usually added by the performer rather than written into the lyric of a song. Skilled vocalists rarely use guttural effects haphazardly or indiscriminately. They are usually used during musical moments where their presence adds emotional emphasis or heightens the emotional drama of the music.

There are two types of shouts commonly used in African American music. The first type may be described as an *intoned* shout; that is, a type of shout that is definite or near definite in pitch (it sounds more like singing than speech). It is frequently used by blues vocalists, and in blues-derived styles. The second type of shout, a *nonintoned shout,* is clearly indefinite in pitch (it sounds more like speech than singing). Rhythm and blues artists like Wilson Pickett were particularly fond of this technique; it is also found in church styles of the 1920s to 1940s. Both types of shouts and screams add to the rhythmic complexity of the performance, because they are often performed on an offbeat or between the beats, as it were, of the musical phrases.

Another technique employed by vocalists is to add (or *interpolate*) additional vocal sounds or even text to a song; some musicologists call this *interpolated vocality.* Like shouts, there are two basic forms. The first type is composed of inarticulate sounds and is generally spoken rather than sung. Its significance is substantially rhythmic.

A second type of interpolated vocality uses a text, but generally not one derived from the lyric. Instead, a new text is introduced, often to restate or extend a theme previously expressed in the lyric. Because the second type of interpolated vocality is verbal, it may also be called an *interpolated verbalism.* Interpolated verbalisms are frequently used by country blues, urban blues, and gospel vocalists. They were also used by popular vocalists of the 1960s and 1970s whose styles were derived from gospel music or the blues: for example Otis Redding, Wilson Pickett, James Brown, and Aretha Franklin. This style is still commonly employed today by popular singers such as Luther Vandross, Peabo Bryson, Howard Hewitt, Stephanie Mills, and Michael Jackson.

Another vocal idiom often used in African American music is called *lyric variation*. It is similar to an interpolated verbalism in that both are used to extend the text or fill in musical moments that would not ordinarily be accompanied by the original lyric. Unlike interpolated verbalism, however, the text of lyric variation is either derived from the lyric, or is used as a basis for embellishing the lyric, or both.

*Falsetto*, or head voice, is common to virtually all African American vocal styles. By employing falsetto, a singer produces a higher-pitched, more intense sound than is possible when singing in a normal or "chest" voice. Falsetto is used sporadically to add emotional emphasis and timbral contrast to songs.

*Blue notes* are common to vocal and instrumental music. Technically, they are microtonal inflections of pitches (changing pitch to levels that fall in between the notes you can play on a piano). In vocal performance they give the impression of pitches being "bent." These notes add to the emotional force of a performance. They also suggest the blues scale—a variant of traditional major and minor scales that we'll be discussing in great depth (see Chapter 3).

*Afro-melismas* are brief vocal extemporizations. They are usually delivered in a rhythmically free fashion and are most often found at the conclusion of melodic motives, phrases, or sections. They are commonly used in gospel or vocal blues styles, or styles derived from them. Afro-melismas are used in a number of creative ways. They may, for example, be used to open a musical work. They are also found as interpolated melodies over repeated instrumental passages. In such cases they often substitute for actual lyrics. A contemporary example is found in singer Whitney Houston's version of "I Will Always Love You," with its many exaggerated and elongated melismatic passages (for example, the way she extends the word "you" in the chorus).

*Lyric improvisation* is the free improvisational development of the text or lyric. It is a prominent feature of gospel music and popular music, especially popular music from the 1960s to the present. The lyric improvisation is usually found in a section of its own, generally located at or near the end of a composition. This section is colloquially known as the *vamp*. The emotional and lyrical freedom that occurs in this section often brings to it a degree of intensity that makes it the emotional climax of musical works.

*Vocal rhythmization* describes a performance where vocal sounds are used mainly for rhythmic purposes. In other words, it is a type of vocal music—sung or spoken—in which the primary emphasis is on rhythm, rather than melody. Vocal rhythmization may be manifested in many ways. It may, for example, occur simply as a brief or isolated passage within an essentially vocal or instrumental composition, or it may constitute the vocal basis of a composition. It may consist of an intoned melody that essentially has no lyric (for example, as in *scat singing*). It may consist of a spoken text given in strict rhythmic phrases, as it does in rap music.

## Rhythmic Features of African American Music

The style features discussed so far are performance idioms that relate mainly to melody, harmony, and structure. The following features address, principally, African American concepts of rhythm and meter. These concepts are of particular importance for understanding the rhythmical uniqueness of African American styles.

### SYNCOPATION

The essential rhythmic characteristic of virtually all African American vernacular styles is *syncopation*: the accenting (emphasizing) of rhythmic patterns on weak rather than strong pulses. In other words syncopated rhythms give a feeling of temporarily contradicting the strong beats of the prevailing meter. Syncopation is the principal means by which African American melodies, or melodic phrases, obtain their distinctiveness. This distinctiveness sometimes results from juxtaposing two or more syncopated motives (see motives 2 and 3 in Example 1.1).

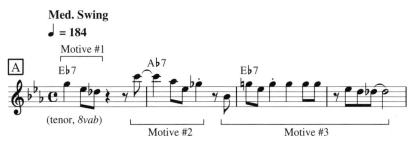

Example 1.1. "Bessie's Blues" (John Coltrane)

The feeling or suggestion of syncopation sometimes results from the placement of a stressed word or syllable on an unstressed pitch, which is followed by a stressed pitch that contains an unstressed word/syllable. In Example 1.2, from Smokey Robinson's "Since I Lost My Baby," the important word "life" begins on G before moving to the "home" pitch of F.

Example 1.2. "Since I Lost My Baby" (William "Smokey" Robinson)

Nonsyncopated motives and phrases also occur in African American music, but seldom for extended periods, unless the underlying accompanying musical events are syncopated. In the Motown classic, "My Girl," the first two phrases are nonsyncopated; the third phrase, consisting of only two notes, is marked by syncopation. The fourth and final phrase begins in a nonsyncopated manner but ends with a syncopated rhythm (Example 1.3).

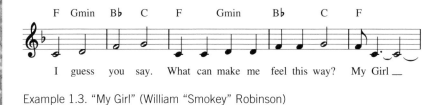

Example 1.3. "My Girl" (William "Smokey" Robinson)

Syncopation in African American melodies usually occurs on several rhythmic levels at the same time. This is called *syncopic stratification*. When diverse syncopations occur in the principal melody the result is *horizontal syncopic stratification*. When diverse syncopations occur in several melodies (or musical events) going on at the same time the result is *vertical syncopic stratification*. Syncopic stratification is one of the principal stylistic attributes that distinguish African-derived styles from most non-black styles. Example 1.4, from "You Don't Know Like I Know" by Isaac Hayes and David Porter, illustrates how syncopic stratification works in African American popular music. In this excerpt, syncopic stratification is evident on at least two levels. The first level, the melody, offers a diverse assortment of syncopations, with many stressed notes occurring halfway between the beats of the underlying pulse. The second level, the bass, consists of a regularly recurring syncopated pattern that mirrors the syncopation of the melody on the second beat of each bar, where there is a silence or a tied note instead of the strong beat implied by the underlying pulse.

Example 1.4. "You Don't Know Like I Know" (Isaac Hayes and Dave Porter)

## RHYTHMIC CONCRESCENCE

African American music often features several highly rhythmic parts played simultaneously. One common effect is to have a highly syncopated melody performed with a nonsyncopated accompaniment: Ragtime is one example of this style; swing is another. In Example 1.4, note the tension that arises when the melody is syncopated and the bass is not, and note the feeling of release or resolution when both parts arrive on a strong beat together (for example, on the words "woman" and "done").

When several melodies (or musical events) occur at the same time they form what we may call a *rhythmic plexus*: an interconnected network of musical events. The events that occur in a plexus are not arbitrary and consequently do not have the same function. Some events merge with other events. When this happens the listener does not hear the individual events, but instead hears the cumulative effect, or union, of all of them. This effect is called *rhythmic concrescence*.

Rhythmic concrescence is a type of rhythmic harmony. It is the rhythmic ideal of most African American vernacular styles. It is also the effect that is implied when terms like *rag, swing, funk, feel,* and *soul* are used to describe the rhythmic affect, or emotional character, of certain styles. In other words, when Duke Ellington suggests that "It Don't Mean a Thing If It Ain't Got That Swing," or James Brown commands an audience to "Make It Funky," they are both alluding to the importance of rhythmic concrescence as a precondition for the enjoyment of the other dramatic offerings of the music.

The particular events of a plexus that create concrescence are constant or mildly variable (they maintain the same basic shape) and generally form ostinatos (patterns that are repeated over and over). Consequently, they are easy to recognize.

## RHYTHMIC TENSION

The other musical events in a plexus are generally highly variable (inconstant) and consequently cannot form ostinatos (repeated patterns). These events create rhythmic tension, like dissonance in a harmony or melody. They therefore make up the conflicting part of the plexus in that they operate against the rhythmic harmony created by the concrescent events. Their presence makes the music more interesting and dramatic.

One way of developing rhythmic tension that is often used in African American styles is *compound rhythm*. A compound rhythm is a single rhythmic line that is heard as two or more distinct lines. It is perceived as more than one rhythm when the timbre or the register of the line is skillfully manipulated. Compound rhythm is a typical characteristic of ragtime (Example 1.5), and occurs sometimes in jazz melodies as well.

Example 1.5. "Maple Leaf Rag" (Scott Joplin)

Rhythms grouped in an asymmetrical pattern in relation to the natural submetrical groupings of the meter are another means of developing tension. An example of this are patterns like 4 against 3, or 5 against 3 in a compound meter; or 5 against 4 in a simple meter (see Example 1.6). Such patterns occur frequently in jazz improvisation.

Example 1.6.

When one repeated rhythm implies a meter different from the underlying beat, the result is *metric syncopation*. Metric syncopation may be defined as the temporary displacement of the underlying meter. In many cases, such as ragtime music, metric syncopation results from compound rhythms in the melody. However, metric syncopation often occurs when two distinct rhythmic parts are performed. Notice for example the second phrase of Duke Ellington's "It Don't Mean a Thing If It Ain't Got That Swing" (Example 1.7), which is distinctly different than the underlying beat.

Example 1.7. "It Don't Mean a Thing If It Ain't Got That Swing" (Duke Ellington)

A phenomenon only occasionally found in African American music is *abstract rhythm*. It consists of one or more patterns that may be perceived metrically in two different ways. For example, the pattern

13

under certain conditions could also be heard as

## RHYTHMIC IMPROVISATION

The most important of all inconstant events in African American music is improvisation. It consists of musical events developed on the spot by the performer. Improvisation in African American music is expressed in three ways:

1. *Extemporization:* The embellishment or variation of a musical event, but not to the point where its original structure is no longer recognizable.

2. *Development:* The manipulation of a musical event to the point where its original structure is no longer perceivable.

3. *Transmutation:* The process of progressing from one recognizable event to another, usually by way of a transformation of the former.

The first type of improvisation is common to folk and commercial styles, although it appears in most other styles at least in short sections. The second type often occurs in jazz styles. The third type is common to contemplative Afro-classical compositions. Inconstancy need not manifest itself exclusively as improvisation. In many styles the inconstant rhythmic aspects of a piece are carefully planned ahead.

We see then that the musical events that shape African-derived rhythmic plexuses group themselves into two opposing forces: (1) those that are designed to *merge* (form the *concrescent* aspect of the plexus), and (2) those designed to *contend* (form the *conflicting* aspect of the plexus). The events of concrescence are constant, symbiotic, and therefore rhythmically harmonious; the events of contention are inconstant, nonsymbiotic, and consequently rhythmically dissonant.

Though both forces operate simultaneously they are not of equal significance. The concrescent events are self-generative and independent. Conversely, the conflicting events depend upon the concrescent events for their aesthetic identity. Without an underlying concrescent background (the swing, or the funk, and so on.) the conflicting events have no definite meaning. Conflicting events are therefore parasitic on the underlying concrescent rhythm.

## Texture and Harmony

African American vernacular styles employ a variety of textures. Common styles include *antiphony* (call and response), *homophony* (melody plus background accompaniment), and *polyphony* (multiple melodic lines of equal importance). Antiphony and *heterophony* (different versions of a single melody performed together) are common to many vocally oriented folk styles. With the exception of vocal folk forms, works are seldom predicated exclusively upon one texture, though one texture may predominate. What occurs more often in nonfolk forms is the juxtaposition of diverse textures or the simultaneous occurrence of several textures. The more technically complicated the style, the more likely the latter will occur.

The predominant harmonic language in African American styles since Reconstruction is vernacular. *Vernacular progressions* are defined in this book as progressions deemed functionally weak by traditional European classical standards. These include diatonic root progressions like V to IV, IV to I, ii to I, ii to vi, ii to IV, iii to I, vi to I, and their minor-key counterparts. Some vernacular progressions occur in styles generally held to be governed by European harmonic conventions—ragtime for example.

European cadential patterns like the V to I authentic cadence and the ii to V half-cadence also occur in African American music, but as a part of a broader set of possibilities. Cadential progressions like IV to I, ii to I, vi to I, ♭II to I, ♭VI to I, ♭VII to I, and V to IV are all common to African American musical styles—particularly black popular styles after 1950. Also a part of the vernacular harmonic lexicon are dominant seventh chords whose roots do not progress (as would normally be the case) to the roots of chords located a perfect fifth below. Progressions like V⁷ to ii, IV⁷ to I, or IV⁷ to I⁷, V to iv, V⁷ to IV⁷ to I⁷, or ♭VII⁷ to IV are all conventional as vernacular root progressions and occur with great frequency.

The interval of the seventh, ninth, eleventh, and thirteenth, occurring within or against chords—whether diatonically or chromatically derived—are not treated as they are in European common practice literature; that is, they are not considered nonchord tones and need not (and frequently do not) resolve downward by step, unless they are clearly incompatible with the underlying harmony (even then, they may not resolve in the expected way). Instead, these pitches are treated with the same freedom as the roots, thirds, and fifths of chords. They may progress up or down by step or by skip. Such pitches are known as *extensions*. Extensions are common to all African American vernacular styles, though not in the same proportion; as a rule, the more harmonically and melodically complicated the style, the greater their occurrence.

African American vernacular melodies show the influence of several types of scales. Pre–twentieth-century African American vernacular music showed a strong bias toward pentatonic melodies (Example 1.8). Though modern melodies use major and minor scales rather profusely the presence of pentatonicism can still be felt. This is particularly true of gospel music, early blues, and the styles derived from them, like soul music of the 1960s and 1970s. It is also true in certain jazz styles, though less so.

Example 1.8. The Pentatonic Scale

Melodies showing the influence of blues scales are not uncommon either. Of all blues scales underscoring black melodies, the hexatonic blues scale appears to be more common in blues-derived styles (Example 1.9).

Example 1.9. The Hexatonic Blues Scale

While the traditional (ecclesiastical) modes were sparsely represented in early African American music, their presence in modern jazz and popular music has increased considerably.

In the ensuing chapters we have much more to say about texture, harmony, and melody and the specific roles they play in the shaping of the various African American styles.

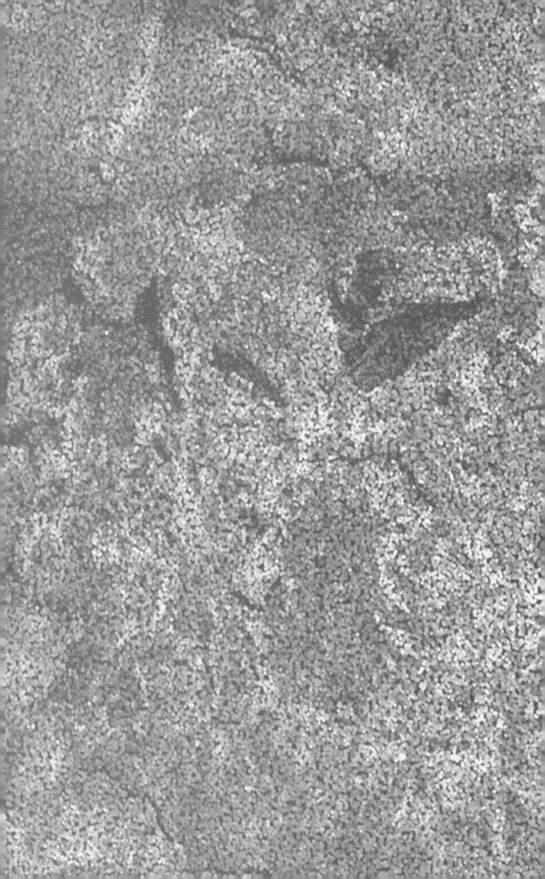

## CHAPTER 2

## WORK SONGS, MINSTRELSY, AND SPIRITUALS

**A**N IMPRESSIVE ARRAY of African American folk and popular genres thrived during the Reconstruction era and immediately afterward (the decades following the Civil War from about 1870 to the turn of the century). Most of the folk forms were either transformed from African roots or were newly developed ones that originated during slavery or shortly thereafter. Such forms included works songs, field hollers, and spirituals, covered in this chapter, and folk blues (see Chapter 3).

### Work Songs

The texts of the work songs generally mirrored the arduous and often unfair conditions under which African Americans lived and labored. They differ noticeably from spiritual texts in that they expressed more the mundane experiences of the people, rather than their religiosity. The types of activities work songs typically accompanied were those that involved the use of large numbers of workers, or work gangs, for example, laying railroad tracks or drilling tunnels. Later, these songs survived in prison camps, where many of them were recorded in the 1930s.

Work songs were functional in that they were used to coordinate the efforts of the workers. Songs were chosen based upon their appropriateness to the work activity at hand. These songs were typically in call-and-response structure. Song leaders coordinated the work activities. Because of the important function they served, song leaders were not arbitrarily chosen. Their selection was based upon their sense of rhythm, their knowledge of the work activity, and their ability to entertain the workers, thereby alleviating the rigorousness and monotony of the tasks.

## Minstrelsy

The most significant of the popular forms to emerge before the Civil War was so-called Ethiopian minstrelsy. Though not developed by blacks, Ethiopian minstrelsy (or simply minstrelsy) was rooted in slave culture. It was a type of staged theatrical entertainment that came about in the 1830s. In such productions, white performers, with faces darkened by burnt cork, entertained their audiences with exaggerated depictions of slave life. Though sometimes pathetic and tragic, these depictions were usually demeaning and grossly stereotypical.

Two caricatures evolved and ultimately became the vehicles through which the minstrels' image of black life was spread. These were Jim Crow, the caricature of an ignorant plantation slave, and Zip Coon, the caricature of an urban slave—a ridiculous, womanizing braggart. The first parody, Jim Crow, traces back to a dance routine first performed by Thomas Dartmouth Rice, a white actor. The idea for Rice's parody purportedly derived from his observation of a dance performed by a lamed Negro. He allegedly adapted this dance into a burlesque that ultimately earned him a fortune. Rice's comic representation, however, was performed at a great cost to the African American. Lerone Bennett Jr. expresses the cost in this way:

> By 1838, Jim Crow was wedged into the language as a synonym for Negro. A noun, a verb, an adjective, a "comic" way of life.
>
> By 1839, there was an antislavery book about him: *The History of Jim Crow.*
>
> By 1841, there was a Jim Crow railroad car—in Massachusetts of all places.

By 1901, Jim Crow was a part of the marrow of America. But he was no longer singing. He had turned mean. The song-and-dance man had become a wall, a way of separating people from people. Demagogue by demagogue, mania by mania, brick by brick, the wall was built. Interracial drinking and interracial dying were banned.[1]

By the mid-nineteenth century, minstrel shows had developed into three-part productions. According to Edward Thorpe, the first part consisted of a comic banter "between the . . . Master of Ceremonies (the interlocutor) and the end-men, Mr. Tambo and Brother Bones."[2] Sentimental songs were then performed, followed by a promenade for the whole company. The second part was called an Olio. It featured singing and dancing, and "verse speaking."[3] The third section was the Finale, which brought back the entire cast.

Although pre-Reconstruction minstrelsy was tinctured with the presence of African Americans, black minstrel troupes and entertainers did not proliferate until after 1864. A prominent black minstrel before 1865 was William Henry Lane, who took on the name of "Master Juba." During the 1840s, Lane was hailed by many as the greatest dancer in the world. Black minstrels offered original and entertaining variations on formats invented decades earlier, stamping the older tradition with the signature of authentic African singing styles and dance conceptions. But the black minstrels did little to usurp the denigrating portraiture of African American culture that the earlier white minstrels had so deeply implanted into the consciousness of mainstream America. The value of minstrelsy, with regard to the tradition of African American music, is best seen seminally in the contributions it brought to black musical theater.

## Spirituals

Spirituals are the earliest body of vernacular folk literature that expresses the religious feelings of African Americans. They are derived from the

African technique of reshaping bits of preexisting songs into new ones. The preexistent material included hymns, folk and popular songs, and minstrel songs. The early spirituals were generally cultivated in religious venues, but only after the formal religious services were over. They were performed in the churches or cabins where services were held for slaves, or in the black quarters of the mass, evangelical revival meetings (called "camp meetings"). Performances of spirituals were frequently accompanied by an African-derived dance known as a *ring shout* (or simply *shout*). This was a type of ceremonial dance in which the participants gathered in the middle of the floor and, with the start of the spiritual, moved or shuffled around in a circle, sometimes for hours. The movement started slowly, then gradually hastened to a point that drove its participants to a frenzied state.

James Weldon Johnson (1871–1938) provides a dramatic description of the ring shout based upon his youthful recollections of the dance:

> The "ring shout," in truth, is nothing more or less than the survival of a primitive African dance, which in quite an understandable way attached itself in the early days to the Negro's Christian worship. I can remember seeing this dance many times when I was a boy. A space is cleared by moving the benches, and the men and women arrange themselves, generally alternately, in a ring, their bodies quite close. The music starts and the ring begins to move. Around it goes, at first slowly, then with quickening pace. Around and around it moves on shuffling feet that do not leave the floor, one foot beating with the heel a decided accent in strict two-four time. The music is supplemented by the clapping of hands. As the ring goes around it begins to take on signs of frenzy. The music, starting, perhaps with a Spiritual, becomes a wild, monotonous chant. The same musical phrase is repeated over and over one, two, three, four, five hours. The

words become a repetition of an incoherent cry. The very monotony of sound and motion produces an ecstatic state. Women, screaming, fall to the ground prone and quivering. Men exhausted, drop out of the shout. But the ring closes up and moves around and around.[4]

The combined experience of the ring shout and the spiritual illustrates several distinctively African features. Among them are:

1. The interconnection of dance and song.
2. Functionality: The music and dance are used to induce an ecstatic state in the participants.
3. Collective participation: The ceremony involves the whole group.

Scholars are not in agreement concerning the origin of the spirituals. Some scholars, for example Eileen Southern, consider the spirituals to have germinated essentially during the nineteenth century. Others, such as Dena Epstein and John Lovell Jr., consider the spirituals to have started much earlier. In any case, it was clearly in the nineteenth century that the spirituals "crystallized" into the form that is known to us today.

## Characteristics of Spirituals

One of the most prominent features of spiritual melodies is syncopation. In the spiritual "Go Down Moses" (Example 2.1), syncopation appears first when the word "down" and the second syllable of "Mo-ses" occur on the weak second beat rather than the strong third beat of the measure. Its next occurrence is on the word "land," in which the singer reaches the closing pitch of F halfway between beats three and four. In the following measure, the word "ole" begins halfway between beats one and two. Two measures later, the second syllable of "peo-ple" begins halfway between beats three and four.

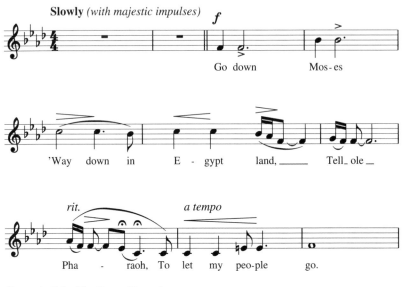

Example 2.1. "Go Down Moses"

A common feature of spirituals is the accenting of syllables that would not be stressed in speech. (This feature often occurs in conjunction with syncopation.) This fact was observed by some of the earliest collectors of African American spirituals. Ethnomusicologist Natalie Curtis-Burlin wrote in 1918:

> Throughout Western Europe and in English and Latin countries, the accents fall as a rule on the stressed syllables of the spoken tongue and on the regular beats of the music. The opposite is the case in Negro songs: here the rhythms are uneven, jagged, and, at first hearing, eccentric, for the accents fall most frequently on the short notes and on the naturally unstressed beats, producing what we call "syncopation" of a very intricate and highly developed order. The peculiarity of syncopation is best explained to the layman by drawing attention to the way in which the natural rhythms of the English language are distorted

to fit the rhythm of Negro music: where the white man would sing, "*Go* Down, *Mo*ses," the Negro chants, "Go *Down*, Mo*ses*."[6]

Many spirituals are based on the pentatonic scale, a scale of five pitches corresponding (roughly) to the first, second, third, fifth, and sixth notes of the standard Western scale. A pentatonic influence or bias is also often evidenced in spirituals based on other gapped scales as well as the Western major and minor scales. The music critic Henry Edward Krehbiel (1854–1923) confirmed this predilection for pentatonic scales, after examining 527 spirituals:

> [T]he tones which seem rebellious to the negro's sense of intervallic propriety are the fourth and seventh of the diatonic major series and the fourth, sixth and seventh of the minor. The omission of the fourth and seventh intervals of the major scale leaves the pentatonic series on which 111 of the 527 songs analyzed are built. The fact is an evidence of the strong inclination of the American negroes toward this scale.[7]

The texts of African American spirituals are usually sung in black dialect—the same as that employed (at one time) by blacks in everyday speech. Though black dialect is subject to regional differences and historical change, the spirituals tend to preserve Southern, black pronunciation as it was around the time of the Civil War. For example, a *d* or *t* sound usually substitutes for *th* sounds in standard English; *that* becomes *dat*, *the* becomes *de*, *thin* becomes *tin*, *death* becomes *det*, and so on. The consonant *g* is dropped in words ending in *ing*. Thus, *doing* becomes *doin'*, *singing* becomes *singin'*, and so on. Many words ending in *er* take the ending sound of *ah*; for example words like *ever* and *better* become *evah* and *bettah*.[8]

Most spirituals are designed as verses followed by refrains. Though completely choral presentations of the verse/choral refrain structure are common today, originally a song leader, or solo vocalist, sang the verse and a chorus handled the refrain, in keeping with the call-and-response pattern discussed in Chapter 1. Natalie Curtis-Burlin described the performance of spirituals as she witnessed them:

> The Negro Spirituals (prayer songs) open with a choral refrain or burthen, followed by a freely declaimed extemporaneous verse or even just a few words of solo sung by a single voice. Then comes the chorus or burthen again; another verse or solo; again the chorus; more verse, and so on, indefinitely, until the song ends with the chorus—a rounded whole.[9]

## Categories of Spirituals

Three common and interrelated ways of categorizing spirituals are presented here. The first system was developed by composer/musicologist Arnold Shaw (1909–1989), which he derived from John Lovell Jr.[10] Shaw isolates three types of spirituals: (1) sorrow songs; (2) jubilees; and (3) cult songs. The sorrow songs, according to Shaw, are slow in tempo and lugubrious in mood, as a result of their emphasis on "the burdens, troubles, and deprivations of slave existence."[11] Examples of this type are "Sometimes I Feel Like A Motherless Child"and "Nobody Knows the Trouble I See." Jubilees, as the name imply, are songs of jubilation. Such songs, according to Shaw, venerate Jesus and God, celebrate heroic figures, and reject Satan. Some of these songs are rendered in a fast tempo, like "Go Tell It On The Mountain" and "Little David (Play On Your Harp)." Cult songs are spirituals that are allegedly named after the "African cult meetings secretly attended by slaves."[12] Such spirituals were used for coded messages, conveying secret meanings to slaves. Spirituals in this category include "Hush, Somebody's Calling My Name" and "North To Freedom."

Before Shaw made his categories, John W. Work (1901–1967) isolated three groups of spirituals: (1) the call-and-response chant; (2) the slow, sustained, long-phrase melody; and (3) the syncopated, segmented melody.[13] Though his categories are similar to Shaw's, Work's categorization is based upon stronger musicological criteria. Work describes the first type of spiritual as rapid in tempo and "characterized by a fiery spirit."[14] The largest body of spirituals fit this category, including "Great Camp Meeting," "Shout for Joy", and "Good Morning Everybody." Work also places "Swing Low Sweet Chariot" in this category but considers it an exception because of its "calmness."

The second group of spirituals isolated by Work is described as slow in tempo and characterized by long, sustained phrases. Some of the most beautiful and popular of all the spirituals belong to this category. Such spirituals include "Deep River," "Nobody Knows the Trouble I See", and "Were You There?"

The third type isolated by Work is usually in a fast tempo and characterized by rhythms, or a rhythmic swing, which induces body movement. He concluded this was the most popular of the three types. According to Work:

> The musical line . . . is often made up of segments or rhythmic
> patterns with a syncopated figure. As to be expected the words
> are usually in short phrase lengths, or one repeated word, rather
> than in complete lines as are "Were You There?" and songs of
> its class.[15]

Work's reference to a "swing that stimulates bodily movement" and "segments of rhythmic patterns with a syncopated figure" are interesting in that they resemble two prominent features of jazz, namely, swing and the riff.[16] Spirituals in this category include "Little David Play on Yo' Harp" and "Shout All over God's Heab'n."

W. E. B. Du Bois (1868–1963) also isolated three categories in his study of spirituals.[17] Du Bois's categories, however, identify the stages of development of the spirituals rather than their technical, thematic, or sociological attributes. The first type of spiritual or slave song, according to Du Bois, is African in its musical character. The example he gives is "March On." The second type is what Du Bois calls Afro-American; "Steal Away" exemplifies this type. The third, according to Du Bois, is "still distinctively Negro and the method of blending original [i.e., indigenous to blacks], but the elements [materials] are both Negro and Caucasian."[18] Conforming to Du Bois's third stage of development are songs like "Nobody Knows the Trouble I See" and "Swing Low Sweet Chariot."

## The Dissemination and Popularization of the Spiritual

In the middle of the nineteenth century interest in the spiritual spread beyond the black communities. This interest was enhanced by the publication of spirituals—singularly and in collections—by touring groups and individual performers and by Euroclassical settings and adoptions.

The first published collection of spirituals was *Slaves Songs of the United States*. It was collected by William Francis Allen, Charles Pickard Ware, and Lucy McKim Garrison and published in 1867. During the next hundred years this work would be followed by literally hundreds of similar anthologies and critical studies of spirituals.

Essays explicating the aesthetic, cultural, and musical import of the spirituals proliferated after 1900. One of the most influential was W.E.B. Du Bois's "Of the Sorrow Songs," an essay from his 1903 book *Souls of Black Folk*. Other important essays followed, such as Alain Locke's "The Negro Spiritual," and the prefaces to James Weldon Johnson's two books of spirituals published in 1925 and 1926, respectively.

The publication of anthologies and scholarly examinations of black spirituals continued well into the twentieth century. Johnson's set of anthologies—titled *The American Negro Spirituals: Books One and Two*—was but one of many. Two other important anthologies were published by Natalie Curtis-Burlin and John W. Work. Henry Krehbiel's scholarly examination of black spirituals was one of the most important of the early twentieth century and brought to the spiritual a level of credibility it had not known beforehand. Collectively, all these efforts validated the spirituals as an exalted and noble folk art—in the eyes of many the best America had to offer—and consequently made them a more palatable resource for concert treatment than any other black idiom.

Touring groups, however, had a much stronger impact upon popularizing the spirituals than published anthologies and analytical studies. The first and most influential of these groups was the Fisk Jubilee Singers. This group was organized by George L. White, the treasurer of Fisk University, for the purpose of raising funds for the institution. Fisk during this time was in urgent need of financial assistance. White's conception of the Jubilee Singers is described by John W. Work:

> White had listened with keen interest to the singing of the students, and in a moment of inspiration stated his belief that if the world could hear these strange songs it would experience the same exaltation which he felt when listening to them, and somehow, out of this, sufficient interest could be aroused to help the new educational experiment.[19]

White's instinct was correct. After organizing the group into a chorus of twelve people, and training them for two years, the group set out on its first tour in 1871. The tour was not only economically successful but brought national and international acclaim to the group and considerably enhanced world interest in the African American spiritual. By 1878 the chorus had raised over $150,000. It was during their first tour that they were given the name The Jubilee Singers and their repertoire identified as Jubilee Songs.[20]

The success of the Fisk Jubilee Singers inspired other groups, including the Hampton Institute choir. This group, comprising sixteen students, was organized in 1873 specifically for the purpose of singing spirituals. Though not as successful as the Fisk Jubilee Singers, within four years of their organization the Hampton choir had earned considerable recognition, built national interest in the spiritual, and raised the funds necessary to build a girl's and boy's dormitory on their campus.

Several European and American classical composers played a significant role in stimulating interest in the spirituals. The most memorable of the European composers was Antonin Dvořák (1841–1904). A world-famous composer who was born in what is now the Czech Republic, Dvořák served as director of the National Conservatory of Music in New York City from 1892–1895. Dvořák's interest in spirituals was aroused, in large part, by one of his African American students, Henry T. Burleigh. Burleigh, a frequent visitor to Dvořák's home, sang spirituals for the great master. "Swing Low, Sweet Chariot" was apparently one of Dvořák's favorites.[21] According to Joseph Horowitz:

> The principal subject of the slow movement [of Dvořák's Symphony #9; his "New World" Symphony]—a tune so resembling a spiritual that it later, as "Goin Home," became one—was entrusted to the English horn, whose reedy timbre, it has been suggested, resembled Burleigh's voice.[22]

Dvořák's interest in American vernacular music, particularly African American slave songs, was shared by Jeanette Thurber, founder of the National Conservatory, and Henry Edward Krehbiel, with whom he corresponded often and who shared with Dvořák his belief that the genesis of an authentic American school of composition resided untapped in the folk music of African Americans. The spirit of African American spirituals is evident in three of Dvořák's most important compositions: his Symphony no. 9 in E minor ("From the New World"), his String Quartet in F major ("the American"), and his String Quintet in E-flat major. The "New World" symphony and the "American" Quartet have become staples of the symphonic and chamber music repertories.

Two other eminent European composers used African American spirituals as a basis for major works: Frederick Delius and Michael Tippett. The influence of the spiritual pervades many of Delius's works, of which the most noteworthy is *Appalachia*. The theme of this work is allegedly based on a slave song. One of Tippett's most important choral/symphonic compositions, and one of the most beloved oratorios of the twentieth century, *A Child of Our Time*, interpolates five African American spirituals into its structure. It is a deeply moving protest against persecution and tyranny that the composer began two days after the start of the Second World War. The specific spirituals he used were "Steal Away," occurring at the conclusion of part one; "Nobody Knows The Trouble I See," "Go Down Moses," and "O, By And By," occurring in part two; and "Deep River," which concludes the third and final part of the composition.

White American composers, for the most part, chose not to take seriously Dvořák's admonishment of using African American folk music as the basis of an American school of composition. Consequently, compositions by eminent white American composers that show serious experimentation with African American spirituals are sporadic and largely minor in significance. One of the few exceptions is Morton Gould's *Spirituals for Strings*.

Samuel Coleridge-Taylor (1875–1912), an Anglo-African, was a disciple of Dvořák, and championed many of his works in England (see Chapter 14). Coleridge-Taylor's interest in African American spirituals, however, did not emanate from Dvořák but rather from a set of concerts given by the Fisk Jubilee Singers in the late 1890s. According to W. C. Berwick Sayers:

> Coleridge-Taylor attended some of the Jubilee concerts, and was deeply affected by the singing; the air, indeed, struck a chord

responsive in him; but in particular it was the quality of the voices that impressed him. . . . Thereafter negro themes occur frequently in his works.[23]

Compositions exemplifying Coleridge-Taylor's interest in the spirituals include: the *Overture to the Song of Hiawatha*, *Twenty Four Negro Melodies*, and *Variations on an African Air*. The *Overture* is based upon a rare version of the spiritual "Nobody Knows the Trouble I See" (Example 2.2).

*Twenty-Four Negro Melodies* was written when the music publisher Oliver Ditson Company of Boston, Massachusetts, asked Coleridge-Taylor to arrange "an album of negro folk songs for the piano."[24] Of the twenty-four songs sent to Coleridge-Taylor, sixteen were African American spirituals.[25] In this latter group were such classics as "Sometimes I Feel Like A Motherless Child," "Steal Away," "Didn't My Lord Deliver Daniel?," and "Wade in the Water." Coleridge-Taylor set each of the twenty-four melodies in theme-and-variations form.

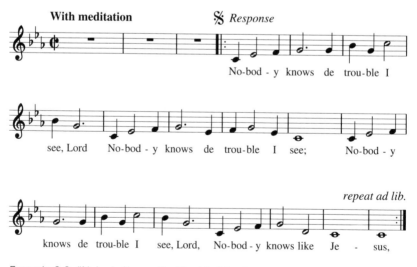

Example 2.2. "Nobody Knows the Trouble I See"

Also included in the original set of twenty-four melodies was a spiritual titled "I'm Troubled in Mind" (Example 2.3), which became the thematic basis for Coleridge-Taylor's *Variations on an African Air*. The composer considered this composition to be one of his best, superior even to his *Song of Hiawatha*. According to Sayers "I'm Troubled in Mind" was based upon a much older melody that was:

> taken from the lips of a slave in Nashville, who first heard it
> from her father. After the aged slave had been flogged he always
> sat upon a log beside his cabin, and, with tears streaming down
> his cheeks, sang this song with so much pathos that few could
> listen without sympathy.[26]

Example 2.3. "I'm Troubled in Mind"

Inspired by the efforts of Dvořák, and particularly Coleridge-Taylor, many African American composers during the first half of the twentieth century undertook the task of writing classical arrangements of spirituals or composing works inspired by spirituals. Among the elite of this group were Henry (aka Harry) T. Burleigh (1866–1949), Clarence Cameron White (1880–1960), Robert Nathaniel Dett (1882–1943), William Levi Dawson (1899–1991), Hall Johnson (1888–1970), William Grant Still (1895–1978), and John Rosamond Johnson (1873–1954).

H. T. Burleigh was a good friend of Coleridge-Taylor. Their friendship was probably inevitable given Burleigh's affiliation with Dvořák, the composer who, by Coleridge-Taylor's own admittance, influenced him more than any other.[27] According to Eileen Southern, Burleigh's 1916 publication of *Jubilee Songs of the United States of America* presented for the first time African American spirituals arranged as art songs.[28] Clarence C. White's contributions include *Bandanna Sketches* (four spirituals for violin and piano), *From the Cotton Fields* (which featured three spirituals), and *Forty Negro Spirituals*, in addition to many articles on the subject of the spirituals.[29]

Composers who arranged or collected spirituals included Dawson, Johnson, Dett, John Rosamond Johnson, and Still. Because they also composed major classical works, we will discuss their influence on classical composers in Chapter 15. Post-1950 composers, arrangers, and conductors who have continued to keep the spirituals alive include George Walker, John Carter, Hale Smith, Adolphous Hailstork, Roland Carter, Nathan Carter, Charles Lloyd, Moses Hogan, and Dianne White.

Like African American and European composers, twentieth-century black concert artists, mainly solo vocalists, have done their share to perpetuate the legacy of the African American spiritual. Some of the most eminent of these artists are Roland Hayes, H. T. Burleigh, Paul Robeson, Mahalia Jackson, Marian Anderson, Leontyne Price, Jessye Norman, Kathleen Battle, Barbara Conrad, and Barbara Hendricks.

Roland Mario Carter

Dianne White

## Spirituals and the Blues

The spirituals share both differences and similarities with the blues. The differences are many. The spirituals, in their original vernacular form, were choral works and were communal. This is in sharp contrast to the solo, individual orientation of the blues. While the blues reflected the physical, mundane universe of African Americans, the spiritual showed their metaphysical concerns. Spirituals, as previously noted, were generally cultivated in religious venues; the blues were cultivated in secular venues. Spirituals were originally performed without instrumental accompaniment; blues artists either accompanied themselves on a solo instrument or were accompanied by an ensemble. The original spirituals grew out of, and consequently reflected, a slave existence; the blues were essentially a postslavery phenomenon. Spiritual harmonizations are generally varied; most blues harmonizations are based on a specific harmonic pattern.

The similarities between the blues and spirituals, however, are no less striking. The formative basis of most spirituals is a verse/choral refrain structure. This structure is a manifestation of the African-derived call-and-response pattern, which is found also in the blues. Second, the call-and-response pattern, even when manifested as a verse/choral refrain chant, is still fundamentally a binary form. To this extent it matches the binary phraseology of the blues, though the manner in which it is manifested differs.

Other similarities also exist. Many of the spirituals, for example, show a strong modal predilection for the pentatonic scale, which is also found in the early blues. Many spirituals use the flatted third and flatted seventh, which were, no doubt, originally vocally delivered microtonal inflections. This same modal phenomenon occurs in the blues in an even more pronounced fashion. The texts of both the spirituals and the blues are rendered in black dialect. This text is musically delivered by the song leader in the spiritual and the soloist in the blues in a recitative style. The lugubrious character of many blues has a precedent in the sorrow songs of the spirituals.

Thus it is clear that the point where the spiritual ends and the blues begins is not firmly fixed. For this reason we cite an aspect of the spirituals—the sorrow songs—as one of the sources of the blues. The blues, however, ultimately developed into a genre independent of the spiritual, and as such took on its own unique structural and aesthetic identity.

## CHAPTER 3

# THE BLUES

## General Attributes

The term *the blues* covers a wide range of musical expressions, from classic country blues to blues-tinged jazz performances. There are many musical elements that define the blues. Typically, blues songs have in common three major elements: an AAB phrase structure; a twelve-bar metrical pattern; and a fixed harmonic formula.

The blues phrase structure typically features an opening phrase that is immediately repeated, sometimes with mild variation, then answered by a contrasting phrase. Thus, the phrase structure constitutes an AAB (or AA¹B) pattern.

> *[A]—When it rain five days an' de skies turned dark as night*
> *[A]—When it rain five days an' the skies turned dark as night*
> *[B]—Then trouble taken place in the lowland that night.[1]*

Because the second phrase repeats the first, the phrase structure of the blues can be regarded as *binary* (two-part).

The second aspect of most blues songs is a fixed metric structure. It is conventionally viewed as a twelve-measure pattern, though patterns less than or greater than twelve measures are not uncommon. What is standard to the metric structure is that it is usually divisible by three; this is because the AAB phrase structure typically divides the metric structure into equal parts.

Underlying the phrase and metric structures is a paradigmatic harmonic formula consisting fundamentally of I–IV–I–V–I, or I–IV–I–V–IV–I. These harmonies occur at specific points within the metric structure, allowing the pattern to function as a harmonic skeleton over which additional foreground harmonies can be added.

The structures of most vocal blues show the influence of call and response on two interconnected levels. First, the B phrase completes the thematic idea introduced in the A phrase. Though not antiphonal in the strictest sense, the antecedent-consequent relationship existing between the A and B phrases makes them strongly reminiscent of call and response. Second, within each phrase, the melody consumes one-half of the metrical phrase and is followed by an instrumental or vocal response. Sometimes the beginning of the response overlaps the ending of the melody.

Like gospel music, the blues include certain vocally derived devices that make possible much of the emotionality, drama, and modality that listeners generally associate with the style. These devices include guttural tones, falsetto, glissandi, blue notes, multiphonics, Afro-melismas, vocal rhythmization (nonintoned rhythmic and arhythmic speech), and a recitative-like vocal delivery (see Chapter 1 for more discussion of these vocal attributes).

The blues form has remained essentially intact since its crystallization during the first quarter of the twentieth century. However, certain deviations in the paradigm do appear from time to time. In some vocal blues compositions, for example, the normative phrase structure is ABC rather than AAB. This type of blues was common in the 1920s in pop songs written in a "blues" style (Example 3.1). The B phrase is often used to deliver the title or hook—in which is stated, or implied, the central idea of the song. This type of phrase structure is ideal for a blues that is not written in verse/chorus structure in that it allows, in however abbreviated a manner, for the presentation of that information usually reserved for the chorus.

Example 3.1. "Hear Me Talkin' to Ya" (Louis Armstrong)

One of the most enduring of all vocal blues, "See See Rider," employs this type of phrase structure (Example 3.2). This traditional blues was recorded in one famous version by the legendary Gertrude "Ma" Rainey (1886–1939), who published the song as her own "composition."

In blues songs written in verse/chorus design, the blues form is often featured in the chorus. The verse often shows the influence of the blues structure without fully conforming to it. Just as often, however, the verse and chorus both follow the blues form. The "Barefoot Blues" and the "Achin' Hearted Blues" are notable examples of the former type of blues song; the famous "Jail House Blues," written by Bessie Smith and Clarence Williams, exemplifies the latter. Another deviation, common to the vaudeville blues, is evident when the phrase structure of the music is AA¹B but the structure of the lyric is ABC.

**Moderate Blues Tempo**

See    See    Rid - er _____    See  what you have  done,_

_ Law'd, Law'd, Law'd,    Made  me love you,    Now your    gal _  has

come, _____    You    made  me    love _  you,

Now    your  gal    has    come, _____

Example 3.2. "See See Rider" ("Ma" Rainey)

Blues composers sometimes chose harmonies different from the standard harmonic pattern. The technique of substituting one harmony for another occurs more frequently with respect to the subdominant chord—IV—than any other. At other times the fundamental harmonic pattern itself is altered. For example, instead of using the I–IV–I–V–IV–I, the progression is altered to I–IV–I–ii–V–I. Charlie Parker was particularly fond of this type of deviation, as was Louis Jordan, the father of rhythm and blues. Its employment, particularly among blues composers, however, predates its use in bebop and rhythm and blues.[2]

Two of the most important and influential elements to grow out of the blues were blue notes and the blues scale.[3] Blue notes, as we know, are microtonal inflections of pitches. As vocal and instrumental devices they can occur anywhere and at anytime in both blues and nonblues styles. They are important for both the emotive eloquence they give and the modal color they introduce—especially in nonblues styles where their use is often sporadic and unexpected.

On instruments of fixed pitch, or in notated scores, blue notes usually are represented as flatted approximations of corresponding natural scale steps. In major key blues, these are typically the flatted third, flatted seventh, and sometimes the flatted fifth. Of the three approximations, the flatted third is the most frequently employed. In W. C. Handy's *Blues: An Anthology*, Abbe Niles describes Handy's method of interpolating the flatted-third blue note into his written songs.

> Handy's convention was the irregular introduction of the flatted third into his scripts. Thus the minor third might share a beat with the major . . . or appear as a grace note to the major . . . or entirely replace the major.[4]

Handy's method of blue note interpolation is evident in his earliest published blues, before the twenties. It was copied by contemporary songwriters of the Tin Pan Alley tradition and surprisingly has remained the preeminent method of blue note interpolation in major key compositions—blues and nonblues—to this day. The influence of blue notes on African-derived harmonies is great. Harmonies like the $I^7$, $IV^7$, $V^7(+9)$, $V^7(+9, -13)$, $I^7(+11)$, $IV^7(-9)$, and the $I^7(+9)$ all show this influence.[5]

Blue notes employed on instruments of fixed pitch, like the piano, are theoretical simulations of the true vocal sounds. The codification of these simulated pitches has resulted in the formation of a six-note (hexatonic) scale known as the blues scale (Example 3.3).

Several harmonies not typically associated with the blues may have been introduced into jazz and popular music by way of the blues. This introduction may have taken place in the early 1920s by way of the vaudeville blues (to be discussed shortly). On beat one of measure six of

Example 3.3. The Hexatonic Blues Scale

"Jail House Blues," for example, a B⁷ chord precedes the expected B♭⁷ chord—V⁷/I (Example 3.4). The B⁷ chord embellishes the resolution of the subdominant to the dominant. The same chord occurs again in measure ten, this time as a harmonic embellishment of the preceding and ensuing dominant structures.

This chord is significant in two ways. First it constitutes what jazz composers and theorists later dubbed a *tritone substitution* (referred to in this book as a *substitute dominant*).[6] Second, it is generated in both cases by a g♭ in the melody—a blue note. The substitute dominant, as we have previously seen, was known and used occasionally by jazz composers during the 1920s. However, in the hands of Duke Ellington, and later Dizzy Gillespie, Thelonius Monk, and Tadd Dameron, it became an important part of the harmonic lexicons of swing and bebop.

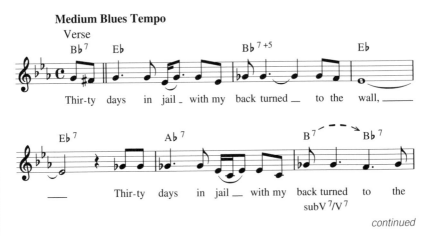

Example 3.4. "Jail House Blues" (Bessie Smith and Clarence Williams)

*continued*

44

Example 3.4. *Continued*

In measure two of the chorus of "Jail House Blues," the blue note g♭ generates yet another chord that bebop composers would later champion. This chord was the dominant-seventh sharp five chord—a functional abbreviation of the dominant-seventh flat thirteen chord.

## Blues Styles

Modern evidence indicates, rather definitively, that the blues probably came into existence in the latter decades of the nineteenth century. Bunk Johnson, one of the pioneers of New Orleans jazz, recalls playing the blues in the 1880s. W. C. Handy (1873–1958) recalls hearing the blues as early as 1892. In this regard he writes:

> While sleeping on the cobblestones in St. Louis ('92), I heard shabby guitarists picking out a tune called *East St. Louis.* It had numerous one-line verses and they would sing it all night.[7]

The work "East St. Louis," Handy admitted, may have influenced the composition of "St. Louis Blues"—a work regarded by many as Handy's signature composition.

Handy also heard a man singing a blues at a Mississippi train station in 1903. According to Handy:

> The effect was unforgettable. His song, too, struck me instantly. . . . The singer repeated the line three times, accompanying himself on the guitar with the weirdest music I had ever heard.[8]

The type of three-lined stanza to which Handy refers equates to an AAA structure:

> *Goin' where the Southern cross' the Dog*
> *Goin' where the Southern cross' the Dog*
> *Goin' where the Southern cross' the Dog.*[9]

Lightnin' Hopkins

AAB patterns were also common:

> *Boll Weevil, where you been so long?*
> *Boll Weevil, where you been so long?*
> *You stole my cotton, now you want my corn.*[10]

The specific type of blues Johnson and Handy observed belongs to a stylistic category known as *country* or *downhome blues*—a style familiar to the Mississippi Delta decades before Handy's awareness of it, though it was probably not identified by the term *blues.*

The features of the country blues are quite specific and differ noticeably from other blues styles. Most country blues performers were individuals accompanying themselves on the guitar. Unlike the highly codified blues songs heard on vaudeville stages, the country blues performers could be highly eccentric in their melodic, harmonic, and rhythmic approaches to a blues song. In a Blind Lemon Jefferson recording of "Black Snake Moan," for example, each of the three phrases is delivered in a metrically free manner, greatly altering the metrical structure. Many country blues performers were known for a fairly rough, loose approach to their performances; Charlie Patton, a denizen of the Mississippi Delta, is perhaps the most famous of these early performers.

The migration of many Delta blues artists to Chicago from the 1920s onward gave rise to the Chicago blues. With this move the style changed from a country blues style to an urban blues style. This new urban style was characterized by new instrumentation and the influence of other urban styles like jazz and gospel music. After 1940 electric guitars and small combos as backgrounds to the soloist also became common. Eminent artists of the Chicago blues tradition include Sonny Boy Williamson, who championed the blues harmonica, Little Walter Jacobs, the legendary guitarist/songwriter/vocalist Muddy Waters, B. B. King (although he was based in Memphis, not Chicago), and Howlin' Wolf.

B. B. King

An earlier type of *urban* blues established itself in the 1920s. This music, in its original form, did not survive the Depression of the 1930s. However, during its heyday it ushered in one of the most influential phases of the vocal blues and set the tone for a continuing tradition of great jazz/blues singers. Its leading exponents were women, many from a vaudeville background, and included such greats as Mamie Smith, Ida Cox, Ma Rainey, Bessie Smith, and Alberta Hunter.

This particular blues style—hereafter designated *vaudeville blues*—was essentially a popular music that reflected either the Tin Pan Alley tradition or the tradition of black songwriters. Some of these black songwriters were prominent personalities in jazz; for example, Louis Armstrong and Clarence Williams. Of the two, Clarence Williams (1893–1965) was particularly prolific as a composer of vaudeville blues. He collaborated with such artists as Joseph "King" Oliver, Bessie Smith, Thomas "Fats" Waller, Sara Martin, and Spencer Williams, and authored

Son Seals

or coauthored such blues as "Mama's Got The Blues," "Achin' Hearted Blues," "Jail House Blues," and "West End Blues."

The vaudeville blues singers were accompanied mainly by small jazz combos consisting of a rhythm section and a front line. In this regard Professor Jeff Todd Titon states:

> the piano marked the beat, and the horns, "commenting" antiphonally, filled in the spaces left by pauses in the vocal, often with improvised lines. If a pianist was the sole accompanist, his stride bass usually marked the beat while his left hand played riffling fills in an elegant style.[11]

An important and highly influential blues style associated principally with the piano was *boogie-woogie*. The term was first used in 1928 as part of the title of a recording by Clarence "Pinetop" Smith called "Pinetop's Boogie-Woogie." The earliest manifestation of the style, however, traces back at least to the turn of the century. Its cultivators were entertainers who serviced the lumber and railroad industries and their off shoots—that is, the turpentine and shipping industries. The venues for these artists were principally barrelhouses and honky tonks. A later venue, one that fostered the development of a more urbanized form of boogie-woogie of the 1920s, was the house rent party.

The earlier cultivators of boogie-woogie—roughly from 1900 to 1930—include such personalities as Hersal Thomas, Jimmy Blythe, Jimmy Yancey, Clarence Lofton, Charles Davenport, Doug Suggs, and Roosevelt Sykes. Great exponents of the boogie-woogie style after 1930 included pianists Meade Lux Lewis, Albert Ammons, and Pete Johnson.

The boogie-woogie piano style featured improvisations over ostinato or quasi-ostinato bass patterns (see Example 3.5). These patterns included four-to-the-bar or eight-to-the-bar walking bass figures, broken octaves, arpeggiations of triads, six chords, or seventh chords, or chordal bass accompaniments. Boogie-woogie improvisations often featured

Example 3.5: Boogie Woogie Bass Patterns

rolls, trills, rapidly repeated notes, extemporized runs, and sharply punctuated chords. These patterns were often meant to represent whistles, honks, bells, chimes, and other musical onomatopoeia that reflected sounds common to the environments of boogie-woogie artists.

From the late twenties to the mid-thirties, boogie-woogie bass patterns contributed to the dissipation of the ragtime-derived oom-pah bass legacy in jazz and simultaneously influenced the development of the jazz walking bass idiom. In addition, boogie-woogie pianists like Meade Lux Lewis, Albert Ammons, and Pete Johnson influenced greatly the development of jazz pianism after 1930. Boogie-woogie bass patterns also factored significantly in the development of rhythm and blues.

The influence of jazz on the development of the urban blues, rhythm and blues, and gospel music was prodigious but not one-sided. From the late fifties onward the favor was returned by way of thrusts like the back to the roots movement, the jazz rock movement, and the fusion movement.

Thus jazz styles and blues styles have traversed collateral developments marked by independent coexistence, symbiosis, and concrescence. The earliest intercourse between the two fused the style of jazz with the form (structure) of the blues, and introduced to American vernacular music the most technically sophisticated of all blues styles—that is, the *jazz blues*.

The *jazz blues* exemplifies a much greater stylistic and harmonic flexibility than what is typically found in other blues genres. A jazz blues

Bessie Smith

may, for example, be written as a swing, a waltz, a bossa nova, a samba, a funk, a ballad, and so on. Jazz blues are commonly written in major and minor keys. They are vocal and instrumental, written for virtually all jazz mediums, and exemplify a far greater harmonic complexity than most other types of blues.

Most jazz blues generally conform to the same paradigmatic structure that governs other types of blues. As with the vocal blues, the paradigmatic AAB phrase structure is sometimes replaced by alternative phrase structures. This is seen in Charlie Parker's "Blues For Alice." Jazz composers experimented with harmonic paradigms other than the basic I–IV–I–V–IV–I. Alternative harmonic patterns include I–IV–I–ii–V–I, and in minor keys i–VI–i–V–iv–I.

## The Blues Principle

In the preceding discussion, we examined the structural features of the blues as shown in specific blues styles. We observed that both the blues *form* and specific blues *characteristics* are quite distinctive. These characteristics, however, are not only heard in classic blues songs. There are few American vernacular styles in which one or more characteristics of the blues are not consistently and noticeably present. We will show how blues elements are heard in songs from the American musical theater tradition, pre-1950 popular songs, jazz, gospel music, black popular music after 1950, white popular music after 1950, European classical music, and Afro-classical music.

## Blues Elements in Jazz

The influence of blues on jazz has a long history; we have already discussed how a separate style, jazz blues, arose when the blues form was joined with jazz style. The blues influence is evident also with respect to the use of alternative phrase structures and with the blues derivation of specific harmonies found in jazz. However, jazz artists from the classic era onward found that only some specific blues elements were needed to provide them with the aesthetic effect they desired. Jazz improvisers, for example, have long known that strategically placed blue notes within their improvisations can transform otherwise bland passages into sublime utterances.

Jazz composers have found that the blues scale—sometimes used in conjunction with the blues form—constitutes a unique and valuable resource in the construction of jazz melodies. The chorus of Duke Ellington's "It Don't Mean a Thing," for example, is based entirely on the blues scale. The same is true of the theme of Gerald Wilson's "Blues for Yna Yna" (Example 3.6)—a jazz waltz predicated upon the blues form—and, with the exception of one note, Nat Adderly's "Work Song."

Ellington's "In a Sentimental Mood" uses patches of three different scale forms, of which the blues scale is one (Example 3.7). Jimmy Giuffre juxtaposes themes based exclusively on the blues scale and the pentatonic scale (heard in some blues and common to gospel music), respectively, in his "Two Kinds of Blues."[12] Quincy Jones skillfully merges generous amounts of the blues scale with a chromatically embellished major scale in the piano opening of his "Blues At Twilight," while the underlying metric and harmonic patterns are based entirely on the blues model.[13] The influence of the blues scale is evidenced strongly in the melody of Stan Kenton's "Artistry in Blues," and is the exclusive basis of the opening of Dave Brubeck's "Take Five."

The creative employment of blue notes is of course standard to the technique of every good jazz improviser. Interestingly, blue notes—either extemporized or written into the melody and sometimes the harmony—were often the only blues elements present in many jazz/blues vocal compositions not based on the blues form but nevertheless identified as "blues." This was as true during the days of the vaudeville blues as it is today.

Example 3.6. "Blues for Yna Yna" (Gerald Wilson)

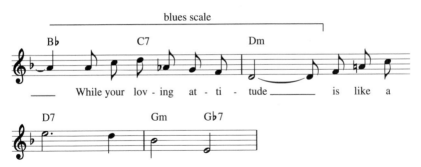

Example 3.7. "In a Sentimental Mood" (Duke Ellington)

## Blues Elements in Pre-1950 Popular Songs

Composers of American musicals frequently interpolated blue notes into their scores. They also occasionally used the blues scale, often in conjunction with the five-note (pentatonic) scale. In the verse of Gershwin's "I Got Rhythm," for example, every pitch of the melody conforms to the blues scale (Example 3.8). Only the absence of one pitch—F, the flat-seventh—prevents the complete expression of the scale. This fact is interesting given that the famous refrain of the same work is based strongly upon the pentatonic scale.

A strikingly subtle use of these scales occurs in Irving Berlin's "Blue Skies." Though not readily apparent, the pitches of the underlying harmonies (G, G$^7$, C$^6$, C$^7$, G minor, and A$^7$) of the first eight measures, when grouped together, give the pitches of the G blues scale and the G pentatonic scale (Example 3.9). The pitches derived from the harmonies are: G, A, B♭, B, C, C♯, D, E, F. The pitches G, B♭, C, C♯, D, and F make up the G blues scale; the pitches G, A, B, D, and E make up the G pentatonic scale. Consequently, while there is no ostensible representation of the blues in the melody, a blues effect is nevertheless present.

| | | | | | |
|---|---|---|---|---|---|
| *Blues Scale* | G | B♭ | C C♯ | D | F |
| | (G, A, B♭, B, C, C♯, D, E, F) | | | | |
| *Pentatonic Scale* | G A | B | | D E | |

Example 3.8. "I Got Rhythm" (George Gershwin)

**Moderately**

I was blue just as blue as I could be. _____
I should care if the wind blows east or west. _____

Ev - 'ry day was a cloud - y day for me. _____
I should fret if the worst looks like the best. _____

Then good luck came a - knock - ing at my door. _____
I should mind if they say it can't be true. _____

Skies were gray but they're not gray an - y - more. _____
I should smile that's ex - act - ly what I do. _____

Blue skies _____ smil - ing at

Example 3.9. "Blue Skies" (Irving Berlin)

Compositions that are based on both the blues and pentatonic scales are common in African American music from the late nineteenth century to the present. When these scales are joined, the pentatonic scale is usually preeminent (Example 3.10). In such instances, the *relative* pentatonic scale generally begins with the second pitch of the blues scale.

Pentatonic Scale

Hexatonic Blues Scale

Example 3.10. Pentatonic/Blues Conjunction

White composers like Irving Berlin, George Gershwin, and Jerome Kern were obviously aware of blues elements and often incorporated them into their music. The craze for "blues" type songs in the 1920s and 1930s led many popular composers to interpolate blue notes and other elements of the blues scale into their compositions, particularly those bearing the word "blues" in the title (even if they were far from being true blues compositions). "Shaking The Blues Away," "Schoolhouse Blues," and "Tokio Blues" are three noted examples by Berlin; Kern's contributions include "Left-All-Alone-Again Blues" and the "Blue Danube Blues."

Blues elements and blues/pentatonic scale conjunctions were also prominent in the music of pre-1950 black songwriters. For example, they occur prominently in the songs of Thomas "Fats" Waller. The famous chorus of Waller's "Ain't Misbehavin'" is a stunning example of a melody based upon a blues/pentatonic conjunction (Example 3.11). Though the piece is based mainly on the C major pentatonic scale—with the exception of the B natural occurring on the last eighth-note in measures three and eleven of the chorus—the E♭, occurring on the second half of beat

Example 3.11. "Ain't Misbehavin'" (Thomas Waller)

three in measures four and twelve, theoretically suggest the blues scale based on the relative minor—that is, a, c, d, e♭, e, g.

## Blues Elements in Pre-1950 Gospel Music

That the presence of the blues is great in gospel music should not be surprising given that gospel's most prominent composers and artists were themselves intimately connected with the blues (see Chapter 4). In notated gospel music of the 1930s we find the blues scale and blue notes prominently represented. The opening of Ezekiel Gibson and Elmer Ruffner's "I Claim Jesus First and That's Enough for Me," for example, is based on a D-hexatonic blues scale, though the composition is written (ostensibly) in F major. This illustrates the same type of blues/pentatonic conjunction seen in Waller's "Ain't Misbehavin'," though the blues element here is much more prominent. In the chorus of Thomas A. Dorsey's "I Can't Forget It, Can You?," the presence of the D blues scale is even more strongly felt, despite the fact that, like the Ruffner compositions, the work is written in F major (Example 3.12).

Example 3.12. "I Can't Forget It, Can You?" (Tommy Dorsey)

## Blues Elements in White
## Post-1950 Popular Music

Blues elements were eminently prevalent in the rhythm and blues of the late thirties and forties, and the post-1950 popular styles based upon the blues. Boogie-woogie bass patterns were heard in early rhythm and blues. Blue notes, the blues scale, and the blues form were also integral aspects of rhythm and blues and virtually all subsequent post-1950 black popular styles.

White commercial styles after 1950 showed the same blues influences as pre-1950 white popular styles. However, blues influences are more apparent in most post-1950 white styles—particularly rock and roll. These influences are seen by way of:

1. a more frequent use of blue notes in singing styles and written compositions;

2. a greater use of blues-derived harmonies and harmonic progressions;

3. the use of boogie-woogie derived bass patterns in rock and roll;

4. a more frequent use of the hexatonic blues scale or melodies showing its influence;

5. the use of the blues form as the basis of compositions or forms derived from it.

Many hit songs of the era were "covers" of R&B numbers by white acts, so they naturally showed blues influences. Even songs written by white songwriters—like Leiber and Stoller, for example—were often written in the style of R&B hits. For example, the duo's "Hound Dog," made popular in 1956 by Elvis Presley, was originally recorded by (and written for) R&B artist "Big" Mama Thornton. It has blue notes written into the melody, uses blues harmonies, and follows the blues form. Other hits of the 1950s written and/or recorded by white artists show some of the same features, for example, "Rock Around The Clock" (1955), "Blue Suede Shoes" (1956), and "Jailhouse Rock" (1957).

The 1960s saw no decline in the use of blue notes and the blues scale by white popular artists and songwriters. The melody of the opening verse of the Beatles' "Love Me Do," for example, is derived from the blues scale, despite the absence of the flatted fifth step. The absence of the pitches A and E (scale steps 2 and 6, respectively), and the presence of $B^\flat$ in measures 18 and 20 against a $G^7$ harmony (a blue note), all strongly imply the blues scale.

With the increased influence of soul and gospel music, blues characteristics became progressively more prominent in the singing styles of white vocalists and in the writing styles of white songwriters. This influence continues to this day.

## Blues Elements in Classical Music

The influence of the blues is seen in the works of three eminent European classical composers—Igor Stravinsky, Darius Milhaud, and Maurice Ravel—principally in their use of blue notes and the blues scale. Of the three composers, Stravinsky's music shows less of this influence. In Milhaud's *La Création du Monde*, however, simulated blue notes are prominent in several sections of the score, particularly the fugue (Example 3.13). The relationship between an interior motive within the countersubject of this fugue and the principal motive of William C. Handy's "St. Louis Blues" is noteworthy. Concerning Maurice Ravel, blues elements are sporadically present in much of the music he composed during the last ten years of his life. They are particularly prominent in his Concerto in G.

Example 3.13. "La Création du Monde" fugue theme (Darius Milhaud)

European-American classical composers since the 1920s have also experimented with the blues, albeit sporadically. In the hands of three composers—George Gershwin, Leonard Bernstein, and to a lesser degree, Aaron Copland—the results have been impressive. Like their European counterparts, the blues/classical experimentations of Gershwin and Bernstein have centered more upon the creative employment of blue notes or aspects of the blues scale within larger symphonic structures. Successful examples of the latter include works like Gershwin's Piano Preludes, *Porgy and Bess*, and *Rhapsody in Blue*, and Bernstein's *Prelude, Fugue, and Riffs*.

The principal black exponent of the blues in classical music was William Grant Still (1895–1978). His most noted work in this genre was his *Afro-American Symphony*. The opening theme of this work is a paradigmatic blues, both in its formative design and its melody—which is derived from the conventional hexatonic blues scale (Example 3.14). Still's orchestration of the theme is suggestive of banjo strumming, an instrument associated with traditional black folk music. Because of these, and other conspicuous Afrocentric features, the *Afro-American Symphony* has remained a popular and frequently performed composition since its creation in the early 1930s.

(Trumpet in B♭)

Example 3.14. "Afro-American Symphony" (William Grant Still)

In Chapter 14 we will discuss the blues influence in Still's *Afro-American Symphony* in greater depth in addition to the blues influences found in the works of other classical composers.

## CHAPTER 4

# GOSPEL MUSIC

**A**FRICAN AMERICAN gospel music is a blues-influenced religious style that was developed sometime between the late 1920s and early 1930s. The composer who influenced its development more than any other was Thomas Dorsey (1899–1993). The musical roots of black gospel music, however, are found in the musical practices of black Holiness and Sanctified churches, and specifically in the musical innovations of the Reverend Charles Albert Tindley.

The Holiness churches (also known as Sanctified, Pentecostal, or folk churches) took a far more liberal attitude toward the performance of African American religious music and the instruments used to accompany the performances than the mainstream Protestant black churches, who considered the cultivation of vernacular performance practices and the use of instrumentation associated with secular styles sinful and inappropriate. The practices encouraged by Holiness churches included:

1. rhythmic hand clapping and foot stomping;
2. unrestrained African vocality;
3. African-derived rhythms, textures, and performance practices;
4. musical accompaniment by piano (or organ), guitar, tambourine, triangle, and drums.

The liberal attitude adopted by the Holiness churches resulted ultimately in their separation from the mainstream black churches; but this same attitude was the reason why these churches were often able to attract large congregations.

## History

The first key popularizer of gospel music was Charles Albert Tindley (1859–1933). Tindley sponsored concerts beginning in 1902 that spread the gospel style and is also credited as the first person to publish gospel songs that included both text and music. Tindley's songs, arranged by F. A. Clark and Tindley himself, were strongly influenced by spirituals (see Chapter 2). In the anthology *Gospel Pearls* his composition "Stand By Me" was published as a spiritual.[1] It was, in fact, the spiritual-like quality of his gospel hymns that contributed to their popularity. Musicologist Jon Michael Spencer writes:

> [I]t was understandable that the gospel hymns of Tindley would be readily and warmly received. Written in the vernacular characteristic of the spirituals, Tindley's hymns captured the mood of disconsolation among the black urban population. They expressed their own ethnic brand of hope, cheer, love, and pity, quite distinct from the classic Methodist hymns.[2]

According to Tilford Brooks, "various Holiness groups used Tindley's songs as models and began to create a repertory of religious songs characterized by free interpolation on the part of the congregation and rhythmic instrumental accompaniment."[3] Tindley's gospel hymns show a strong pentatonic influence (Example 4.1). This is a feature they share with spirituals, in addition to their mood and the vernacular manner in which they were performed. The harmonizations of Tindley's works are consistent with later gospel arrangements. The harmonies are mainly based on Western common practice conventions with emphasis on the primary chords: I, IV, and V. Secondary domi-

Example 4.1. "Leave It There" (Charles Tindley)

nants occur sporadically, the most common of these are V⁷/IV and V⁷/V; the vernacular root progression IV to I is common. In notated form, however, Tindley's melodies are not syncopated and only rarely feature the accenting of normally unstressed syllables or words—as spirituals and gospel music typically do. A single rhythm pattern (homorhythm) governs chords and melody; contrapuntal lines in these compositions are rare. Neither are the texts of Tindley's melodies based upon black dialect, as are spirituals.

The second key name in the history of gospel music is Thomas Dorsey. His career as a blues pianist began in Atlanta when he was about ten years old. As a teenager Dorsey honed his skills by playing in stomps, bordellos, and house parties, ultimately developing for himself a considerable reputation among his colleagues—one that earned for him the nickname "Barrelhouse Tom." He left for Chicago in 1916 with the hope of enhancing his musical career and settled there permanently in 1919.

Dorsey's blues background prepared him for the innovations he would later bring to gospel music. He survived in Chicago as a relatively obscure artist who championed a conservative, gutbucket style of blues pianism. He came into prominence in 1923 as a blues composer when Monette Moore recorded two of his compositions: "I Just Want a Daddy I Can Call My Own" and "Muddy Water Blues." In the same year Joseph "King" Oliver recorded Dorsey's "Riverside Blues." Between 1923 and 1926 Dorsey toured with Gertrude "Ma" Rainey as her accompanist and arranger. In 1928, under the name "Georgia Tom," Dorsey wrote and recorded a blues titled "It's Tight Like That," which became a huge hit.

Dorsey showed no interest in religious music before September 1921, when he heard Professor W. M. Nix render a soul-stirring performance of "I Do, Don't You" at the National Baptist Convention.[4] Inspired by Nix's performance and by the gospel hymns of Charles Tindley, Dorsey began writing gospel songs. His first gospel composition, "If I Don't Get There," was copyrighted in 1922 (Example 4.2). After 1930 Dorsey left the world of the blues and turned to gospel composition exclusively.

Dorsey's contributions to the evolution of black gospel music are many. Gospel music historian Michael W. Harris notes that Dorsey is the principal person responsible for shaping the solo gospel blues idiom and popularizing it through his published arrangements.[5] He is also credited with merging blues performance practices with existing Afro-vernacular vocal practices. Other contributions credited to Dorsey include coining the term *gospel song*, co-organizing the first gospel chorus (1931); cofounding the National Convention of Gospel Choirs and Choruses (1932); and establishing the first publishing company dedicated to the sale of gospel music: the Dorsey House of Music (1932). Among Dorsey's most memorable compositions are "Precious Lord, Take My Hand," and "There'll Be Peace in the Valley."

Example 4.2. "If I Don't Get There" (Thomas Dorsey)

*continued*

Example 4.2. *Continued*

## Performance Traditions in African American Gospel Music

African American gospel music is expressed by way of three performance traditions: solo, quartet, and choral styles. The solo gospel style is characterized by the prudent use of the attributes of African vocality, particularly turns, melismas, hollers, moans, and other guttural effects, and microtonal inflections (blue notes). As previously mentioned, the solo gospel tradition, as a blues-influenced idiom, traces back essentially to Thomas Dorsey. The popularity of solo gospel singing increased during the 1930s and 1940s with the rise of professional gospel vocalists like Mahalia Jackson (1911–1972) and Rosetta Tharpe (1921–1973). Tharpe was among the first gospel singers to sign with a major record company. Great solo gospel vocalists, families, and groups who came into prominence after 1950 include James Cleveland, Andrea Crouch, Shirley Caesar, Edwin Hawkins, Al Green, Take Six, the Winans, and Kirk Franklin.

The gospel quartet tradition also came into prominence during the 1920s and 1930s. Gospel quartets during this time were generally a cappella ensembles and were typically male. Male quartets usually consisted of a first and second tenor, a baritone, and a bass. Their repertoires included hymns, jubilee songs or spirituals, popular songs, and newly composed compositions sung in the popular-harmony tradition (such as later used by secular groups like the Mills Brothers), accompanied by percussive effects like rhythmic hand clapping.

The melody of quartet-style gospel songs was most often sung by the first tenor; sometimes, however, the melody was taken by the baritone or bass. The lead vocalist generally rendered the melody in an extemporized, highly emotional style.[6] The other voices generally supplied a simple rhythmic or sustained harmonic accompaniment to the melody. These accompaniments often consisted of a phrase derived from the text of the composition, either reiterated constantly or mildly embellished. The text for sustained harmonic backgrounds was often based on a vowel sound; the vowel *o*, as in wh*o*, was quite common.

The quartet tradition continued to evolve through the 1940s, 1950s, and 1960s, but was not always rendered literally by a four-voiced vocal ensemble; quintets and sextets also became common. Instrumental combos comprising piano or organ, guitar, and bass accompanying the vocal groups became progressively more common. As the vocal ensembles became more secularized and commercialized, the harmonic, melodic, and rhythmic aspects of their styles became increasingly more reflective of jazz and other Afro-vernacular influences.

From their proliferation in the 1930s to the present, the popularity of gospel choirs never waned. We've previously noted some of the organizational contributions Dorsey made to the development of the gospel chorus tradition in the 1930s. Dorsey's musical contribution to choral gospel music, however, seems to be the same as his contribution to solo gospel singing; that is, the introduction of blues-derived performance techniques.[7]

Gospel choral singing is generally rendered homorhythmically (a single rhythm governs all parts). Sometimes the chorus serves as an accompaniment to a solo vocalist. At other times, the chorus is the featured medium and is itself accompanied by piano. The popularity of choral gospel singing from the mid-1970s onward is reflected in the steady increase of gospel choirs affiliated with college and university music departments. From the 1970s to the 1990s gospel choirs began appearing increasingly with noted symphony orchestras, usually in conjunction with pops programs or programs featuring Afrocentric or vernacular repertoires.

## Characteristics of Black Gospel Music

Gospel melodies are sung in an extemporized or improvisational style. Turns, blue notes, melismas, and guttural effects are common among solo vocalists. Melodies of notated gospel scores from the 1930s through the 1960s show strong pentatonic influences. The hexatonic blues scale is also frequently present or implicated in many of these scores.

The harmonic language of gospel music through the 1950s consists essentially of standard chords based on the key in which the piece is written, embellished by diminished and secondary dominant chords and occasional chromatic progressions. Vernacular root progressions are common, particularly IV to I (or the blues-derived IV[7] to I), and less frequently ii to I (Example 4.3). Modulations generally do not occur, though gospel compositions written in minor keys sometimes reference the relative major in ways that suggested a brief modulation. Harmonies that venture beyond the key occur as a result of blue notes in the melody or passing tones in the inner voices or the bass. These chords are usually borrowed from the parallel minor—for example, the iv or $^{\flat}$VI in major.

In the late 1940s more radical harmonic progressions began to appear, influenced by contemporary developments in jazz. In measure

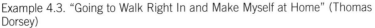

Example 4.3. "Going to Walk Right In and Make Myself at Home" (Thomas Dorsey)

four of Thomas Dorsey's "He Is the Same Today" (copyrighted in 1949), for example, the tonic chord—G major—progresses to an $E^\flat$ dominant seventh in the following measure (Example 4.4), a *substitute dominant.* The substitute dominant was a common part of the harmonic lexicon of bebop (see Chapter 3), the jazz style in vogue during the time Dorsey's composition was written. Thus the presence of the $E^{\flat 7}$ chord in Dorsey's composition suggests a contemporary jazz harmonic influence.

The augmented-seventh chord—also known as the minor-seventh sharp-five, **7(+5)**—was also an established part of the jazz and blues harmonic lexicons by 1950. Its presence in gospel music, however, was atypical before this time. In Mary G. Rubin's "His Name Is Ev'rything to Me," copyrighted in 1950, this chord is used often. The augmented-seventh chord is unusual because it may serve either a dominant or non-dominant function, depending upon how it is employed. The presence of the augmented-seventh chord confirms the jazz influence in that it too was a chord often used by contemporary jazz composers. Augmented-

Example 4.4. "He Is the Same Today" (Thomas Dorsey)

seventh chords, irregularly resolving diminished chords, substitute dominants, and other advanced chords are found sporadically in many published gospel compositions written during this period.

Published gospel scores from the 1930s through the 1960s were commonly written in verse/chorus form. Typically the verse preceded the chorus, but the opposite arrangement was not infrequent. Special choruses, optional choruses, and codas were sometimes added.

The tempos of published gospel scores varied. Some were sung fast, some in a moderate tempo, others slowly, and others in a free-rhythmic fashion. Expressions like *ad lib.*, *slowly ad lib.*, *rubato*, or *recitative* indicated an arrhythmic approach to the song. In some cases several tempos were called for in the same composition. Typically, such compositions began with a slow or recitative-like introduction, then changed to a fixed tempo with the start of the verse or chorus. Gospel works written in a recitative or free rhythmic style sometimes called on the piano or organ to supply improvised embellishments. These embellishments took the form of interpolated chords, scalar passages, arpeggios, broken chords, and so on. In some gospel compositions the *ad lib.* function of the piano was specified.

Gospel compositions up to the mid-1960s were generally written in duple meters. Simple duple meter appears to be more common than compound duple meter. Many works written in simple duple meter, however, were often performed in compound duple meter; that is, works written in meters like $\frac{2}{4}$ or $\frac{4}{4}$ were often performed with an underlying feeling of $\frac{6}{8}$ or $\frac{12}{8}$. Compositions in simple triple meter—for example, $\frac{3}{4}$ and $\frac{6}{4}$—were written less commonly, but do exist.

## Other Gospel Composers

Lucie Campbell (1885–1963) was a contemporary of Charles Tindley and Thomas Dorsey. Her career as a gospel composer extended from around the late teens through her death. "The Lord Is My Shepherd" (Example 4.5) was copyrighted in 1921, a year earlier than Dorsey's first

### The Lord Is My Shepherd

*Dedicated to my Mother, June, 1919.*

Example 4.5. "The Lord Is My Shepherd" (Lucie Campbell)

*continued*

Example 4.5 *continued*

copyrighted work.[8] As suggested by the title, the text was inspired by the Twenty-third Psalm. It is written in a homorhythmic style, similar to those of Tindley. However, the composition contains many instances of syncopation in the melody and accentuation of normally unstressed syllables. Its harmonies are also unusual for this early period: vernacular progressions and root position and inverted diminished passing chords are all characteristic of later gospel writing.

Another eminent gospel composer was the Reverend Dr. William Herbert Brewster (1897–1987). Brewster's compositions, according to Eileen Southern, are distinctive for their use of "melismatic cadenzas, vivid biblical images, and tempo changes."[9] One of Brewster's most outstanding compositions is "How Far Am I From Canaan" (Example 4.6). This work is, in effect, a gospel tone poem based upon a story suggested by the title. Brewster wrote:

> The title of this song was suggested by a friend—It was suggested from an imaginary picturesque scene of the Children of Israel after 40 years wandering in the wilderness arriving at the Jordan river. Tired, weak, footsore, and weary, they must have asked the question—"How Much Farther?"—"We've been on this journey so long"—"How far are we from Canaan?"[10]

The "wandering in the wilderness" nature of the work is aptly depicted by the slow, *ad lib.* tempo. This feature, in conjunction with the imagistic text and the exclusively pentatonic melody, makes it a strongly convincing work. Brewster was well qualified to treat gospel music in this manner, for in addition to being a composer of considerable gifts, he also wrote religious plays and poetry. These talents merged to produce biblical pageant plays in which compositions like "How Far Am I From Canaan" were often featured.

"How Far Am I From Canaan" is important for other reasons. During the late 1940s, Sam Cooke, while on tour with the gospel group the Highway QC's, visited Brewster in Memphis. Daniel Wolff writes of Brewster's claim that Sam Cooke "would come around to be 'lectured' on composition."[11] Brewster further claimed that "How Far Am I From

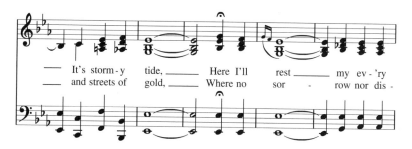

Example 4.6. "How Far Am I From Canaan" (W. Herbert Brewster)

Canaan" was a composition that Cooke came to Memphis to learn. The piece would later be used in a sing-off between Cooke and LeRoi Taylor to test which of the two young singers would be best qualified to become a colead singer with the Soul Stirrers, one of the gospel world's most renowned vocal ensembles at that time.[12] Cooke not only won the position over Taylor, but a short time later began his career with the group by performing the same composition.

Other outstanding gospel composers between 1930 and 1960 include Sallie Martin (b. 1896), Roberta Martin (1907–1969), and James Cleveland (1931–1991).

## Derivative Influences

Modern gospel styles are virtually indistinguishable from contemporary secular commercial styles. Highly stylized arrangements featuring elaborate jazz voicings, complex chromatic harmonies, adventurous modulations, and lush, sophisticated orchestrations are common. The complex nature of contemporary gospel harmony is evidence in the opening phrases of Kirk Franklin's "Savior, More Than Life" (Example 4.7). Supporting the unison melody is a harmonic language characterized by the use of diatonic and chromatic progressions in which upper extensions are common. Making the progressions all the more dramatic are the frequent occurrences of syncopated harmonic rhythms. These syncopated harmonies sometimes match the melody rhythmically and other times contrast with it. The principal difference between contemporary gospel styles and their secular commercial counterparts lie mainly in their texts—the former obviously being religious.

Since the 1970s gospel influences have found their way into genres not traditionally associated with gospel music, like television and movie scores, musicals, vernacular cantatas and oratorios, and, less frequently,

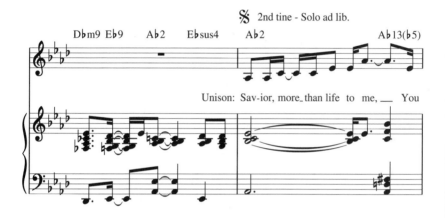

Example 4.7. "Savior, More Than Life" (Kirk Franklin)

classical music. For example, the musical score for the acclaimed 1970s television miniseries *Roots*, authored by Quincy Jones and others, featured an original gospel composition titled "What Shall I Do?" This composition was coauthored by Quincy Jones and gospel legend James Cleveland. In the late 1980s a new genre known as gospel rap emerged (see Chapter 13).

Gospel musicals since the 1980s have grown in popularity. *Mama I Want to Sing* and *Born to Sing* are two recent examples of successful off-Broadway musicals. Gospel influences in vernacular cantatas have also proliferated. An example of the latter is Valerie Caper's *Sing About Love*. Gospel choirs appear regularly in music videos as background choral groups for pop singers—black and white. For example, Madonna's at the time scandalous video for her song "Like a Prayer" prominently featured a gospel choir.

Gospel influences are rare in extended vernacular and classical compositions, but they are occasionally found. An excellent example in an extended vernacular composition is *Handel's Messiah: A Soulful Celebration*. This work, appearing in 1992, was a vernacular reworking of George F. Handel's *Messiah* and featured an impressive gathering of contemporary jazz, popular, gospel, and rap artists. Different vernacular styles (jazz, rap, ragtime, big band, gospel, and so on) were used as a basis of the new arrangements of Handel's music but because the text was religious, the general musical effect, however unintentional, was consistent with contemporary gospel music. The recording project was conducted by Quincy Jones and coproduced by Norman Miller, Gail Hamilton, and Mervyn Warren. The participating artists included George Duke, Stevie Wonder, Howard Hewitt, Patti Austin, Tramaine Hawkins, Dianne Reeves, and Take Six.

Unlike spirituals and the blues, true gospel influences are rarely used by African American composers as a basis for, or as an integral structural aspect of, their style. An important exception is found in the music of Diane L. White (b. 1963). Her background as a gospel composer, singer, and conductor is reflected in her classical compositions by the use of harmonic color and by the rhythmic intensity and character of her music.

# The Jazz Aesthetic

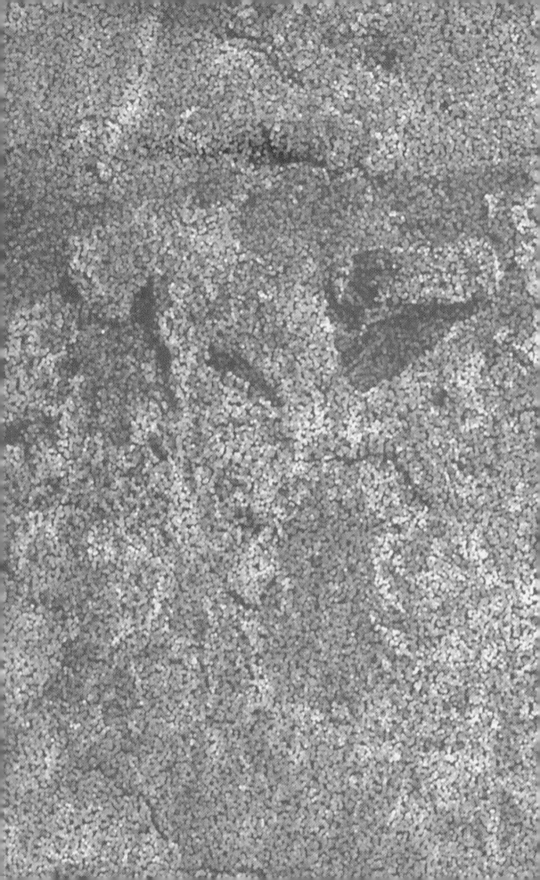

## CHAPTER 5

# THE EMERGENCE OF RAGTIME

**T**HE TWO MOST significant indigenous stylistic developments to emerge before 1900 were the folk blues (see Chapter 3) and *ragtime*. Ragtime came into existence shortly after the Civil War, essentially as a folk form. It did not, however, begin its ascent towards national and international prominence until the early 1890s. Ragtime resulted from a synthesis of specific African-derived melodic, rhythmic, and textural idioms with European-derived harmony and form. The so-called classic ragtime of the 1890s through the 1920s was primarily written for and played on the piano, although it was adapted to other instruments and ensembles.

Ragtime style consisted essentially of a syncopated melody, in duple meter, which moved against a nonsyncopated bass. The harmonies occurred alternately with the bass on the weak pulses of the measure. The syncopated melody moved twice as fast as the nonsyncopated bass and the harmony. It is this rhythmic stratification (or layering) that is the strongest African element in ragtime.

The form of most notated rag compositions consisted of from four to six sections that grouped themselves into a higher binary design. These sections were expressed as either ABA | C; ABA | CD; ABA | CDE; or ABA | CDC.[1] The completion of the repeated A section concluded the first part of the binary structure. Sections consisting of sixteen bars were common, though sections of greater length did occur. All but the recapitulated A section were usually repeated. Contrasting sections were sometimes written in related keys.[2]

## Types of Ragtime

There are three types of piano rag compositions. The first is a folk-based, improvisational approach that resulted in a style sometimes called *jig piano* by its practitioners. The second was the most popular form of the music, one we may label *commercial rag*. The third constituted an artistic approach to ragtime, resulting in a style that became known as *classic rag*.

Folk ragtime, or *jig piano rag*, was ragtime's first manifestation. It was cultivated principally by self-taught black itinerants who performed in bawdy houses, saloons, and honky-tonks in small towns and larger cities throughout the Eastern seaboard, and in the South, Southwest, and Midwest. The jig pianists provided music that accompanied the highly syncopated black dances prevalent in these regions.

Most of this music was not "written down," but improvised on the spot. Sometimes popular songs or folk songs served as a basis for the improvisation. That jig pianists provided music principally for entertainment purposes suggests that their harmonic language was a simple one. The melodies too, in their preimprovised form, were probably simple in their structure and based upon (or strongly influenced by) common five-note (pentatonic) scales. Given the diversity in the structure and pace of the popular black dances, it is reasonable to assume that jig piano rag may have been performed in a broader set of tempos than those used by subsequent ragtime styles.

Given its improvisational nature, form in jig piano rag was undoubtedly variable, not conforming to the structural models that characterized later rag styles—at least not consistently. To this extent most jig piano rags probably had a single theme and consequently expressed only one emotion. Modulation was probably not a common feature.

Unlike jig piano music, *commercial ragtime* compositions were notated and published. They consisted of multiple sections, with each section featuring two-phrase or four-phrase themes that were often repeated.

Sections were often contrasted by different keys and modalities, that is, major versus minor. Melodic phrases were usually symmetrical. The harmonies were principally simple major/minor chords corresponding to the key of the melody but were embellished occasionally by secondary dominants or leading tone chords. Chromaticism was used incidentally and more with respect to melody than harmony. The melodies of commercial rag compositions were tuneful and rhythmic, their character often shaped by lilting, highly syncopated rhythmic motives. Unity and coherence were often imparted to these melodies by the frequent repetition of the motives.

Though commercial rag compositions emphasized directness and simplicity in all their technical aspects, except perhaps rhythm, this simplicity did not necessarily result in a simple product. Effectively composed commercial rags often showed profound aesthetic and compositional elegance. A good example of one of the better commercial rags is Tom Turpin's historic "Harlem Rag" (Example 5.1). It was the first ragtime composition published by an African American composer, appearing eleven months after William H. Krell's "Mississippi Rag," the first published ragtime composition.

The "Harlem Rag" opens with two symmetrical, four-measure phrases that are repeated. The first two measures introduce a motive that provides the basic harmonic and rhythmic shape for the entire opening theme. Although the second phrase opens with a new melodic idea built around the pentatonic scale, it returns to an altered version of the opening motive in its concluding two measures.

The harmonic structure of the opening theme is simple and predictable, but its harmonic rhythm is not. The normal, leisurely half-note harmonic rhythm heard in much ragtime is established in the first four measures. It doubles in measure five to movement in quarter-notes. After a brief pause in measures six and seven, the harmonic accompaniment returns with movement in eighth-notes, just in time for the arrival of the

Example 5.1. "Harlem Rag" (Tom Turpin)

final cadence. This methodically composed acceleration of the harmonic rhythm greatly contributes to the rhythmic pacing of the theme.

The most artistically exalted expression of nineteenth- and early twentieth-century ragtime was called *classic rag*. Like its commercial rag counterpart, it was a literate, multithematic style. Its technical and aesthetic features, however, were more sophisticated. The melodies, for example, were not only highly syncopated but also offered intricate and varied motives and were generally richer in their lyrical breadth—often to the point of exhibiting an introspective quality. Folk elements were

Tom Turpin

still present in classic rag melodies but were treated in a more disguised or abstract manner.

The opening theme of Scott Joplin's "Maple Leaf Rag" demonstrates many of these features (Example 5.2). The theme is in A♭ major and consists of four phrases, structured abcc; that is, the second phrase contrasts with the opening phrase and is followed by yet another contrasting phrase which is repeated. This curiously asymmetrical pattern contributes much to the uniqueness of the theme.

Joplin packs the opening theme with drama. A catchy melody consisting of two, two-measure motives constitutes the first phrase, a. The second phrase, b, occupies the next four measures and introduces new material that serves as a transition for the final two phrases. The second part of phrase two (the second motive) begins in the bass register with an arpeggiated minor triad. But by successively repeating this arpeggio at the next octave, the motive is launched to the highest registral point in the opening theme, where it meets seamlessly with the third phrase, c. The fourth phrase, c¹, is a near verbatim repetition of the third, but at an octave lower. With the exception of the sporadic occurrence of the pitch c♭, the melody notes of the last two phrases outline an A♭ pentatonic scale (a♭, b♭, c, e♭, and f). To enhance the harmonic drama of the work, Joplin embellishes the essentially diatonic structure of the theme with secondary leading tone chords, and chords borrowed from the parallel natural minor.

Thus, by way of the skillful use of diverse but highly unified motivic material, prudently delivered harmonic and melodic chromaticism, and folk scalar material, Joplin in sixteen brief measures constructs an impressively dramatic opening theme. He also lays the foundation for material presented in other parts of the composition. For example, the second theme—beginning in measure seventeen—is clearly derived from the opening theme. The rhythmic structure of both themes is almost identical, and there is also, noticeably, a similarity of contour between the opening motive of the first theme and that of the second theme. Similar rhythmic interrelationships also exist in subsequent themes.

*continued*

Example 5.2. "Maple Leaf Rag" (Scott Joplin)

Example 5.2. *Continued*

There are other features that distinguish classic rag from commercial rag. For example, classic rag generally exemplifies greater textural variety. This often results from a greater use of counterpoint (two melodies stated at the same time) and generally from a stronger focus on the melodic development of the composition. Classic rag composers also were more daring in their use of harmony. Consequently, chromatic, unexpected, and extended progressions (such as ninth and sixth chords) and daring chromatic modulations are all common features of classic rag.

Classic ragtime is generally associated with three individuals: Scott Joplin, James Scott, and Joseph Lamb—the latter a European-American composer. Other notable contributors to the literature include Scott Hayden, Artie Matthews, Arthur Marshall, Louis Chavin, and Eubie Blake. Though James Scott's works do not show the same level of complexity as those of Joplin, his skillful use of upper extensions in the melody, resulting in implied ninth, eleventh, and thirteenth chords, brings to his works an unquestioned elegance and uniqueness. The use of these extensions in such an early work is noteworthy in that it foreshadows their later use in jazz. For example, in his "Frog Legs Rag" (Example 5.3), Scott emphasizes his unusual thirteenth-note extension by placing it on the syncopated second note of measures one, five, nine, and thirteen.

Scott's harmonic language in "Frog Legs Rag" is essentially diatonic, with a sparse use of secondary structures. He makes the harmonies more

Example 5.3. "Frog Legs Rag" (James Scott)

interesting by occasionally presenting the chords in one of their inversions before stating them in root position. The harmonic effect is enhanced further when the inversion in the bass occurs simultaneously with an extension in the melody, as it does in measures seventeen and eighteen. Scott also uses inversions to maintain harmonic motion—usually quarter note movement—during periods when the harmonic rhythm is longer.[3]

The better rag compositions of Arthur Marshall (1881–1968), a younger contemporary of Joplin and his first student in Sedalia, were often characterized by their harmonic and rhythmic ingenuity. In "Kinklets" (Example 5.4), for example, the abab symmetry of the opening theme is counterbalanced by diverse motivic material that shapes each phrase. At no point in either phrase is a motive immediately repeated. The results are phrases striking in their rhythmic interest and activity.

Symmetry in the construction of classic rag themes was not an axiom followed by every noted rag composer, as Marshall's "The Pippin" demonstrates. The phrase structure of the opening theme is abcadc[1]; in other words, there are six phrases, with the last phrase, c[1], repeating the opening of the first c phrase but employing a different conclusion. These phrases also move between the key of F minor and A♭ major, adding to the contrasting natures of the individual melodies.

The design of "The Pippin" is also quite interesting. It consists of four sections; not the typical five or more that characterize the rags of Joplin. The form is ABCA. The final A section, however, restates only the last three phrases of the opening A section, then repeats the last phrase of the theme, resulting in an abcc phrase design. The A and B sections are in the tonic key of A♭ major; the C section is in D♭ major; the final A section returns to the original key.

The ragtime compositions of Artie Matthews are noteworthy for their pianistic virtuosity and for the elegance of their melodic and harmonic chromaticism. Nowhere are these attributes better exemplified than in his "Pastime Rags" (Example 5.5). He composed five of them

**Introd. Moderato**

*Two Step*

Example 5.4. "Kinklets" (Arthur Marshall)

Example 5.5. "Pastime Rags No. 1" (Artie Matthews)

between 1913 and 1918. These rags mirror a number of common styles of the day; the third is particularly interesting for its Spanish-tinged melody and rhythms.

## Scott Joplin

The central figure in rag music was Scott Joplin (1868–1917). Joplin was born in Texarkana, Texas. His mother played the banjo and his father the violin. Joplin's musical gifts became evident when he was a child. To encourage his development, his mother purchased a piano for him, and he taught himself to play. Joplin subsequently studied with a piano teacher living in the area who taught him to read music. As Joplin's skills matured so did his interest in becoming a professional pianist. This fact, coupled with his growing interest in the infectious vernacular musical influences around him, motivated him to leave Texarkana during his adolescence.

Joplin arrived in St. Louis in 1885 and made his living for the next eight years as a jig pianist while intermittently traveling to other cities. In 1893 he met Otis Saunders in Chicago. Saunders, and later the Turpin brothers, encouraged Joplin to write down and publish his compositions. The theoretical training Joplin received at the George-Smith College for Negroes after 1897 facilitated his growth as a composer.

Joplin's first big compositional success came with the publication of "Maple Leaf Rag" in 1899. This composition—probably Joplin's first true ragtime masterpiece—was followed by dozens of other masterfully composed piano works, including "The Entertainer" (1902), "The Chrysanthemum" (1904), "Bethena" (1905), "Gladiolus Rag" (1907), "Solace" (1909), and "Stoptime Rag" (1910).

"The Entertainer" is, among other things, a superlative example of how Joplin used texture and registration to contrast successively stated motives—in a manner reminiscent of call and response. As previously noted, the opening motive of the first theme is given as a single melodic line (measures five and six), but is *answered* by the second motive doubled at the third and octave (measures seven and eight).[4] This pattern continues for the next two phrases. The same technique is used in the second theme but with the pattern reversed. It is also found in subsequent themes, though in a less obvious manner. Another striking feature is the D♭–F–G♯–B chord, found near the end of the third theme (measure fifty-six), which bears a striking sonic resemblance to a chord later known as a tritone substitution (substitute dominant) when applied to the early blues, and to swing, bebop, and postbebop styles (see Chapter 3).

The "Chrysanthemum"—subtitled "an Afro-American Intermezzo"—is noteworthy for the perfect symmetry of its form, the elegant manner in which each theme is given unity and coherence, and the manner in which the various themes interrelate. The work is written in an expanded binary form constituted by an ABA | CDC structure. In each of the two larger parts of the form the contrasting theme—B of part one, and D of part two—modulate to a different key but return to the key of the preceding theme simultaneously with its recapitulation. The recapitulated A and C themes are stated in their entirety but are not repeated. The most conspicuous difference between the sections is a result of the fact that the D theme is in a minor key, in contrast to the major key of the B theme.

"Gladiolus Rag" and "Euphonic Sounds" are exquisite examples of Joplin's mature style. This mature phase of Joplin's development was characterized by the occasional de-emphasis of the oom-pah bass pattern, the profuse use of chromatic harmony, and the use of unexpected and surprising chord progressions. The 1909 composition, "Solace," exemplifies Joplin's stylistic flexibility. This work is subtitled "A Mexican Serenade" and, by way of its tango-like oom-pah pattern, exemplifies beautifully Joplin's interest in Latin musical influences.

Scott Joplin's greatest musical achievement was his opera *Treemonisha*. This work was the second of two operas and the last of a set of extended compositions that began with his ballet *The Ragtime Dance.* To consider *Treemonisha* an operatic masterpiece would be somewhat irresponsible, because the work is replete with dramatic frailties. But as a purely musical and philosophical endeavor Joplin's effort is singular. In this regard we may cite his elegant use of African American references in the opera. He referred to various traditional dance forms, including a ring-play and a Corn Huskers dance (in section three). The music of the Corn Husker's dance exemplified the call-and-response pattern, as it also did in the section titled "Good Advice" (section nine) where Parson Altalk's *call* is answered by the the congregation.

His use of the pentatonic scale is striking in several sections, beginning with the principle theme of the overture (Example 5.6). The opening motive of this theme is identified by Joplin as "The . . . principal strain in the Opera," and "represents the happiness of the people when they feel free from the conjurors and their spells of superstition."[5] The choral response given to Parson Altalk's call in section nine of the opera is also based on a pentatonic motive.

Also impressive is Joplin's use of black dialect in the opera. The use of black dialect as a rhetorical device was common in the poetry, novels, and short stories of early-twentieth-century African American writers, and remains so today. Like his literary contemporaries, Joplin used black dialect for characterization, but he used it selectively. The protagonist, Treemonisha, uses no dialect at all. Those educated by her use black dialect sparingly, while the antagonists, led by Zodzetrick, speak almost

Example 5.6. *Treemonisha* (Scott Joplin)

exclusively in dialect. It would appear that Joplin employed black dialect to rank his characters intellectually and morally in that the thickness of the characters' dialect corresponded to their degree of ignorance, inculcated superstition, and, in the case of the antagonists, their social parasitism and criminality.

The true value of Joplin's *Treemonisha*, however, is perhaps better seen from a different vantage point. *Treemonisha* constitutes one of the first large-scale African-derived musical compositions to admonish blacks to rise beyond the beliefs, values, and attitudes that inhibit their development. Few other contemporary efforts of similar scope were so morally and musically prodigious. The work also demonstrated the artistic, aesthetic, and dramatic potential of black music in that it did not, like so many other contemporary black efforts of similar scope, offer circumscriptive constructions of either black identity or black musical intellectuality. Instead it showed how the European/African duality of the African American could, when properly accessed, serve as a powerful vehicle for the loftiest of black musical and dramatic expressions.

## CHAPTER 6

# CLASSIC JAZZ

**R**AGTIME, as an autonomous style, continued well into the 1920s, concluding perhaps with the late efforts of Joplin's principal successor, James Scott, and transitional titans like James P. Johnson and Eubie Blake. Decades before its demise, however, ragtime—in conjunction with other folk influences—seeded the first manifestation of America's most important twentieth-century vernacular development: jazz.

The first jazz style is called *classic jazz.* It had two phases. The first came into existence in New Orleans, Louisiana, sometime before 1897 and lasted until about 1917. Job opportunities for New Orleans's musicians opened up in other parts of the country as news of the style spread and an audience for it grew. This was particularly true in Chicago, Illinois, after 1917, giving birth to what is often called the Chicago style or the second phase of the classic jazz era. This phase lasted until about 1930 before being completely usurped by the rapidly crystallizing trends that ushered in the next jazz era.

## Stylistic Attributes

Louis Armstrong considered folk songs and spirituals to be, in great measure, the source of jazz. There may be more to this claim than what has previously been suspected, particularly if we add popular styles to the mix; that the classic jazz style contained elements drawn from other popular, African American styles is unquestionable.

But what specifically constitutes the classic jazz style? The absence of recordings and other documented evidence makes impossible a definitive definition. However, based upon recordings by New Orleans artists after 1917, and the narrative accounts many artists have provided, we may surmise with relative assurance the following style features.

Though larger ensembles existed, the typical New Orleans group was a small ensemble, or combo, usually consisting of from five to seven players. The ensemble consisted of two parts: a rhythm section and a front line. The front line was usually composed of a trumpet, a clarinet, and sometimes a trombone. The trumpet improvised the main melody; the clarinet often provided a faster-moving, accompanying counter-melody. The trombone either offered a countermelodic accompaniment in a lower register or functioned as the bass instrument when no other bass was present. These parts were said to be "collectively improvised"; that is, the players would make up their parts as they performed, listening carefully to what the other lead parts were offering, so as to form a coherent whole. Solo improvisations were often extemporized or orna-mented versions of the basic melody rather than full-blown transforma-tions of it, as would be common in later periods. Thus, the improvisations by classic jazz artists were less evolved than those of later jazz artists.

In the front line, we see again the African-derived notion of melodic and rhythmic stratification, in that the simultaneous statement of three polyphonic *voices* existed on different levels of rhythmic density. However, besides rhythmic stratification, which also occurs in piano rag-time though on a less-sophisticated level, classic jazz offered registral (voices in different octaves) and timbral (voices with different sound qualities) stratification as well. The simultaneously stated melodies did not create a cacophonous or contentive effect. To the contrary, the aes-thetic mandate of each artist was to improvise his melody in a manner conducive to the realization of a type of rhythmic harmony or oneness with his coimprovisers.

It was the job of the rhythm section to counterbalance the polyphonic front line with a relatively constant rhythmic and harmonic accompaniment. The rhythm section consisted of (1) a fretted instrument (banjo or guitar); (2) a bass instrument (tuba, double bass, or trombone); and (3) a trap drummer. The piano was not an integral part of small ensembles in the New Orleans styles, though solo pianists were well represented. After 1917, however, the role of the pianist in the small ensemble became more prominent.

The bassist usually provided the rhythmic, harmonic pulse on the strong beat of the measure, often outlining the roots and fifths of harmonies and occasionally filling the interval between the two pitches extemporaneously. The fretted instrument often strummed all four beats of the measure, usually filling in the beats with the appropriate harmonies.[1] The drummer supported the other instruments with corresponding rhythmic patterns.

Form in classic jazz shows the influence of ragtime, the blues, and occasionally popular song structure. *Ragtime-influenced* classic jazz compositions are multisectional, with some sections modulating to related keys. Multi-improvisational sections were sometimes contrasted with sections in which a single soloist was preeminent, or a solo vocalist was introduced, or sectional playing in the front line was featured. Sectional playing was sometimes rendered in a duet-based, single-rhythm style, forecasting its similar use in swing.

The *blues* effect in classic jazz compositions is often realized more by their underlying I–IV–I–V–I or I–IV–I–V–IV–I harmonic patterns and twelve-bar metric structures than by the expected AAB blues phrase structure. This is particularly so in cases where the melody is rendered in a polyphonic improvisational style, which sometimes made the phrase structure hard to hear. In other instances, the blues melody is given in typical call-and-response fashion, but the answer is rendered by a polyphonic improvisation. The latter technique is typical of, but not exclusive to, vocal blues compositions.

The classic-jazz harmonies were basically diatonic, embellished sporadically by secondary structures and occasionally by upper extensions (sevenths, ninths, elevenths, and thirteenths) occurring in or against the underlying harmonies, and especially in extemporized renderings of the melody. In Louis Armstrong's performance of Lil Hardin's "Struttin' with Some Barbecue," for example, he strongly emphasizes the thirteenth extension in his solo in measures five and six (Example 6.1). Another occurrence of a thirteenth extension is in the harmony in measure eight—in this case the flat thirteenth—adding poignancy to the final cadence through this nondiatonic harmony (a harmony that is not found in the key). Another unusual touch is found in measure seven, where the player in effect performs an arpeggio of the supertonic chord (based on the second step of the scale), including the minor seventh and major ninth extensions.

As has been previously stated, though classic jazz was realized objectively in simple duple meter, the true metrical basis of classic jazz was really compound meter. That is, jazz was generally written (when written) in meters like $\frac{4}{4}$ or $\frac{2}{4}$, but stylistically interpreted in meters like $\frac{12}{8}$ or $\frac{6}{8}$.

Example 6.1. "Struttin' With Some Barbeque" (Lil Hardin)

106

## Early Cultivators

New Orleans jazz developed between 1897 and 1917 principally in the "pleasure houses" of Storyville, a red-light district in New Orleans created and legally ordained in 1897 to contain and thereby circumscribe the activities of prostitutes to a sectioned-off part of the city.[2] Two groups were principally responsible for the creation of this music: one was the blacks, the other the creoles of color.

The colored creoles—as a group distinct from both blacks and from whites of French and Spanish descent—trace their legal origin back to the early eighteenth century with the passage of the *Code Noir* of 1724, a black code that provided for the discretionary freedom of slaves by their white owners.[3] This law in effect gave a legal identity to the children born from liaisons of slave women and white slave owners. The period between 1725 and 1860 marked the economic and social rise of the creoles of color. By the first quarter of the nineteenth century, this group had amassed a prodigious economic power base, in comparison with the so-called negro (or pure black) population. Some owned cotton and sugar plantations; they were also well represented in most of the respectable professions. Some creoles, particularly those educated in France, acquired individual distinction in the sciences and the arts.

The Louisiana Legislative Code No. 111 effectively halted the economic ascension of the creoles of color by designating as "black" any person of African ancestry. This law provided, in effect, a moral license for the dismantling of the creoles' vast business interests and consequently facilitated the collapse of their economic and political power. As a result, creoles turned to other ways of making a living (specifically music making) which at one time had been merely hobbies or avocations for them.

The higher classes of creoles performed music of the Western classical tradition. Their approach to music making was refined, literate, contemplative, and governed by European aesthetic taste. But even these high-class creoles were aware of the music that was being performed by their darker-complexioned counterparts. Such a music had long been a feature of New Orleans culture. One highly prominent example was the music that accompanied the voodoo influenced dances of the blacks at Congo Square—a spectacle that didn't end until 1885.[4] Black vernacular music was also a prominent part of the church and social activities of the people, principally in the form of the spirituals and the blues.

These powerful black folk influences greatly transformed the popular music forms in vogue in New Orleans during the last quarter of the nineteenth century, creating a new musical style. The precise period of gestation for this new sound is not yet known, but its first manifestation as a style noticeably distinct from the constituent styles that shaped it is said to have occurred around 1894, when cornet player/bandleader "Buddy" Bolden gave a now-famous performance. Jack Buerkle and Danny Barker describe the event in this way:

> In the summer of 1894 [Buddy Bolden] got up in front of a crowd at Globe Hall and turned his cornet into an extension of his very soul as he wailed a blues number. His playing had some of the Congo Square ease and flavor, but it was something more, something new.[5]

Charles "Buddy" Bolden (1868–1931) was undoubtedly one of the most influential musicians in New Orleans up to about 1907. He played with a number of bands, and he played for all types of events in the black community. He is reputed to have been a cornetist of extraordinary power and volume, but his reign was unfortunately a brief one. Apparently suffering a mental breakdown, he was committed to an asylum around 1907 and remained there until his death. Before his illness, however, he had helped lay the foundation of a tradition that would be perpetuated and expanded by a host of his contemporaries and followers. This prestigious vanguard included artists like Bunk Johnson, Papa Celestin, Jelly Roll Morton, King Oliver, Sidney Bechet, Freddie Keppard, Kid Ory, Jimmy Noone, and later Daniel Louis Armstrong.

Willie Geary "Bunk" Johnson (1879–1949) was one of the earliest pioneers of New Orleans jazz. He is known for his exceptional cornet playing and his abilities for leading a band. He was highly respected by his fellow musicians, even if during his lifetime he did not achieve the same degree of fame as some of his colleagues. Johnson was rediscovered as a result of the Dixieland jazz revival in the 1940s, and returned to performing before his death.

Like Johnson, Oscar "Papa" Celestin (1884–1954) was also an early pioneer of the New Orleans jazz style. He was a bandleader of considerable note, having formed and led some of the most important bands in New Orleans, including the Original Tuxedo Orchestra in 1910 and the Tuxedo Brass Band in 1911. He worked with many of the leading black musicians of the period, including Clarence Williams, Jimmy Noone, and Louis Armstrong.

Sidney Bechet (1897–1959) was one of the giants of the early New Orleans school. He was the first jazz performer to gain fame on the soprano saxophone. In 1919, Bechet moved to New York and joined the Southern Syncopated Orchestra, with whom he traveled to Europe. While there he came into contact with European composers, who reportedly became interested in his playing. This fact is important considering the large number of jazz-influenced classical works that came into prominence after 1920. After his return to the United States in 1921, he recorded with Clarence Williams, Mamie Smith, and later with Duke Ellington. Bechet remained active in Europe and America until his death in Paris.

Ferdinand Joseph Morton, also known as Jelly Roll Morton (1885–1941), was the most important and influential of all the New Orleans jazz pianists, despite the relatively short period in which he was active there. He left New Orleans permanently in 1907. Morton's piano style exemplifies beautifully the early consolidation of ragtime and the blues. He was also one of the first great jazz composers—if not literally the first—to have written a number of jazz classics while active as a Storyville musician. His classics include the "New Orleans Blues," the

"King Porter Stomp," the "Jelly Roll Blues," and the "Wolverine Blues." Morton settled in Chicago in the teens and became a bandleader of note, recording with his group, the Red Hot Peppers, in the 1920s. Morton's band compositions were among the first full-scale arrangements for jazz band; his band members did not improvise, but followed his written parts. In this way, he forecast the sophisticated arrangements of Duke Ellington.

Like Morton, Edward "Kid" Ory's (1886–1973) talents extended into the compositional arena. His most noted composition is the "Muskrat Ramble," originally recorded by Louis Armstrong in 1926. Ory, however, is better known for his performance innovations on the trombone, which established him as the greatest of the New Orleans "tailgate" trombonists. He is believed to be the first trombonist to use the instrument for fills, glissandi (slides), and rhythmic effects. Ory also took a band of New Orleans jazz players to Los Angeles around 1918, helping to spread the style to the West Coast.

Joseph "King" Oliver (1885–1938) is generally known as the mentor of Louis Armstrong, and because of this, he is often overshadowed by his more historically significant protégé. The truth is, however, that Oliver was a great musician in his own right. It must be remembered that Oliver played with and led some of the best and most prestigious groups in New Orleans before his departure for Chicago in 1918. His influence in New Orleans as an improviser on the cornet—as Armstrong himself testified—was singular and continued subsequent to his arrival in Chicago through the 1920s. Oliver's Creole Jazz Band was the first black ensemble to record jazz pieces, recording forty-two numbers in 1923. Sadly, after the mid-1920s, Oliver was unable to change his style to keep up with new developments in jazz and was virtually forgotten by the time of his death in 1938.

The most prominent figure of the classic jazz era was Daniel Louis Armstrong (1900–1971). Armstrong was born and raised in New

Louis Armstrong

Orleans, Louisiana. He was introduced to the trumpet at the age of thirteen while serving a brief sentence at a reformatory school for misfiring a pistol. His real progress on the instrument, however, began after Joseph Oliver took him on as his student. Armstrong became Oliver's replacement in Kid Ory's band upon Oliver's departure for Chicago in 1918.

Armstrong spent a brief stint aboard a riverboat called the *Dixie Belle*, with a band organized by Fate Marable in 1918. This was Armstrong's first trip away from New Orleans. In 1922, Armstrong was summoned to Chicago by Oliver, where he joined Oliver's group as his second cornetist. With this move, Armstrong entered the most influential phase of his life. During this decade Armstrong transcended the innovations of his mentor and his competitors and emerged as the quintessential improviser of the classic jazz era, setting new standards for the still relatively embryonic art of jazz improvisation.

Armstrong appeared on Oliver's first recordings and soon was leading his own groups on record, notably the Hot Five and Hot Seven combos. These legendary groups—featuring stellar musicians Lil Hardin (then Armstrong's wife) on piano, Kid Ory on trombone, Johnny Dodds on clarinet, and "Baby" Dodds on drums—set the standard for small combo jazz recordings. Armstrong began to feature his own trumpet solos on these recordings, breaking away from the collective improvisation model to highlight his own stunning creativity as an improviser. Later in the 1920s, he enlisted pianist Earl Hines into his band, whose modern harmonic sense pulled the music into an even more sophisticated direction.

Armstrong's contributions did not stop at this point. He popularized a new style of jazz singing called scatting. This was a very rhythmic form of singing that used nonsense syllables as the text. Armstrong's strong sense of phrasing, expressed equally in his scatting and his trumpet solos, was particularly impressive to other musicians. Because of his incredible talent, he became the first great jazz soloist and set the stage for the virtuosic players of the 1930s and beyond.

## The Chicago Style

After the closing of Storyville in 1917, many prominent New Orleans musicians left the city. Many ended up in Chicago. As previously mentioned, Jelly Roll Morton left New Orleans much earlier. He had been actively involved in the musical activities of black Chicago years before the arrival of colleagues like King Oliver in 1918 and Louis Armstrong in 1922. These New Orleans invaders, along with indigenous musicians from Chicago's South side, founded the Chicago style.

There is little evidence to suggest that the Chicago phase of classic jazz was radically different from the earlier New Orleans style. Some scholars suggest that the tempo of Chicago style jazz may have been faster.[6] It has also been suggested that the Chicago style featured a four-to-the-bar interior rhythm preeminently, in contrast to the alleged two-to-the-bar pattern of the New Orleans style. The former pattern did occur with great frequency among Chicago ensembles on existing recordings; however, the two-to-the-bar pattern, though less common, is also heard.

Though the saxophone was occasionally used in the New Orleans style, particularly as a solo instrument, its prominence in small classic jazz ensembles grew considerably in Chicago-style jazz during the 1920s. The piano also grew in prominence during this same time in Chicago-style jazz.

Two other major changes occurred in Chicago. The repertoire of the jazz bands grew to include many more popular song and dance pieces. As a cosmopolitan city, Chicago had little appetite for the more folk-flavored musicians of the South. Even Armstrong, when he first arrived, was ridiculed as a country bumpkin because of his thick accent and rural dress. Fancier outfits, more lavish arrangements, and smoother sounds were quickly the order of the day. Second, white Chicago musicians were deeply impressed by the music of the New Orleans transplants. They began performing a style of jazz that would become highly influential in the Midwest among other white musicians. Their hero would be trumpeter Leon "Bix" Beiderbecke (1903–1931), born in Davenport, Iowa, and leader of the Wolverines, a band that gained great popularity in the mid-1920s in Chicago. Beiderbecke's incredibly pure tone and his melodic imagination gained him numerous fans, including black musicians like Louis Armstrong, who performed with him at least on one occasion. Jazz was quickly becoming a two-way street for black and white musicians.

## CHAPTER 7

# THE EMERGENCE OF SWING

**T**HE EARLIEST USE of the term *swing*, as it relates to jazz, was as an aesthetic notion alluding to the ideal manner of performing a classic jazz composition. Specifically, it referred to the peculiar type of rhythmic effect that occurred when all the parts of the composition blended perfectly and effortlessly. This effect was achieved when the members of the front line *played off* of each other in a manner that produced a perfect, polyphonically delivered, rhythmic harmony between them; and second, when the front line as a whole blended synchronously with the underlying rhythm/harmonic forces of the rhythm section (see Chapter 6).

When the swing effect was properly rendered by a big band, the result was the swing style. In his autobiography, *Swing That Music*, Louis Armstrong provides wonderful insights into the phenomenon of swing as it applied to the jazz orchestra of his time.

> For a man to be a good swing conductor he should have been a swing player himself, for then he knows a player is no good if the leader sets down on him too much and doesn't let him "go to town" when he feels like going. That phrase, "goin to town," means cuttin' loose and takin' the music with you, whatever the score may call for. Any average player, if he's worth anything at all, can follow through a score, as it's written there in front of him on his instrument rack. But it takes a swing player, and a real good one, to be able to leave that score and to know, or

"feel," just when to leave it and when to get back on it. . . . It is just that liberty that every individual player must have in a real swing orchestra that makes it most worth listening to. Every time they play there is something new swinging into the music to make it "hot" and interesting. . . .

You will think that if every man in a big sixteen-piece band had his own way and could play as he wanted, that all you would get would be a lot of jumbled up, crazy noise. This would be and is true with ordinary players, and that is why most bands have to play "regular" and their conductors can't dare let them leave their music as it is scored. The conductor himself may decide on certain variations, . . . but the players have to follow that scoring. But when you've got a real bunch of swing players together in an orchestra, you can turn them loose for the most part. "Give 'em their head," . . .They all play together, picking up and following each other, "swinging," all by sheer musical instinct. It takes a very fine ear and some years of playing to do that.

So if you have been hearing about swing music, but have not known much about the difference [between groups that swing and those that don't], listen closely when you hear one of the big "regular" orchestras . . . and then listen carefully to a swing orchestra. . . . [W]hen you listen to a swing band, you will begin to recognize that all through the playing of the piece, individual instruments will be heard to stand out and then retreat and you will catch new notes and broken-up rhythms you are not at all familiar with. You may not have known the melody very well but you will never have heard it played just that way before and will never have heard it just that way again. Because the boys are "swinging" around, and away from, the regular beat and melody you are used to, following the scoring very loosely and improvising as they go, by ear and musical feeling.[1]

The type of swing style that was produced by the jazz orchestras was in some ways different from that rendered by previous classic jazz ensembles. This new orchestral swing featured sections interacting with each other and with soloists in ways that allowed for far greater textural and timbral variation than what was previously possible with smaller classic jazz combos. These attributes, and the nuanced manner of their presentation, will be discussed in greater depth later in this chapter.

The third use of the term *swing* concerns the period in which the swing style was commercialized and mainstreamed. Swing, when used in this context, refers to the swing era—an era that reached its full bloom by the mid-1930s.

The three meanings of the term *swing* are not only interconnected but also relate to the development of jazz. The *swing effect* or aesthetic, as it relates to jazz, begins with the New Orleans phase of classic jazz. The *swing style* proper was worked out during what is generally referred to as the preswing era, which began during the mid-1920s. The *swing era*, however, crystallized in the following decade.

An important qualification should be interjected at this point. Swing, as an abstract aesthetic phenomenon, was (and is) not exclusive to jazz and existed in African American folk styles before jazz. James Weldon Johnson wrote in 1925 about the presence of swing in spirituals:

> I have said that the European concept of music, generally speaking, is melody and the African concept is rhythm. It is upon this point that most white people have difficulty with Negro music, the difficulty of getting the "Swing" of it. White America has pretty well mastered this difficulty; and naturally, because the Negro has been beating these rhythms in its ears for three hundred years. But in Europe, in spite of the vogue of American popular music, based on these rhythms, the best bands are not able to play it satisfactorily. Of course, they play the notes cor-

rectly, but any American can at once detect that there is some-thing lacking. The trouble is, they play the notes too correctly; and do not play what is not written down. . . .

In all authentic American Negro music the rhythms may be divided roughly into two classes—rhythms based on the swing-ing of head and body and rhythms based on the patting of hands and feet. Again, speaking roughly, the rhythms of the Spirituals fall in the first class and the rhythms of secular music in the second class. The "swing" of the Spirituals is an altogether subtle and elusive thing. It is subtle and elusive because it is in perfect union with the religious ecstasy that manifests itself in the swaying bodies of a whole congregation, swaying as if responding to the baton of some extremely sensitive conductor. So it is very difficult, if not impossible, to sing these songs sit-ting or standing coldly still, and at the same time capture the spontaneous "swing" which is of their very essence. . . .

Later on, Johnson adds:

We were discussing the "swing" of the spirituals, and were say-ing how subtle and elusive a thing it was. It is the more subtle and elusive a thing because there is a still further intricacy in the rhythms. The swaying of the body marks the regular beat or, better, surge, for it is something stronger than a beat, and is more or less, not precisely, strict in time; but the Negro loves nothing better in his music than to play with the fundamental time beat. He will, as it were, take the fundamental beat and pound it out with his left hand, almost monotonously; while with his right hand he juggles it. It should be noted that even in the swaying of head and body the head marks the surge off in shorter waves than does the body. In listening to Negroes sing their own music it is often tantalizing and even exciting to watch a minute fraction of a beat balancing for a slight instant on the bar between two measures, and, when it seems almost too late, drop back into its own proper compartment. There is a close similarity between the singing and the beating of the big drum and the little drums by the African natives.[2]

Though the Armstrong and Johnson quotes refer to two different black musical styles, notice how similar they are in their description of swing. It should also be noted that the swing effect was evident in some blues styles and in some of the pre-1950 derivatives of spirituals and blues, like gospel music.

## Swing Style and the Big Band

Although the principal medium for the swing style was the big band, or jazz orchestra, the big band was not unique to swing. Big bands, in one form or another, existed before jazz. As brass bands, or concert bands, they were the mediums for much American dance music in the nineteenth century. With the popularity of ragtime in the late nineteenth century, these bands quickly expanded their repertoires to include cakewalks, two steps, and other ragtime compositions. In other words, with the arrival of ragtime and related Afro-vernacular expressions, brass bands were transformed into syncopated bands. In Sedalia, Missouri, in the 1890s, such bands were known as "jig bands."[3] Scott Joplin reportedly led several such bands, and used these bands to perform his music locally.

By the first two decades of the century, syncopated dance bands were common throughout the country and by way of tours were spreading their rhythmic gospel throughout the United States and Europe. In 1917, for example, James Reese Europe (1881–1919) had taken the seventy-one piece 369th Infantry band on an extensive tour of French cities.[4] His repertoire is said to have included "jazz" numbers. Composer/bandleader

Will Marion Cook took his Southern Syncopated Orchestra on a tour of Europe that lasted until 1922.[5] Other important exponents of syncopated dance music during the teens and early twenties included Ford Dabney, Wilbur Sweatman, and the legendary W. C. Handy.

Large ensembles, we know, were an integral part of early jazz during its inception. Groups like the Onward Brass Band and the Tuxedo Orchestra played a significant role in the development of the New Orleans jazz style. Large jazz ensembles were featured on riverboats in the late teens and twenties. Fate Marable's riverboat orchestras were prime examples. As mentioned earlier, Louis Armstrong was recruited by Fate Marable to perform with a twelve-piece orchestra aboard the *Dixie Belle* in 1918. This group afforded Armstrong his first opportunity to leave New Orleans.

Dance bands, particularly white bands, were quite active in Chicago and on the East Coast in the 1920s. The most famous of these bands was led by Paul Whiteman. Their playing styles often featured contemplative syncopated music, but their performances were generally rigid, rhythmically and harmonically dull, and not oriented towards improvisation. Some of these bands, however, were skillful and inventive in their handling of instrumental sections, particularly reeds, and in this regard had much to teach the black bands.

For the true swing effect to manifest itself in a large ensemble, several aesthetic and technical hurdles had to be overcome. First, the technical control it takes to handle a large number of musicians implied to some degree a more developed view of musical structure than what was required for small New Orleans ensembles. Factors such as texture, timbre, density, and formative design brought to the forefront the creative skills of arrangers, composers, and conductors. Second, the spontaneity, fluidity, smoothness, blues orientation, and swing of the New Orleans jazz improvisers, and the perfect sense of rhythm that underlay these skills, had to be incorporated into swing arrangements and compositions in a manner that brought them into balance, aesthetically and architectonically, with the other elements of the work. Thus big band swing required the reconciliation of two seemingly opposite approaches to jazz—one eminently contemplative, the other consummately spontaneous.

From 1923 to 1927, two men, Fletcher Henderson (1897–1952) and his arranger Don Redman (1900–1964), attacked and substantially surmounted these aesthetic hurdles, and in so doing laid the foundation for big band swing. Other eminent bands of the twenties and early thirties built upon and expanded the foundation laid by Henderson and Redman. These bands included the Earl Hines Orchestra, Bennie Moten's Kansas City Orchestra, the Tiny Parham Orchestra, McKinney's Cotton Pickers, and the Luis Russell Orchestra. Swing would reach its highest expression, however, in the music of William "Count" Basie (1904–1984), Jimmy Lunceford (1902–1947), and the quintessential Edward Kennedy "Duke" Ellington (1899–1974).

## Elements of Swing

The principal medium of expression for swing was the big band or jazz orchestra. This ensemble consisted of reeds, brass, and a rhythm section. The reeds in the black swing bands of the 1920s were clarinets and saxophones. Though the number of reeds varied from group to group, three reed players generally constituted the norm. Often clarinetists doubled on saxophones, giving the reed section a flexible timbral palette. The Fletcher Henderson band, one of the pioneer big bands led by the great pianist/arranger, recorded his early classic "Stampede" on May 14, 1926, featuring three reeds: Buster Bailey on clarinet, Coleman Hawkins on tenor saxophone, and Don Redman doubling on alto saxophone and clarinet. During the 1930s, reed sections became more focused on the alto and tenor saxophones.

Fats Waller

The brass section consisted of trombones and trumpets. Many of the early black bands often used only one trombonist. This number increased to as many as three by the mid-1930s. However, three trumpeters were not uncommon in black bands of the twenties. The tuba, though a brass instrument, functioned generally as the bass.

The rhythm section generally consisted of a fretted instrument (banjo or guitar), a bass instrument, drums, and piano. The banjo was still present in early swing ensembles; during the late twenties and thirties, however, the guitar became more common. The fretted instrument played both two-to-the-bar and four-to-the bar chord patterns. The specific pattern chosen by the banjoist or guitarist may have been based upon factors like the tempo, the style, the swing of the composition, or perhaps some combination of all three.

The bass part in earlier black bands was frequently taken by the tuba. It generally rendered a two-to-the-bar oom-pah pattern, sporadically embellished. However, by the 1930s four-to-the-bar walking bass lines became more prominent. The double bass became the standard bass instrument after 1935, though it too was employed by some of the earlier bands.

The piano was a key part of the rhythm section of early black swing ensembles and remained so throughout the swing era. In the earlier bands of the 1920s, the pianist often played highly extemporized accompaniments, which sometimes constituted embellished versions of the main melody—particularly when accompanying other improvisers. This improvised accompaniment helped to differentiate the piano functionally from the banjo/guitar, and contributed to the swing of the rhythm section. Also, by functioning as a variable instead of a constant aspect of an arrangement, the piano frequently appeared as a middle ground—or quasicontrapuntal element—in relation to themes, solos, and other foreground elements. The music of Fletcher Henderson, Bennie Moten, and Earl Hines frequently exemplified this type of pianism.

As the swing style evolved from the mid-twenties through the thirties, black bands, from Fletcher Henderson onward, developed techniques designed to organize and control the manner in which the various sections of the ensemble interacted with one another and with soloists. In this way, these bands were able to effect a timbral and textural palette of considerable complexity and diversity. The textures commonly used by brass and reed sections were homorhythmic (a single melody line expressed by the entire section), antiphonic (call and response), and polyphonic (two or more melody lines) in various combinations. Two- or three-part harmonies were often employed as well as repeated riffs (short melodic motives) played by a section, often building to a climax when the entire band played a final chord or cadence. The timbral combinations were virtually infinite.

Count Basie

Unlike previous ensembles, the swing band offered the clear possibility of a foreground, middle ground, and background presentation of musical events. The foreground was usually reserved for the melody; the middle ground for countermelodies and/or harmonies; and the background for rhythmic/harmonic support. With such enormous textural possibilities, density (the number of voices sounding at once) inevitably became a factor in the creation of drama in swing compositions.

Swing melodies were widely diverse in their character. Some swing melodies consisted of nothing more than literal or varied repetitions of essentially one rhythmically distinctive motive (the riff; see Example 7.1). Count Basie (1904–1984) was particularly fond of this type of melody. So was Melvin James "Sy" Oliver (1910–1988), as exemplified by his 1943 classic, "Opus One."

**Bright Bounce Tempo**

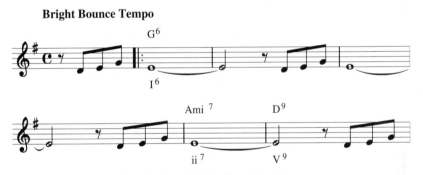

Example 7.1. "Jumpin' at The Woodside" (Count Basie)

Some melodies, or significant parts of them, were constructed from scales other than the major or minor scale. For example, "Jumpin' at The Woodside" is based on an incomplete G pentatonic scale, and as such was typical of many African American folk and popular melodies of the period. The opening of "It Don't Mean a Thing If It Ain't Got That Swing," by Duke Ellington, among the best-known of all swing melodies, is based entirely upon a hexatonic blues scale (Example 7.2).

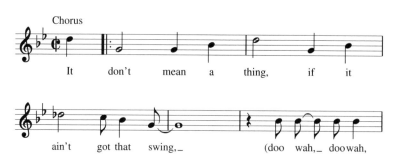

Example 7.2. "It Don't Mean a Thing If It Ain't Got That Swing" (Duke Ellington)

The swing classic "Tuxedo Junction" (Example 7.3) also shows the influence of the blues scale. This composition was pieced together during a recording session in 1939 by Erskine Hawkins (1914–1995) and members of his band in their search for an additional tune to record. If it were not for the singular occurrence of an E♭—the last eighth-note tied over from measure twenty-three to the dotted quarter that begins the ensuing measure (not shown in the following example)—the entire melody would be predicated exclusively on the hexatonic blues scale.

Example 7.3. "Tuxedo Junction" (Erskine Hawkins, William Johnson, and Julian Dash)

Melodies showing the influences of more than one scale were not uncommon during the swing era. Here again, Duke Ellington provides the paradigm for masterful melodic writing in this vein (Example 7.4). "In a Sentimental Mood" is a study in the conjunctive use of the major scale with African-derived scalar resources. The elegance, taste, and

Example 7.4. "In a Sentimental Mood" (Duke Ellington)

sophistication of this melody are surpassed by few others in the history of American vernacular music. The melody opens with a passage that outlines, note for note, the F pentatonic scale (see measures five and six). The F major scale governs the melody in the following two measures but then changes again with the beginning of a passage based upon a blues scale in D in measure eight. The remainder of the melody returns to the major scale.

The harmonic language of swing was broad, ranging from the use of simple diatonic structures, sometimes embellished by upper extensions, to the use of secondary dominants and more exotic harmonizations like extended dominants (dominant seventh chords that resolve normatively to nondiatonic harmonies), secondary and extended substitute dominants (sometimes called tritone substitution chords; see chapter 3), and

Duke Ellington

diminished and augmented triads and seventh chords. Eleventh and thirteenth chords were also quite common.

"Jumpin' at the Woodside" by Count Basie illustrates the employment of a simple diatonic progression. The composition is in the key of G major. The $I^6$ underlies the melody for the first four measures. A $ii^7$ is introduced in measure five. It resolves to $V^9$ in the ensuing measure, completing a diatonic two-five progression. The inevitable resolution of the dominant ninth to $I^6$ in measure seven begins a four-chord turnaround progression consisting of $I^6$-$vi^7$-$ii^7$-$V^9$.

Two factors make this progression interesting. The first is the employment of the $I^6$ and $V^9$ structures rather than their simple triadic counterparts. The extensions on both chords—emanating from the same pitch—are inspired by the quasipentatonic melody these chords harmonize. The second factor is the harmonic rhythm that, over the eight-measure duration of the theme, accelerates from four measures, to one measure, to a half measure in length.

Secondary and extended substitute dominants are beautifully featured in Ellington's 1933 masterpiece "Sophisticated Lady" (Example 7.5). The second measure of the melody is harmonized by three successive substitute dominants, the last of which resolves to the $V^7$ ($E^{b7}$). The entire succession serves only to embellish—that is, structurally prolong—the essential two-five progression that begins with the $b^b$ in measure three and concludes with $E^{b7}$ in the following measure.

| $ii^7$ | {subV$^7$/F$^7$ | subV$^7$/E$^7$ | subV$^7$/V$^7$ . . . |
| | extended | extended | secondary |
| | substitute dominant | substitute dominant | substitute dominant |

A succession of substitute dominants occurs again in measure six. In this instance all three substitute dominants are extended. The last, $G^{b7}$,

Example 7.5. "Sophisticated Lady" (Duke Ellington)

resolves to F⁷—the dominant of the V⁷/V⁷. Diminished and augmented structures and other chromatic progressions are exemplified in other Ellington masterpieces composed during the swing era, for example, "Mood Indigo," "In a Sentimental Mood," "Prelude to a Kiss," and "Take the A Train."

The formative basis for swing works in the mid to late 1920s were often song form or blues structures. Highly nuanced interactions between instrumental sections were not yet well-developed. Simple, unified rhythmic writing, harmonic highlighting (used as a counterpoint to the melody), and simpler forms of antiphony (call and response) were techniques frequently used by arrangers. Within this small arsenal of techniques, however, arrangers of early black bands often rendered strikingly interesting and imaginative works.

The 1926 Fletcher Henderson recording of the Ager-Yellen classic "Ain't She Sweet" is an early example of creative swing-band arranging. The work begins with an eight-measure introduction, after which the melody enters with the opening theme (A) in three-part design (that is, aaba). The first part of the opening theme—a—is given by the reeds in a quasi-homorhythmic style. After the customary repetition of a, the b section enters, with the melody carried by the reeds but answered antiphonally by the trumpets. The opening a then returns without a repeat. A contrasting sixteen-measure theme (B) consisting of two new sections follow, this time featuring the trumpets with the lead, answered by the reeds. The original theme (A) returns but with a trumpet improvisation. A clarinet soloist usurps the trumpet improviser in the b section and continues throughout the ensuing a section.

A brief two-measure transition (or bridge) based on the opening motive of the melody and delivered homorhythmically by the brass and reeds launches the theme into a new key. The a section is again rendered homorhythmically by the reeds, this time rhythmically highlighted by the trumpets. The following b section showcases the reeds without polyphonic or antiphonal assistance. The a section repeats with the same orchestration as before and is followed by a brief retransition that ushers the composition back to its original key.

In the final statement of the theme a slightly varied a section is delivered by a trumpet, which engages in a polyphonic dialogue with a trombone in quasi–New Orleans style. The reeds provide a harmonic accompaniment in even half notes against the trumpet/trombone dialogue. The saxophone soloist takes center stage in the ensuing b section. The previous a section in quasi–New Orleans style, returns to conclude the composition.

Thus, through clever arranging, a basic AB pattern is made more interesting through varying the voicings and manner in which the melodies are stated and also by introducing brief passages and key changes to offer variety throughout the composition.

By 1932 the techniques of pitting instrumental sections against one another and against soloists had grown to a highly nuanced art. This fact, along with the relative standardization of the instrumentation of the swing band, brought the swing era almost to full bloom. The sectional playing of the greatest bands was subtle, crisp, rhythmically articulate, and, in the best arrangements, always balanced in its display of timbral and textural elegance. Nowhere is this to be better observed than in Sy Oliver's arrangement of "Battle Axe" as performed by the Jimmy Lunceford Orchestra in 1943.

This emphasis on sectional writing did not preclude the evolution of the solo improviser. Often arrangements were constructed in such a way as to maximize the contributions of talented improvisers without sacrificing a sense of overall formal balance in the composition. In Earl Hines's "Cavernism," for example, three interior sections in which various instruments are featured performing improvised melodies are framed by the theme, which is heard at the opening and closing of the work. Duke Ellington was particularly noted for arranging his compositions in ways that took advantage of his soloists. Such arrangements were often constructed as head arrangements, that is, quickly prepared, unnotated arrangements that were worked out on the bandstand.

## Great Improvisers

As we have seen, swing brought about radical changes to the structure of jazz composition. Swing, however, also introduced radical changes in improvisational style. Improvisation generally became more fluid and rhythmically dramatic and consequently more lyrically nuanced. Many new improvisational greats came to the fore during the swing era, becoming icons in their own right and laying the foundation on which some of the highest improvisational innovations in jazz were to be built. Among the most renowned and creative of these artists were Art Tatum, Lionel Hampton, Charlie Christian, Coleman Hawkins, and Lester Young.

Art Tatum (1910–1956) was born in Toledo, Ohio. He began his career in the 1920s and by the early 1930s was actively involved in night club engagements and recordings. His mastership and influence had become so great that by the mid-1930s he had won the acclaim of the most reputable jazz and classical artists of his time. Tatum employed rich harmonies in the manner of the great Romantic pianists. His flawless execution and improvisational inventiveness was so amazing that it frequently inspired jazz and classical artists to visit the clubs where he was performing, including the great classical pianists Arthur Rubinstein and Vladimir Horowitz.

The premiere vibraphonist of the swing era was Lionel Hampton (b. 1913). He was born in Louisville, Kentucky, but raised in Birmingham, Alabama, and Chicago, Illinois. He began his career as a drummer but did not encounter the vibraphone until 1930, during a recording session with Louis Armstrong. The vibraphone during this time was still relatively new and unpopular. Hampton popularized the instrument and in so doing became the first in a line of great jazz vibraphonists.

The swing era introduced to the world of jazz several great masters of the tenor saxophone, four of which were Chu Berry, Ben Webster, Coleman Hawkins, and Lester Young. Of these four, the latter two emerged as the preeminent tenor icons of the era.

Coleman Hawkins literally began the tradition of the great tenor saxophonists, and to this extent may justifiably be regarded as the father of the tenor saxophone. He was born in Kansas in 1904. By the early 1920s Hawkins was a featured artist with the Fletcher Henderson orchestra. Hawkins was to the tenor saxophone what Lionel Hampton would become to the vibraphone in the next decade; the tenor saxophone, like the vibraphone, was a relatively novel instrument that had little application outside of marching bands before its adoption as a jazz medium.

Hawkins's style during his early tenure with Henderson was characterized by a huge, rough sound punctuated by a so-called slap-tongued improvisational technique. The slap-tongued technique was a quasistaccato method of articulating notes. Usually the first of a regular grouping of two pitches was accentuated and followed by a short, choppy pitch.

The effect was that of a dotted eighth-note followed by a sixteenth-note. Though now considered antiquated, this slap-tongued style contributed greatly to Hawkins's uniqueness as an improviser. But its was only the first of several styles Hawkins would ultimately unveil during his evolution as a tenor saxophonist. According to trumpeter Rex Stewart, Hawkins's slap-tongued style ended in the late 1920s after hearing an Art Tatum performance in Toledo, Ohio. A more mature style unveiled itself in the late 1930s after Hawkins returned from a four-year stint in Europe. Though still big, his sound was tempered by a greater lyricism, greater control and technical facility, and a more enriched harmonic vocabulary underlying his improvisations.

Hawkins's influence was underscored by his affiliation with bebop greats like Thelonius Monk, Dizzy Gillespie, Miles Davis, Fats Navarro, and Max Roach. These and other bebop artists performed in Hawkins's ensembles early in their careers. In the 1950s Hawkins's influence was evident in the early playing style of Sonny Stitt. Hawkins's musical evolution continued until well into the 1960s, during which time he absorbed aspects of the new styles that emerged; he died in 1969.

During the 1930s a young saxophonist name Lester Young introduced an alternative approach to playing the tenor saxophone—one that would have a great impact on saxophonists (and other instrumentalists) in the ensuing decades. Young was born in Woodville, Mississippi, in 1909. His early training traces back to his father, Willis Young. He eventually performed with some of the most innovative of preswing and swing bands, such as the Original Blue Devils, King Oliver, Fletcher Henderson, and Count Basie.[6]

Young replaced Coleman Hawkins in Fletcher Henderson's band in 1934. His improvisational style during this time was often ridiculed by some of his colleagues in the band. These musicians were used to the big, rough growl of Coleman Hawkins and considered Hawkins' sound the model for tenor saxophone playing. Young's approach was nearly the opposite. His sound was light, not big. His style was characterized by a relaxed lyricism, as if singing through the horn. According to Billie Holiday, Young was initially perturbed by the absence of a larger sound and did peculiar things to enhance the volume of his sound. However, he eventually came to appreciate the uniqueness of his own sound and style; so did the next generation of tenor saxophonists. His style gradually eclipsed that of Hawkins as the favorite among the tenor saxophonists of the 1940s and 1950s, and beyond.

Also memorable and influential were Young's humor and wit, and particularly his mastership of *jive*.[7] In this latter regard Professor Douglas Daniels notes that Young's "language, shared by musicians, entertainers, and [those] knowledgeable of hip public, considerably influenced American slang."[8] However, it would be Young's profound and unique lyricism that would constitute his greatest and most enduring contribution to jazz. Billie Holiday saw in this attribute a justification for assigning to Young a sobriquet befitting the greatest master of his instrument, so she anointed him "president" of the tenor saxophone. This sobriquet in its abbreviated form—"Prez"—has stuck with Lester Young ever since. Lester Young died in 1959, following a lengthy bout with alcoholism.

The story of Charlie Christian is, once again, the story of a visionary who understood and brought to light the possibilities of a relatively new instrument, the electric guitar, and thereby laid a foundation that ensuing luminaries would build on. Charles Christian was born in Dallas, Texas, in 1916. and came into national prominence after joining Benny Goodman. Though Christian was not the exclusive cultivator of the electric guitar, he was the first to show its capacity for rapid runs, sophisticated harmonies, and lyrical subtlety within improvisational contexts. These attributes endeared him to bebop guitarists, who saw Christian's new experimental style as eminently compatible with the pyrotechnical dictums of their newly emerging jazz thrust. Christian's reign as the pre-eminent guitarist of the swing era was tragically short. He died of tuberculosis in 1942, at the age of twenty-five.

## CHAPTER 8

## BEBOP

**W**HILE SWING was initially an adventure-some and innovative new style, once it achieved mass popularity, many second- and third-rate bands jumped on the swing bandwagon. The innovative techniques of call-and-response and swinging rhythms soon became hackneyed in the hands of lesser arrangers and players. Younger and more serious jazz musicians felt that the swing style had reached an artistic dead end. These artists saw themselves as proponents of a more adventurous music, and between 1939 and 1945 they brought into reality their new stylistic conception. The style they crafted shared some of the musical attributes of swing but expanded considerably its harmonic, melodic, rhythmic, and improvisational character. The new music came to be known as *bebop*, though it is debatable whether most of these artists initially referred to it by this term.

These musicians—commonly called *beboppers*—were outspoken concerning their political and philosophical beliefs, particularly those that pertained to racism, economics, and the artistic merits of black music and black musicians. The beboppers, for example, regarded themselves as artists and their music as an art form—in the highest sense of the term. Though they were not opposed to musicians making money from their efforts, they did not look favorably upon musicians who commercially exploited the music with no concern for its artistic merit. Neither did they look favorably upon musicians who attacked the new music. Attacks from musicians anchored in previous jazz styles were frequent.

The beboppers were not appreciative of black musicians who presented themselves in traditional stereotypical images to make themselves marketable to nonblack audiences. Such images had their source in nineteenth-century minstrelsy and—by way of vaudeville acts, movies, white musicals, white productions of so-called black musicals, and radio—continued to portray black people in a racially demeaning and denigrating fashion. The beboppers felt that the perpetuation of these images by black artists hampered their efforts to bring about a much-deserved respectability for bebop—and jazz. Eminent black musicians who subscribed to such images were not beyond the open criticism of bebop artists. Dizzy Gillespie, a leading bopper, said:

> I criticized Louis [Armstrong] for . . . his "plantation image." We didn't appreciate that about Louis Armstrong, and if anybody asked me about a certain image of him, handkerchief over his head, grinning in the face of white racism, I never hesitated to say I didn't like it.[1]

It is sad that one of the greatest innovators in jazz, Louis Armstrong, was shunned for stage mannerisms that were by the late 1940s outdated, at least among the younger black performers. Armstrong in his day had been a strong image of a proud black performer who was greatly admired by all musicians, white and black. By the late 1940s, he was playing in a mixed-race, small band, a powerful statement in and of itself, even if he had to occasionally "grin . . . in the face of racism." In later years, Gillespie would admit his admiration for Armstrong the musician.

It is generally held that the beboppers desired to create a music that would be exclusive to themselves. There is no great amount of evidence to substantiate this claim. Though the beboppers were an insular fraternity, the natural current of business and the growth in the popularity of their new style inevitably brought them into contact with nonbeboppers and nonblack musicians—as well as white journalists and audiences.

What is more evident is that the beboppers were aware of the parasitic relationship that nonblack commercial forces had historically had with jazz and other black popular styles. The results of this relationship were seldom favorable to the black artists who created the music, either economically or with regard to proper recognition. Thus, we see that the beboppers were initially and justifiably guarded concerning the dissemination of their music. Pianist/composer Mary Lou Williams recalled:

> I went to Minton's [a Harlem nightspot said to be the original home of bebop] every night. When the thing started, Thelonious Monk and the others had a little band going. They were afraid to come out because they were afraid that the commercial world would steal what they had created. So they stayed in Harlem, at Minton's, and the downtowners began to come up, writing their notes on their little pieces of paper and everything, you know. . . . I heard some of the guys speak about not wanting to play downtown or play in the open so everybody could take it from them. Because you know the black creators of the music have never gotten recognition for creating anything.[2]

Concurrent with the inception of bebop was a rising Muslim movement. This movement influenced the beboppers and their music in several ways. First, it inspired some modern black musicians to convert to Islam. Doing so, some felt, was a way to escape segregation. Others converted because they believed that Islam did not discriminate among its followers. Still others saw Islam as less contradictory and less hypocritical in its practices than Christianity. Second, the impact of Islam is evident in the names of some of the bebop classics; "A Night In Tunisia" and "Dance of The Infidels" are two well-known examples.

Much has been written about the alleged antiwar sentiments of the beboppers. While it is true that some beboppers were pacifists, their reaction against World War II went deeper than their intrinsic dislike for human genocide. The beboppers were unappreciative of the social injustices to which black soldiers were often subjected when they returned home from the war. They also found it difficult to reconcile risking their lives for a country that treated African Americans so badly. John Birk "Dizzy" Gillespie (1917–1993) put it this way:

> They started asking me my views about fighting. "Well, look, at this time, in this stage of my life here in the United States whose foot has been in my ass? The white man's foot has been in my ass hole buried up to his knee in my ass hole!" I said. "Now, you're speaking of the enemy. You're telling me the German is the enemy. At this point, I can never even remember having met a German. So if you put me out there with a gun in my hand and tell me to shoot at the enemy, I'm liable to create a case of 'mistaken identity,' of who I might shoot."[3]

## Schools of Bebop

According to Dizzy Gillespie, bebop developed in two settings in the early 1940s: "In those days we had several means of access to experience: big bands were one, jam sessions were another. I tried to get plenty of both."[4] The principle venue for jam sessions between 1939 and 1945 in New York was a place called Minton's Playhouse. Musicians of the new musical vision—which included trumpeter Gillespie, pianist Thelonious Monk, bassist Oscar Pettiford, drummer Kenny Clarke, alto saxophonist Charlie Parker, and others—often met after their regular jobs and engaged each other in spirited but diplomatic improvisational exchanges on the bandstand. By trading their ideas, freely and openly, they crafted the new music.

The main cultivators of the style each provided distinctive contributions. Dizzy Gillespie's contributions included the introduction of an expanded harmonic vocabulary; a new rhythmic conception, which led to the introduction of Afro-Cuban influences; an innovative style of trumpet playing that influenced virtually all of his contemporaries and successors, including Miles Davis, Theodore "Fats" Navarro (1923–1958), Clifford Brown, Lee Morgan, and Freddy Hubbard; and an entirely new big band conception. Gillespie was also a wonderful showman; with his goatee, hipster clothes, and beret, he became a symbol of bebop for the 1950s.

From Thelonious Monk (1918–1982) bebop inherited a new piano conception that changed forever the style of *comping*. Comping is a style of piano accompaniment to a soloist where chords are dropped in at strategic places; the beboppers made this far more rhythmic and percussive than had previously been the case, preferring to insert chords on the offbeats and in surprising places and often offering extended and unusual harmonies. Like Gillespie, Monk also expanded the harmonic vocabulary of bebop. His most lasting contribution, however, appears to be his compositions. These works constitute many of the enduring bebop classics and are probably performed more consistently than the compositions of any other bebop composer, with the exception of Gillespie and Parker.

Kenny Clarke (1914–1985) seeded a new style of jazz drumming, one in which the bass drum provided accents at specific points rather than regular two-beat patterns. In Clarke's style the basic pulse was kept by the cymbals. This allowed the bass drum to accent in a manner that complimented other aspects of the band. These unexpected accents were called by musicians bombs, literally because of the booming sound of the bass drum which often surprised and shocked the listeners.

From Oscar Pettiford a new type of bass improvisation evolved. Pettiford's style, said to have been influenced by jazz guitarist Charlie Christian, featured a melodic type of bass improvisation that de-emphasized the roots of harmonies.

Charlie Parker (1920–1955) is generally remembered as perhaps bebop's most distinctive improviser. It is true that Parker's improvisational style, and the influence it had (and continues to have) on later musicians,

Thelonious Monk

is one of bebop's greatest legacies. His style was characterized by speed of execution, his creative use of syncopation and blues elements and accents, his penchant for interpolating quotes from other compositions, and generally his profound melodic lyricism. But in addition to his improvisational gifts—or maybe because of them—Parker forged a compositional conception that became one of the principal melodic models for bebop.

Of all the bebop big bands of the late forties, Dizzy Gillespie's were the most influential and the source of most bebop big band innovations. As previously stated, these innovations were both harmonic and rhythmic. The musicians who entered Dizzy Gillespie's big band were immediately introduced to the new harmonic language of bebop and to a unique big band sound. Charlie Rouse comments about his experience with Dizzy Gillespie's first band in 1945:

> It was something that you weren't used to. They were playing harmonics [harmonies] that no one was playing before . . . Bird and Dizzy and Thelonious had created a new set of harmonics. And it was scary, man, at first. But everybody was showing each other different things. It was like a school. It was really a school within the band.[5]

Dizzy Gillespie's big band sound was original, due in great part to his arranger Walter Fuller. In some instances Gillespie supplied Fuller with only the melody with a specific set of underlying harmonic progressions and additional information about the format of the piece. This left the job of orchestration, texturing, and voicing to the creative imagination of Fuller. The distinctiveness of Gillespie's sound, according to Walter Fuller, was a consequence of his voicing techniques:

> In Dizzy's band, I used all open harmony for the saxophones all the way through, then close harmony for the trumpets, and spread out the three trombones. That's what gave the brass that big fat sound, with the close harmony in the trumpets.[6]

In situations where the band played standard tunes the sound of the band was still unique because Gillespie would often reharmonize the tunes. That is, he kept the original melody of a song but changed its underlying harmonic structure. These new harmonies often startled the members of the band.

> When we did, like, say, "One Bass Hit," you had a thing in there where he went into the bridge, and the saxophones came in and hit a flatted fifth, or raised eleventh. Everybody was looking saying, "What the hell is that?"[7]

Despite its insular beginnings bebop became the first international jazz language. This did not happen immediately, however; for bebop during its time reflected aesthetic and political values very much to the left of mainstream America and as such made inevitable a stylistic reaction from those excluded from it.

## Elements of the Bebop Style

The titles of bebop melodies showed the wide-ranging, intellectual interests of the musicians as well as being full of inside jokes meant to appeal to the fraternity of boppers. Some paid or implied homage to certain individuals—for example, "Sid's Delight" (Tadd Dameron), and "Blues For Alice" (Charles Parker). Some titles attested to the macabre, baroque, or surrealistic nature of the music: "Real Crazy" and "Prelude To A Nightmare" (Babs Gonzales), and "'Round Midnight" (Thelonious Monk). Charlie Parker's nickname (Yardbird) offered many opportunities for creative tune-naming ("Yardbird Suite" and "Ornithology" are two examples). Others were based on the sounds of the melodies themselves; Gillespie's famous "Salt Peanuts" was named for the rhythm of the six-note refrain, which seems to call out "Salt Pea-nuts/Salt Pea-nuts."

Virtually all upbeat bebop melodies shared one common feature—the *bebop motif*. (The word *motif* is employed here to describe a characteristic or stereotypical musical figure that recurs frequently. It should not be confused with the word *motive*, which refers abstractly to a musical figure that combines with other figures to make phrases.) This motif was a small melodic fragment consisting generally of two consecutive eighth notes, seeming to express the sound "be-bop." The fragment usually occurred on a downbeat. The last eighth note was either followed immediately by a rest or tied to the ensuing note, both resulting in a syncopational ending. The bebop motif sometimes occurred at the end of motives or phrases (Example 8.1); in some melodies, it occurs as an isolated fragment (Example 8.2).

Describing bebop melodies is a difficult task, for despite common characteristics, talented bebop composers were able to stamp their melodies with their own distinctive voices. Consequently, melodic contour, range (tessitura), phrase length, and even the rhythmic construction of motives varied widely. In fast bebop melodies, however, two paradigms occurred with great frequency. The first may be called the *Dizzy Gillespie paradigm* (Example 8.3). In this particular type of melody a brief phrase—usually two measures in length—opens the A section of the theme. The phrase usually consists of one highly rhythmic motive that often ends with the bebop motif. The phrase is then repeated twice, either literally with slight variation or in a sequence. The final phrase contrasts with the previous three by introducing different motivic material, which brings closure to the A section. The resultant structure is reminiscent of a call-and-response pattern in that the last phrase gives the impression of answering the previous three:

A    a    2-measure phrase, rhythmic motive ends with bebop rhythm

      $a^2$    a repeated, literally, slightly varied, or in sequence

      $a^3$    as above

      b    different motivic material, closing the section

**Medium (Up) Swing**

Example 8.1. "Well You Needn't" (Thelonious Monk)

Solo on [A] ; After solos
D.S. al Coda.

Example 8.2. "Blues for Alice" (Charlie Parker)

The motivic and rhythmic character of the B section are noticeably different from that of the A section—and the ensuing recapitulative section, if one is present. It may simply constitute repetitions of the same motive over a changing harmonic scheme, as it does in "Night In Tunisia," or a more elongated phrase design, as it does in "Woody'n You." (Example 8.3). The Gillespie paradigm, in its economical use of

Example 8.3. "Woody'n You" (Dizzy Gillespie)

motivic material, exhibits features strongly reminiscent of the music of Sy Oliver and Count Basie.

The second type of melodic paradigm may be termed the *Charlie Parker paradigm*. This generally constitutes an elongated melody made up of many diverse motives, sometimes riff-like and syncopated, which are often interrupted by rests. Independent phrases exist but are often difficult to perceive. This is because the motives that constitute each phrase are generally asymmetric in length and variable in their character and their number per phrase, and they are seldom literally repeated (Example 8.2).

In Charlie Parker's "Blues For Alice," for example, the blues structure mandates the perception of three phrases. The character of each phrase, however, differs radically. Of the three phrases, the second and third are more closely akin, due in large part to the similar motivic construction of the last two bars of each phrase. Phrase one consists of two motives seamlessly joined by a tie connecting the last eighth note in measure six to the first quarter note in the ensuing measure. The phrase ends, predictably, with the bebop motif on beat two of measure eight.

The eighth-note rest, on the first quarter of the ensuing beat, confirms the ending of the previous phrase and simultaneously prepares the pickup to the next phrase. The second phrase contains four syncopated motives; the first motive is separated from the second by an eighth-note rest; the second motive is joined to the third by a tie; and the third is separated from the fourth again by an eighth-note rest. Each rest occurs at corresponding points in their respective measures, making the points of demarcation between the motives very clear.

The third phrase offers still more contrast by introducing new motivic material. The last two measures, however, are rhythmically identical to the last two measures of the previous phrase. This, along with (1) the sporadic occurrence of ties that connect motives and which introduce the opening phrase; (2) the similarity in the contour of the beginning of all motives (with the exception of the motive that opens the third phrase); and, of course (3) the sporadic occurrences of the bebop motif—helps considerably in imparting a sense of coherence and unity to this theme.

Perhaps a third melodic paradigm was introduced by Tadd Dameron (1917–1965), one of bebop's greatest composers. Dameron's concept of melody was more lyrical and rhythmically tempered than those of Parker and Gillespie. That is, his melodies are not always fragmented by interpolated rests as they are in Parker's melodies, nor are they characterized by the constant repetition of phrases, as sometimes occurs in Gillespies melodies. They are, however, no less elegant or original in their employment of syncopation or the bebop motif. (Listen, for example, to Dameron's "Sid's Delight" and "Focus.") Dameron's arranging and orchestrational skills often show a craftsmanship superior to his colleagues, though these skills did not fully mature until the 1950s. As an orchestrator, Dameron was particularly astute in his treatment of flutes and woodwinds. Dameron the composer contributed many masterpieces to bebop literature. Among them are "Lady Bird," "Hot House," "Sid's Delight," "Focus," "Our Delight," "Good Bait," "If You Could See Me Now," "Fountainebleu" (an extended composition), and "Dial B for Beauty."

When the harmonies of bebop are abstractly compared to those of swing, the differences are not as great as they were once assumed to be. Chords like the minor sixth (a minor triad with an added major sixth), various types of ninth and thirteenth chords, and the so-called tritone substitution (substitute dominant) are common to the harmonic lexicons of both swing and bebop. Yet when you listen carefully to bebop music, you clearly perceive a harmonic language noticeably different from that which governs swing. What specifically constitutes this difference?

In one sense, the difference is more in the degree to and manner in which certain chords are used, particularly chromatic chords. In other words, bebop features a much greater use of chromatic progressions (progressions outside of the key). The expanded use of chromaticism was melodic and harmonic and in both cases decorative (used to embellish essentially diatonic contexts). The harmonic use of chromaticism is nowhere better illustrated than in the beboppers' use of the two-five progression. A two-five progression occurs when a minor seventh chord is immediately followed by a dominant seventh whose root is located a perfect fifth below the root of the minor seventh. Two-five progressions may be primary (for example, $d^7$ to $G^7$, in the key of C major), secondary (for example, $e^7$ to $A^7$ as it relates to the key of C major = the related two of the $V^7/d^7$), or extended (for example, $| a^{b7}$ to $D^{b7} | G^{b7} |$ as it relates to the key of C = the related two of the dominant of the subV$^7$/IV). This progression, already a well-established practice before bebop, was often used by bebop composers in a more extended fashion. That is, minor seventh chords (or minor sevenths with a lowered fifth) often progressed downward a perfect fifth to the roots of dominant-seventh chords that did not resolve diatonically. In bebop and postbebop literature, these progressions often occurred in sequences:

$$ \| \; g^7(\text{-}5) \mid C^7(\text{+}9, \text{+}5) \mid f^7(\text{-}5) \mid B^{b7}(\text{+}9, \text{+}5) \mid e^{b7}(\text{-}5) \mid A^{b7}(\text{+}9, \text{+}5) \mid D^b(\text{+}7) \; \| $$

The above progression is taken from the first eight measures of Dizzy Gillespie's "Woody'n You," written in D$^b$ major. In measures two through seven, identical two-five progressions occur, the last of which resolves to the tonic in measure eight. Interestingly, none of the two-five progressions are diatonic to the key.

The same composition also illustrates the melodic use of chromaticism, which is largely a consequence of the chromatic harmonies. For example, note the G natural on beat three of measure one, and the pitches C$^b$ and E natural, which occur as the first and last eighth-notes in measure six. However the D natural, occurring on the first half of the fourth beat of measure seven, is not harmonically derived.

The extensions used in this chord progression are also noteworthy in that they too reveal a peculiarity of bebop. While all the chords leading to the tonic are chromatic to the key, the extensions employed against the first, second, and fourth chords are, ironically, derived from the key of $D^b$ major. In using diatonic extensions against these chromatic harmonies, Gillespie subtly relates them to the key of $D^b$. These same diatonic extensions enhance the intrinsic dissonance of the chords to the extent that in each case they are nonindigenous to the chord to which they are applied.

However, Gillespie keeps the listener off guard by following the first four chords with two additional chromatic chords, embellished this time by chromatic extensions. The lowered fifth in the $e^{b7}(-5)$ chord and the raised ninth and raised fifth extensions against the $A^{b7}$ structure are not derived from the key of $D^b$ major. They are derived from $D^b$ minor—the parallel minor; to this extent these chords must be classified as *borrowed chords*.[8] Because of the prodigious use of chromaticism, the types of two-five progressions used by the beboppers became more varied than those used by swing arrangers.

Indirect resolutions of dominant chords are a common feature of bebop harmony. An indirect resolution occurs when the resolution of a dominant-seventh chord is interrupted by the interpolation of the related two of the chord to which the dominant resolves. Thus, indirect resolutions are applicable to both secondary and extended dominants and substitute dominants. For example, in measures twelve, thirteen, and fourteen of Charlie Parker's "Blues for Alice," $D^{b7}$ (the subV$^7$/V$^7$) resolves ultimately to the dominant, but not before the interpolation of the supertonic or ii$^7$.

$$\ldots\ldots\,|\,a^{b7}\quad D^{b7}\qquad\qquad|\,g^7\qquad\qquad\qquad|\,C^7\ |\ldots\ldots$$
$$\qquad\qquad\ \ \text{subV}^7/\text{V}^7\quad\ \ \text{ii}^7\ (\text{supertonic})\qquad\text{V}^7$$

The technique of writing a sequence of chromatically descending, substitute dominants was introduced during the swing era in compositions like Duke Ellington's "Sophisticated Lady." The beboppers seized upon and abstracted this technique. Though Ellington used the technique to embellish or prolong the resolution of the supertonic to the dominant and the tonic to the V$^7$/V$^7$, the beboppers required no such functionality to validate the employment of sequences of dominant structures. Consequently, they *sequenced* dominant sevenths in any manner they chose.

In Thelonious Monk's "Well You Needn't," for example, the B section begins with a whole-step transposition of the last phrase from section A (Example 8.1). Appropriately, a $G^7$ chord is used to harmonize it. The next phrase constitutes a transposition of the same phrase a semitone higher; the underlying harmony is transposed correspondingly. The harmonic and melodic transposition continues its semitonal ascent for another one and one-half measures, in a rhythmically accelerated fashion. It then begins a half-step descent for the next two measures, in a manner reminiscent of Ellington's previous use of the technique, cadencing finally on the subV$^7$/I$^6$ in measure sixteen.

There was at least one chord the beboppers highlighted in the harmonic lexicon of jazz, if in fact they did not introduce it: the augmented-eleventh chord. It was used both compositionally and improvisationally. Dizzy Gillespie was apparently the first bebop musician to realize the improvisational and harmonic ramifications of the augmented eleventh—known to him as the flatted fifth. He remarks about how he first became aware of the flatted-fifth:

> Edgar Hayes had this arrangement, a ballad arrangement, and the chord was an E-flat . . . and I heard this A concert going up a scale, and I played it, and I played it again, played it again, played it again. I said, "Damn! . . . Listen at this, man!" Before that time, until 1938, that was not a part of my musical conception.[9]

Later Gillespie notes:

> From doing this, I found that there were a lot of pretty notes in a chord that were well to hold, instead of running over them. That's what Rudy [Powell] taught me. . . .There are a lot of

pretty notes in a chord, and if you hold them for an extended time, it adds a hue . . . to your solos.[10]

The interval of the augmented eleventh was often used with substitute dominant chords by Dizzy Gillespie, Thelonious Monk, and Tadd Dameron; the augmented-eleventh interval was also occasionally used within nondominant structures. The tonic chord with an added augmented eleventh is one notable example. This chord given at the conclusion of compositions had a particularly striking effect. The augmented eleventh as an extension, and the other extensional possibilities inspired by Gillespie's discovery of the sharp eleventh extension, had a profound impact on bebop improvisation and changed the sound and nature of jazz improvisation forever.

A chord commonly known to swing musicians as a minor-sixth chord was borrowed by the beboppers and used in a more expanded fashion. Gillespie attributes this innovation to Thelonious Monk, who, according to Gillespie, used the chord typically with the minor sixth in the bass. An example of the expanded use of this structure has already been cited in Gillespie's "Woody'n You."

As already noted, improvisational style in bebop was based on a more expanded harmonic chromaticism than swing. This fact, coupled with the fact that bebop improvisers gave greater emphasis to the higher extensions in chords, resulted inevitably in a more dissonant improvisational style. In addition, the improvisation style of the beboppers was more variably rhythmical and syncopated, and in upbeat compositions, more technically rigorous.

Speed of performance—that is, the rapid deliverance of musical ideas—in upbeat bebop compositions was something the beboppers valued highly, to the extent that it showed the improviser's technical command of his instrument and powers of invention. Consequently, rapid sixteenth-note runs interspersed with highly syncopated riffs and the skillful placement of rests (which often framed and defined the runs and riffs) were quite common. Because bebop compositions often exploited more difficult keys than those of swing, the bebop improviser was required to have a stronger knowledge of major and minor scales than his earlier counterparts.

The beboppers often used the harmonic format of preexistent songs and pop tunes as the basis of improvisations. When the underlying harmonies (*changes*, as they are frequently called by jazz musicians) were not, in their original form, suited to the taste of the improvisers, they often reharmonized them. Reharmonization was also a tool the beboppers used in jam sessions to test the improvisational skills of outsiders.

Form in bebop composition was not given a great deal of attention. In small combos, the music generally began with the melody or theme played in unison or octaves by front line musicians. This opening section of the work was immediately followed by a series of improvisations that varied in length. The theme was recapitulated after the improvisations, bringing the composition to a close. In big bands, the theme was often introduced by one or more instrumental sections usually in a homorhythmic or quasi-homorhythmic fashion. When an introduction preceded the theme, the texture and orchestration of the theme was generally different. Improvisations followed the theme but were usually circumscribed in their length, as they were in swing bands.

In larger band settings, various types of instrumental (sectional) accompaniments were employed. Sometimes these instrumental accompaniments were texturally complex, sometimes they were sparse, and at other times they were completely absent, leaving the job of solo accompaniment to the rhythm section. Several solos presented consecutively were usually followed by a section in which the instrumental choirs were featured in fanciful or inventive textural interplay with each other or with the rhythm section. The recapitulation of the theme usually signaled the ending of the work.

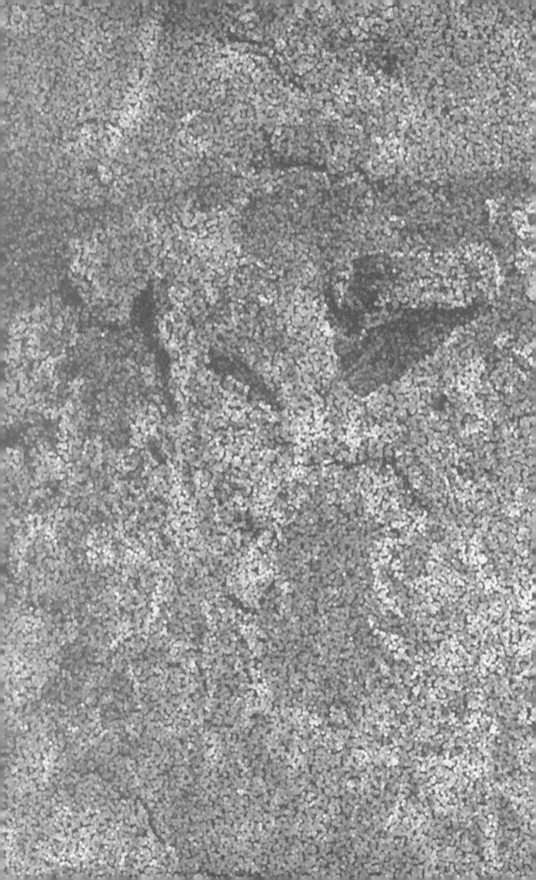

## CHAPTER 9

## JAZZ: 1950 TO 1970

JAZZ CONTINUED its evolution through the fifties and sixties, though its popularity was ultimately usurped by the rise of R&B, soul, and other styles. The fifties witnessed an unusually broad mixture of influences, all of which had prodigious philosophical, aesthetic, and economic impacts on later developments in jazz. The reigning stylistic influence going into the fifties was bebop. In the hands of some of its most uncompromising representatives, it continued to develop, despite its waning popularity, the deaths of two of its most articulate exponents—Charles Parker (due to drug abuse) and Clifford Brown (in an automobile accident)—and its usurpation by new influences.

One of these newer influences was called *cool jazz*. It crystallized in the early fifties and for a brief period not only became the dominant jazz style but also influenced other movements, like *West Coast jazz* and *third stream*, the latter a style founded by classical composer Gunther Schuller that was based upon the merging of elements from jazz and Western classical music. Cool jazz was a reaction to the hyperintensity and speed of bebop; these players were more reflective, and tended to favor slower tempos. The use of muted instruments was also a trademark of cool, particularly of the trumpet. Among the leading exponents of cool was trumpeter Miles Davis, saxophonist Gerry Mulligan, pianist Lennie Tristano, and arranger Gil Evans.

In the late fifties, a back-to-the-roots reaction to cool wrestled back the allegiance of many former beboppers who, for various reasons, had previously defected to the cool jazz camp. This style was known as *hard bop* (sometimes referred to as *soul jazz*). Like bebop, it was a powerful, emotional music; but, unlike bebop, it was based on African American folk forms, including gospel and blues. Hard bop tried to restore to jazz its folk roots and make it once again a popular music. Concurrent with the inception of hard bop was the germination of an even more controversial style—one that would push jazz seemingly to the very limits of its technical and aesthetic identity. For reasons to be given later we may call this movement *avant-garde nationalism* (many other writers call this style *free jazz*).

The aesthetic and philosophical lines demarcating these styles were not always clear. Many bebop musicians, for example, outwardly professed their admiration for classical music and openly acknowledged the contributions some of their conservatory-trained compatriots made to the style. Conversely, many cool artists wrote or performed music that evidenced conspicuous bebop influences. In addition, several eminent exponents of cool jazz made meaningful collaborations with bebop artists; George Shearing and Charlie Parker is one of several such collaborations. Despite their aesthetic and philosophical interconnections, however, the distinctiveness of these styles justify their independent examination, along with the role played in their development by individual musicians.

## Cool Jazz

Cool jazz meant different things to different people. For some artists it was the means by which the smoothness, relaxed elegance, structural pristineness, and clarity exemplified by improvisers like Lester Young and composers like Duke Ellington could be expanded into a general aesthetic approach. For others, cool jazz was a way to incorporate Euro-classical aesthetic ideals into jazz in a manner more convincing than those attempted by artists of earlier periods. For many of its white cultivators, cool was the stylistic answer to a long search for a personal expression, one independent of imitating black models. For other adherents, particularly those intimidated by bebop, cool jazz constituted a necessary reaction to the musical tension and alleged philosophical and political radicalism of the beboppers. Conversely, for some of its detractors cool jazz was a style designed to validate those artists who could not compete with the pyrotechnical improvisational skills of their bebop counterparts.

Whatever one's point of view, cool jazz was a viable and powerful movement that lasted as a dominant thrust for about a decade. Though its range of expression was somewhat broad, certain common features can be identified. Cool melodies, for example, tend to be symmetrically constructed. They are generally less syncopated than bebop melodies and noticeably do not use silences (rests) in the complex manner characteristic of bebop style.

However, the influence of bebop is unequivocally evident in the harmonic language of cool. Major and minor ninth and thirteenth chords, added-note chords, as well as augmented-eleventh chords are commonly employed. The harmonic rhythm of many cool compositions, however, is often slower than that of bebop. This fact contributes to the perception of a more relaxed style.

Improvisations by cool artists were generally less virtuosic than those of bebop artists. In cool-oriented big bands, improvisations were often more restrained and, like swing, functioned more as part of a broad array of dramatic devices than as a vehicle for personal showmanship and invention. Generally cool improvisations, as exemplified by performers like Miles Davis, emphasized economy of statement rather than technical prodigality.

In many ways, form in cool resembled form in swing, in that emphasis was often placed on the overall structure of the work and how the individual sections fit together into the total picture rather than on the technical inventiveness that occurred incidentally within individual sections. In large ensembles, counterpoint played a more prominent role than in bebop big bands and served to complement other textural devices employed to dramatize the music.

Classical associations were an integral part of the cool aesthetic. These associations were exemplified in several ways: (1) a trend for cool artists to study with or associate with classical artists; (2) an involvement by classical artists in cool jazz and in writing compositions for cool jazz ensembles; (3) the titles of cool compositions, particularly those written by white arrangers and composers, that often alluded in some conspicuous way to Euro-classicism—for example, "Opus in Beige" (Gene Roland), "Riff Rhapsody" (Gene Roland), "Artistry in Blues" (Stan Kenton); and (4) experimentation by cool artists and their disciples and associates with the merging of jazz with classical genres, forms, and procedures—for example, jazz-influenced musicals, blues operas, symphonic jazz, and so on.

Eminent black artists who wrote or performed music conforming to the cool aesthetic, however loosely, included Miles Davis (1926–1991), Quincy Jones (b. 1933), and John Lewis (b. 1920). It must be noted, however, that black artists, particularly composers, who wrote exclusively in the cool style were rare. What seems to be more in evidence are composers who incorporated aspects of cool in a continuing but declining swing tradition or who blended cool elements with those of bebop. The Quincy Jones masterpiece "Quintessence" constitutes a good example of the latter (Example 9.1). While it conforms in many ways to style features characteristic of cool ballads, the second phrase, which begins with a sixteenth-note arpeggiation of an F-minor chord, is strongly reminiscent of a similarly shaped pattern that forms the motivic basis of Thelonious Monk's "'Round Midnight." Linking this piece even more to Monk's "'Round Midnight" is the extemporized manner in which this ballad is typically performed and its frequent half-note and quarter-note harmonic rhythms.

Jones's original orchestration of the melody, however, typifies the lushness that characterizes cool arrangements of the fifties.[1] The solo melody performed on the saxophone begins in measure three, following

Example 9.1. "Quintessence" (Quincy Jones)

a brief introduction featuring four successive imitations of the opening motive, each orchestrated differently. As the saxophone expresses the main theme, the mood is nuanced from section to section by instrumental accompaniments that vary from slowly moving backgrounds of varying volumes to quasicontrapuntal intrusions of the opening motive to voluminous outbursts by combined instrumental sections.

Another exceptional cool performer/composer was Miles Davis. While his style is said to have epitomized cool improvisation, some of his compositions, interestingly, show a mixture of cool and bebop influences. When he first arrived in New York to study at the Juilliard School, a prestigious classical music conservatory, Davis played with Charlie Parker and other boppers, and their influence remained in his work despite his subsequent allegiance to the cool school. His composition "Boplicity," as correctly suggested by the title, contains elements that are decidedly of the bebop tradition; for example the prominence of the

Miles Davis

bebop motif, and the highly diversified and highly syncopated motivic constitution of the theme. Its mood, however, is generally more relaxed than that of most pristinely bebop melodies.

More typical of cool melodies are compositions like "Django," written by John Lewis (Example 9.2). Lewis, as pianist and arranger for the Modern Jazz Quartet (MJQ), set the style of one of the most popular jazz groups of the 1950s and 1960s. The MJQ took a classical model—the string quartet—and adapted it to jazz, performed in concert halls, and emphasized in the presentation of their music the seriousness of their approach, just as classical musicians performed. They even recorded an album of jazz arrangements of Bach, a clear wedding of classical themes with jazz techniques. Illustrating Lewis's penchant for third stream is his composition *European Windows*. This work, written in six parts and orchestrated by the composer, was recorded in Germany in 1958 by members of the Stuttgart Symphony Orchestra. The composition constitutes a "series of sound perspectives on European music and culture."[2]

While many black jazz artists participated in varying degrees in the development of cool jazz, the evidence suggests that its dominant cultivators were in fact white artists. Some of the more superlative of this cadre included Woody Herman, Gil Evans, Dave Brubeck, and Stan Kenton.

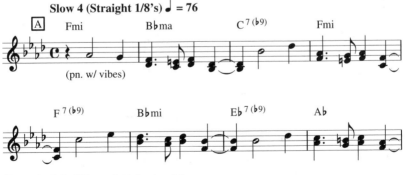

Example 9.2. "Django" (John Lewis)

## Hard Bop

In the mid-fifties, two interconnected trends destined to challenge the primacy of cool became evident. The first of these trends laid the foundation for what was to become *avant-garde nationalism* in the following decade (to be discussed shortly); the second trend was known as *hard bop*. One school of hard bop constituted essentially a refinement and expanded development of the bebop style. Not surprisingly, its principal cultivators were from the forties bebop camp and included artists such as Fats Navarro, Dizzy Gillespie, Thelonious Monk, Max Roach, Art Blakey, Clifford Brown, Tadd Dameron, and Jackie McLean. To the extent that this aspect of hard bop did not transmute the parameters of bebop into a new style the designation *bebop* is still applicable to it. An exquisite example of 1950s bebop is the Art Blakey composition "Transfiguration," initially recorded in 1957.

However, the major thrust of hard bop was in effect a "back-to-the-roots" movement. The "roots" referred to by its cultivators were African American folk and popular vernacular styles, for example, blues, spirituals, and gospel music.[3] Its leading innovators included alto and soprano saxophonist Julian "Cannonball" Adderley (1928–1975), trumpeters Nathaniel Adderly, Cannonball's brother (b. 1931), Donald Byrd (b. 1932), and Lee Morgan (1938–1972), tenor saxophonist Theodore "Sonny" Rollins (b. 1930), pianist Horace Silver (b. 1928), and organist James "Jimmy" Smith (b. 1928).

Hard bop melodies were basically simple in their motivic construction, singable, generally symmetrical, and exhibited conspicuous black vernacular influences. The works were generally formatted like bebop compositions. That is, the pieces opened with a statement of the melody followed by a series of improvisations and concluded with a recapitulation of the original melody by the ensemble. Two of the great classics from this genre are Lee Morgan's "Sidewinder," and Horace Silver's "Song For My Father" (Example 9.3). Though embellished somewhat by

Example 9.3. "Song for My Father" (Horace Silver)

the sixteenth-note triplet patterns, the opening four bars of "Song For My Father" are predicated on an F-minor pentatonic scale, a feature that also links this melody strongly with contemporary black popular elements and of course gospel roots.

Hard bop continued through the sixties. The commercial success of several of its principal exponents—such as Cannonball Adderley with "Mercy, Mercy, Mercy," Lee Morgan with "Sidewinder," and Horace Silver with "Song For My Father"—did much to seduce many other musicians into at least a partial involvement with the style. By the late sixties hard bop had expanded its borders to include more black popular influences, as exemplified by Ramsey Lewis's *jazzed* versions of popular and soul music hits in 1967 (for example, "Alfie," "Soul Man," "Respect," and "I Was Made to Love Her") arranged by Richard Evans.[4]

## Avant-Garde Nationalism

As previously noted, concurrent with the development of hard bop was an experimental thrust that laid the foundation for a radically new jazz aesthetic, one that crystallized in the 1960s. This new style was dubbed *avant-garde nationalism* by some and *free jazz* by others. Neither term adequately describes this movement, though both relate, in spirit, to the period that gave impetus to the style. Three of the earliest cultivators of the style were Sun Ra (1915–1996), Charlie Mingus (1922–1979), and Cecil Taylor (b. 1933). Among its most noted cultivators during the 1960s were Eric Dolphy (1926–1964), Ornette Coleman (b. 1930), Archie Shepp (b. 1934), Cecil Taylor, John Coltrane (1926–1967), Albert Ayler (1936–1970), and Don Cherry (1936–1995).

Though New York was the epicenter of the new music, by the mid-1960s its influence had spread to many areas around the country and in varying degrees was evident in the styles of many jazz musicians. Eminent artists from Chicago who pioneered the new music in the middle and late 1960s included Richard Abrams and Fred Anderson; from St. Louis, Missouri, Oliver Lake and Julius Hemphill; from Los Angeles, Horace Tapscott among others; and from New Orleans, such artists as Edward Blackwell, Alvin Batiste, and particularly Edward "Kidd" Jordan.

Avant-garde nationalism was in great measure a reflection of the political and cultural nationalism championed by radical black artists and intellectuals of the period, and many of its aesthetic and stylistic attributes are best seen in these terms. The 1960s was a particularly turbulent and violent era that for black Americans resulted in a great political, psychological, cultural, and historical reassessment and redefinition. African Americans were no longer content to view the world or themselves purely in Western European terms. For many blacks a new definition of freedom was necessary in order to transcend the notion of simply being accommodated by a historically hostile or indifferent society. It entertained, and for many endorsed, the viability of complete cultural and philosophical autonomy.

Radical black historians began to reassess and dismiss Eurocentric notions of black history—particularly African history. This gave rise to a new revisionist historical literature, one decidedly Afrocentric. Black nationalist writers wrote novels, poetry, and plays that openly and unapologetically attacked Eurocentric assumptions of black identity. Such literature frequently reflected the vehemence, anger, and rage of the period. A classic example of the latter is *Dutchman*, a play written by LeRoi Jones (who later took the name Amiri Baraka), one of the most important and influential African American playwrights and poets of his generation. One of the lead characters in the play expresses this hostility:

> I'll rip your lousy breast off! Let me be who I feel like being. Uncle Tom. Thomas. Whoever. It's none of your business. You don't know anything except what's there for you to see. An act. Lies. Device. Not the pure heart, the pumping black heart. . . . You fuck some black man, and right away you're an expert on black people. What a lotta shit that is. . . . They say, "I love Bessie Smith." And don't even understand that Bessie Smith is saying, "kiss my ass, kiss my black unruly ass."
>
> Charlie Parker? Charlie Parker. All the hip white boys screamed for Bird. And Bird saying, "Up your ass, feebleminded ofays! Up your ass." And they sit there talking about the tortured genius of Charlie Parker. Bird would've played not a note

of music if he just walked up to East Sixty-seventh Street and killed the first ten white people he saw. Not a note![5]

Litigators and particularly activists challenged on every front laws and practices that previously circumvented or circumscribed the implementation of the constitutional rights of black Americans. Nationalist artists and intellectuals forged new alliances with groups from other parts of the African diaspora and the Third World. From such alliances were derived interests in new philosophies, new ideologies, non-Western mythologies, non-Western mysticism, and non-Western religions.

The musical manifestations of avant-garde nationalism were many. Rhythm, for example, began to be conceived in more liberal ways. This manifested itself in a greater use of African- and Asian-influenced rhythms, and in the increased use of asymmetric meters, changing meters, free meter, and ultimately no meter. For some artists, the absence of rhythmic synchronicity between the various members of an ensemble was an aesthetically acceptable and inevitable notion.

Old and new scales were investigated and ultimately adopted. From African American traditional music came the pentatonic scale. From early European music came the ecclesiastical or church modes. Each mode has its own pattern of intervals, giving it a unique character but making transposition from mode to mode impossible. Miles Davis was one of the first artists to begin experimenting with using modes as a basis for composition (on his famous 1959 album, *Kind of Blue*). John Coltrane, under the influence initially of Davis, took modal experimentation to an even higher level, as did Pharoah Sanders, Yusef Lateef, and Alvin Batiste. Some musicians turned to non-Western music, such as the rich tradition of the music of India, drawing from these sources many exotic scales. Others turned to the work of twentieth century composer/theorist Arnold Schoenberg, who developed twelve-tone music, where all twelve chromatic notes are freed from their traditional tonal and harmonic functions. These new scale patterns made possible new harmonic resources and introduced a broader tonal spectrum to jazz, one that ranged from expanded tonality, to bitonality, to atonality.

New instruments were introduced, along with instruments that had previously been underutilized. Alice Coltrane's creative ventures with the harp helped greatly in demonstrating its potential as an improvisational instrument. Other such instruments were the violin, alto flute, and exotic instruments like the kora (African harp) and mbira (African thumb piano). Such instrumentation redefined from this point forward the role timbre and timbral mixtures played in the contemplative and improvisational construction of jazz composition.

New performing techniques were also introduced. Such techniques included multiphonics, that is, the production of two or more sounds from the same sound generator. This technique was manifested either by simultaneously humming the melodic pattern played by the instrumentalist, at the unison, octave, fifth, or some other interval; or by exploiting the extreme register of the instruments—overblowing—creating at times eerie, screeching sounds. Pharoah Sanders's improvisational style in the 1960s often made use of this technique; see for example his composition "Upper Egypt." Another noted performer was saxophonist/flautist Rahsaan Roland Kirk, who often played two or more instruments simultaneously as well as using other techniques to produce multiple sounds.

One interesting outgrowth of the avant-garde nationalist movement was the emergence of the multitalented jazz artist. The intellectual, political, and creative concerns of many jazz artists were no longer expressed exclusively by way of music. A number of these artists became proficient in other artistic modes of expression and generally treated these nonmusical modes as extensions of the same creative process. Archie Shepp is one noted example. His drama *Junebug Graduates Tonight* is subtitled *A Jazz Allegory*, and contains many musical interpolations.[6] By the early 1970s, it was no longer unusual to find eminent contemporary jazz artists who were also adept as poets, painters, or playwrights. The trend continues to this day.

The creativeness of the new music notwithstanding, it was clear to its cultivators from the beginning that their music was not destined to receive any great stamp of approval from the social or business establishment. The absence of such acceptance and support worked against the music ever becoming economically viable. Job offers, consequently, were not plentiful. When jobs were available, the conditions under which the artists worked were often not hospitable. Musicians were sometimes forced to play on inadequate in-house instruments (badly tuned pianos, for example) or suffer public indignities from owners whose concern for making money far transcended their interest in the musicians' art.

In an attempt to improve the economic viability of their music, ensure its continuation, and foster its acceptance among the people, many of its cultivators organized self-help efforts. Such efforts frequently took the form of arts guilds or arts associations. These guilds began to emerge around 1960, though they were preceded by efforts that began in the early 1950s. In his book *Fire Music: A Political History of Jazz*, Rob Backus enumerates a number of such organization. including: (1) *The Jazz Artists' Guild*, established in 1960 by Charles Mingus, Max Roach, and Abbey Lincoln; (2) *The Jazz Composers Guild*, which included Sun Ra, Bill Dixon, Cecil Taylor, Archie Shepp, and others; (3) *The Jazz Composer's Orchestra Association* (JCOA) established in 1965; and (4) *The Underground Musicians Association*, cofounded by Horace Tapscott in 1964 in Watts.[7]

The most influential of all the self-help organizations to emerge between 1965 and 1975 were the *Association for the Advancement of Creative Musicians* (AACM) and the *Black Artist Group* (BAG). The Association for the Advancement of Creative Musicians was founded on May 26, 1965, in Chicago. It offered to inner-city students (of all ages) applied classes in various instruments and classes in music theory. From this association emerged such legendary artists as The Art Ensemble of Chicago, an experimental group that consisted of Joseph Jarman, Don Maye, Lester Bowie, Malachi Favors, Roscoe Mitchell, Richard Abrams (cofounder of the organization), and composer Anthony Braxton. The AACM remains active today. It now has two branches, the original branch in Chicago and one subsequently created in New York.

The Black Artist Group (BAG) came into being in 1968.[8] Its cofounders included Julius Hemphill, Oliver Lake, and Floyd Le Flore. The organization originated after a trip Lake made to Chicago to meet with members of the AACM. He was impressed by the AACM's organization and by the classes they offered. Inspired by what he had seen, Lake set out to organize the creative black talent active in St. Louis. Before the inception of BAG, musicians met only within professional contexts or during jam sessions. Initially, Lake considered creating another branch of the AACM but, after speaking with Julius Hemphill, opted instead for the creation of an independent organization—one that would merge not only the talents of musicians, but also of actors, visual artists, poets, and others. Such multi-artistic resources enabled BAG to install theater, dance, literary, and visual arts components in addition to music. They gave concerts on weekends, which often brought the various components of the organization together in collaborative efforts.[9] An artists exchange program eventually emerged between BAG and the AACM in which artists from the AACM would perform at BAG concerts and vice versa. BAG folded in the early 1970s, but some of its musicians went on to exert an enormous influence on contemporary experimental jazz, an influence that continues to this day.

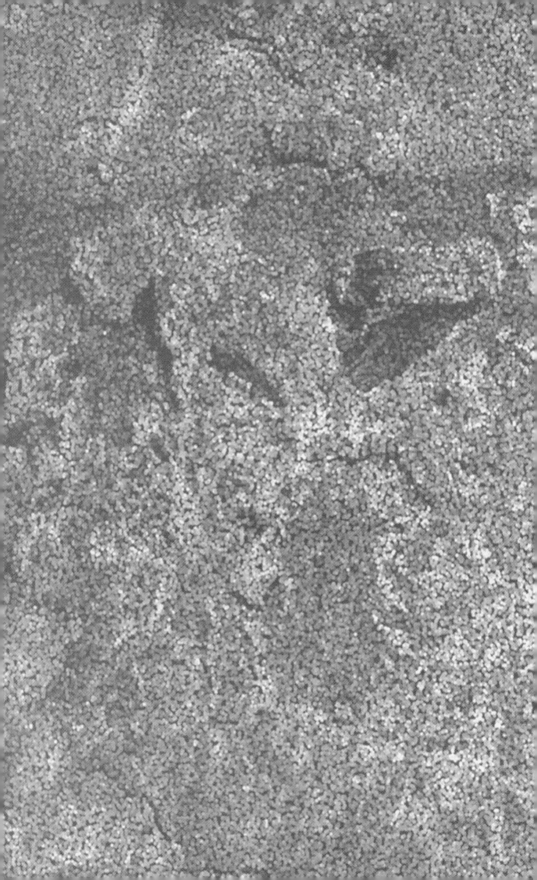

## CHAPTER 10

# JAZZ: 1970 TO THE PRESENT

**J**AZZ CONTINUED branching off into many different directions after 1970. The result was a highly diverse array of jazz styles spanning a range that breached the boundaries of popular music at one end and Western classical music at the other. Thus, since the 1970s, jazz, as a genre different from the other vernacular and non-vernacular expressions, has become increasingly difficult to define. Of all the styles that fit under the rubric of jazz, however, four have been well-represented by black jazz artists: jazz rock/fusion; third stream; experimental jazz; and neo-bebop. But even here the lines separating these styles, and the artists who cultivate them, are not always clear.

## Jazz Rock and Fusion

Both R&B and 1960s rock were influential in the formation of *jazz rock* (also called *fusion*), a type of hybrid resulting from a mixture of jazz with contemporary popular music. The popularity of some black jazz rock artists was, in fact, the result of their jazz or quasijazz adaptations of contemporary popular songs, for example "Broadway" as performed by vocalist/guitarist George Benson, "Ain't No Sunshine When She Gone" as performed by saxophonist Grover Washington, Jr., and Earl Klugh's rendition of "Could It Be I'm Falling In Love." Original compositions, however, were not beyond the purview of jazz rock artists, as Eric Gale's "Nezumi," and Ralph MacDonald's "Lookin' Good" bear testimony.

Just what exactly constituted a 1970s jazz rock composition was not always clear; many of the artists who wrote jazz rock tunes also wrote

Grover Washington Jr.

"straight ahead" pieces (that is, in a more mainstream jazz style), and often placed both types of jazz on the same album. In the works of some artists, the two styles became so intertwined that their differences are not easily discernible. Though some jazz rock works featured a lead vocal, most were instrumental. In their clearest manifestation, jazz rock compositions were unpretentious in their use of popular elements; this usually meant they included tuneful, singable melodies, funk or funk-influenced rhythms, and transparent, usually uncomplicated harmonies of the type common to popular compositions. The theme was usually followed by one or more instrumental solos. Simple duple meter predominated. Tempos were generally danceable.

The more complicated jazz rock pieces were mainly instrumental, written in simple duple meter and song-form structure, sometimes featuring free-rhythmic, cloudlike introductions. They sometimes were based upon African or non-Western rhythmic backgrounds and always featured one or more improvisations. The melodies were rhythmically sophisticated, and though often attractive, they were generally not light or singable. The harmonies were characterized by the use of higher extensions and chromatic progressions.

Both forms of jazz rock continued into the 1980s and 1990s, but were identified more by the term *fusion*. The simpler, more popular paradigm, performed by artists like Grover Washington Jr. and George Benson, predominated. New artists like Najee, Gerald Albright, and Walter Beasley emerged in the late 1980s and brought to popular jazz rock/fusion their own unique signatures. Often the styles of the more popular fusion artists were so close to contemporary rhythm and blues that distinguishing the two was virtually impossible.

## Free Jazz after 1970

The free jazz movement of the 1960s also continued into the 1970s and beyond but became increasingly more marginalized by its own esotericism, which made it difficult to compete with the more lucrative, vernacular-based jazz and nonjazz styles. The patronage of universities, art institutions, and foundations rescued a few of the free jazz artists from economic ruin, but the trek for many, to this day, remains unjustly difficult. Nevertheless, their experimentation continued, resulting in new techniques and procedures, like (1) the development of new systems of notation; (2) expanded timbral and textural exploitations; (3) the use of electronic instruments and computers as improvisational mediums; (4) experimentation with multimedia forms and notions; and (5) new approaches to conducting.

Another result of post-1970 free jazz experimentation was the greater role played by the performer in the creation of musical composition; by the late 1970s, this role would be dominated by the performer. This movement established improvisation as every bit as viable as the

Western-based notion of contemplative composition, if not more so, and effectively dislodged the primacy of the latter.

New artists came into critical (if not popular) acclaim, as did previously established but unrecognized talents that emerged during the late 1960s, including Anthony Braxton, Oliver Lake, George Lewis, Douglas Ewart, and Edward Jordan. The most popular of the experimentalists of the 1970s was Anthony Braxton (b. 1945), who came out of the AACM school of avant-garde jazz performers/composers (see chapter 9). Braxton's music shows influences from both the Western classical avant-garde tradition and the free-jazz tradition. Ronald Radano notes that:

> Braxton's affinity for modernist music, together with his philosophical attachment to vanguardist artistic principles, calls to mind a particular realm, the world of experimentalism, which, under the aesthetic leadership of John Cage, became this half-century's musical emblem of intellectual crisis and uncertainty. But unlike previous experimentalists . . . Braxton, in a multitude of ways, has drawn from the African American legacy. His articulation of a vital, dynamic art that referred to the modernist legacy but in a distinctly African American creative voice signaled the appearance of a dramatically new kind of musician: the black experimentalist.[1]

Oliver Eugene Lake (b. 1942), founder of the Black Artists Group (BAG), was also (and remains) a member of the acclaimed World Saxophone Quartet, an organization he cofounded. Its original membership consisted of alto saxophonists Julius Hemphill and Lake, tenor saxophonist David Murray, and baritone saxophonist Hamiet Bluiett. Since the death of Julius Hemphill in 1995, the group has added soprano saxophonist John Purcell.

Like many contemporary jazz artists, Lake shuns labels like avant-garde, but much of his work reflects the experimentation initiated by

Oliver Eugene Lake

BAG and AACM. His composition "Eraser of the Day" for alto saxophone solo (copyrighted 1980), for example, is a highly expressive work that is written essentially without a meter, employs interpretive improvisational symbols and directions, and interpolates a brief $\frac{3}{4}$ passage for metric contrast (Example 10.1). Lake has also written works for orchestra, string quartet, and string trio. An example of the latter is *Spaces*, a suite for violin trio, which, despite the traditional instrumentation, uses experimental techniques as well.

Flautist/composer Douglas Ewart (b. 1946) was born in Kingston, Jamaica. He came to Chicago in 1963 and became a member of the AACM in 1967. He has remained affiliated with this organization, serv-

Example 10.1. "Eraser of the Day" (Oliver Lake)

Douglas Ewart

ing as its president from 1979 to 1986. Ewart cites a long list of jazz innovators—Thelonious Monk, Charlie Parker, Charles Mingus, Eric Dolphy, Ornette Coleman, Fred Anderson, the Art Ensemble of Chicago, Turk Burton, and Anthony Braxton—as musicians who influenced his early development.[2] Yet when hearing Ewart's music one is struck by a truly unique voice that, despite its experimental nature, is at times strikingly sensuous, tranquil, aesthetic, and dramatic. His earlier compositions include "Difta Dolphy" (ca. 1969), "Jila" (1975), and "Black Jesus" (ca. 1978).

Ewart's compositional style in the 1980s began to show his interest in planetary notions, with titles like "Fire This Time," "The Unfolding," and "Mars Blues." The latter work was written for mixed ensemble, as music integral to a play called *Mars*, for Paul Carter Harrison.[3] An important composition from the 1990s is "Boukman." Boukman, according to Ewart, was a Jamaican slave who ran away to Haiti and later inspired the Haitian revolution.[4]

Trombonist George Lewis is, like Ewart, a member of the AACM. He joined the AACM in 1971 and his earlier compositions reflect its influence. An example of Lewis's seventies compositional voice is a work called "Shadowgraphs," a set of five pieces for jazz orchestra. The fifth "Shadowgraph" is described by Lewis as " a big piece of paper with sixteen minutes of bebop heads on it." The members of the ensemble interpret these heads then "take off . . . on their own way. They'd also have to listen to everyone who was doing whatever they were doing, but you didn't have to say, 'now you have to listen to everyone else.'"[5] This statement underscores one of the important differences between so-

George Lewis

called free-jazz improvisation and Western classical notions of improvisation, that is, free jazz improvisers listen intently and responsively to one another and never play randomly unless such an approach is specified. Thus, modern experimental jazz improvisation is not "free" in the sense of encouraging aimless playing.

Lewis's compositions from the 1980s onward reflect his interest in computer-oriented music and his penchant for using various media. An example of the latter is "Changing with the Times," which in addition to music features poetry, fiction, and an actor who presents an autobiographical depiction of the life of Lewis's father, George Lewis, Sr.

Among his colleagues, Edward "Kidd" Jordan (b. 1935) is one of the most highly respected masters of the free-jazz school. Jordan was born in Crowley, Louisiana, but since 1955 has lived in New Orleans. He has performed with such noted artists as Sun Ra, Muhal Richard Abrams, the Art Ensemble of Chicago, and Fred Anderson. Jordan's style is rooted in the free-jazz experimentations of the 1960s, but has since matured into a unique, sensitive, and highly personal voice. Specifically, his style is based upon the free development of a theme, but the theme itself may constitute a melody, a melodic or rhythmic motive, a timbre, a sound not emanating from a musical instrument (the sound of a fan, for example), or even a feeling. Jordan sometimes derives his ideas from unusual scale forms.

Jordan factored significantly in the creation of the World Saxophone Quartet. The group's creation emanates from an invitation Jordan extended to four New York saxophonists—Julius Hemphill, Oliver Lake, David Murray, and Hamiet Bluiett—to perform a concert organized by Jordan initially at Southern University in New Orleans and a performance the following night at the noted New Orleans jazz spot, Lu and Charlie's (now defunct). During these concerts the group was paired with a rhythm section that included drummer Alvin Fielder, bassist Elton Heron, and bassist London Branch. The audience response to the

Edward "Kidd" Jordan

group was so favorable that it inspired them to remain together. They originally called themselves the New York Saxophone Quartet but changed this name on discovering the existence of another group with the same name.

## The Neo-Bebop Aesthetic

Many artists—black and white—could not relate to the experimentations of free-jazz artists, but they also rejected fusion music as too commercial in its orientation. They felt jazz should return to its "roots," in this case the bebop stylings of the 1950s. This new mainstream style (also known as neoclassicism) was, and continues to be, led by trumpeter/composer Wynton Marsalis (b. 1961), son of jazz pianist Ellis Marsalis (b. 1934). Other eminent artists include Wynton's brother, saxophonist Branford Marsalis (b. 1960), trumpeter Terence Blanchard (b. 1962), flautist Kent Jordan (b. 1958), trumpeter Roy Hargrove (b. 1969), pianist Marcus Roberts (b. 1963), and pianist/composer Donald Brown (b. 1954).

From the beginning, Marsalis has been a charismatic and articulate spokesman for this new thrust, stressing the traditional virtues of technique, theory, aesthetics, an understanding of form and structure, and an appreciation for and understanding of jazz history and literature. His commitment to such lofty musical values has led some his detractors to label him a "purist." But Marsalis validates these values with his consistent display of a formidable performance technique—one that brilliantly accommodates the most rigorous demands of both the jazz and Western classical repertoires. More recently Marsalis has showcased another side of his creativity, the writing of extended compositions in the jazz idiom, and has admirably completed several major projects. One of his most impressive is the score for a ballet choreographed by Peter Martins and the New York City Ballet, entitled *Jazz: Six Syncopated Movements*. Other dance scores include *Jump*, written for the American Dance Theatre, and *Griot*, written for the Garth Fagan Dance Company. In 1997, Marsalis won the Pulitzer Prize for his composition, *Blood on the Fields*. He was the first jazz composer to win this award.

Terence Blanchard and Roy Hargrove are two prominent trumpeters who came into national prominence after Marsalis. Blanchard performed with Lionel Hampton in the early 1980s and with Art Blakey in the mid-1980s. With the latter master he became an important and influential artist, displaying a style that, though highly distinctive, is strongly anchored in the hard bop tradition. Blanchard has also distinguished himself as a composer of film scores. Of the better known are the scores for producer/director Spike Lee's *Do The Right Thing, Mo' Better Blues*, and *Malcolm X*.

Roy Hargrove surfaced with the assistance of Wynton Marsalis but has since distinguished himself as one of the most astounding jazz artists of the 1990s. Hargrove attended the Berklee College of Music in Boston. In 1995 he won the *Down Beat* Readers Poll. Hargrove's style is also rooted in the hard bop tradition but has quickly matured into a unique trumpet voice that leaves little trace of its derivation.

In the 1980s Kent Jordan emerged as the most brilliant flautist of the neo-classical tradition. Jordan, like Marsalis, descends from a highly respected aspect of the New Orleans jazz aristocracy. He is the son of saxophonist Edward Jordan, the brother of noted trumpeter Marlon Jordan, jazz vocalist Stephanie Jordan, and classical violinist Rachel Jordan, and the nephew of clarinetist/composer Alvin Batiste. Jordan is a graduate of the New Orleans Center for the Creative Arts and the Eastman School of Music. He has recorded and performed with Wynton Marsalis, Kevin Eubanks (guitarist and director of the Tonight Show orchestra), Elvin Jones, Bheki Mseleku, and Delfayo Marsalis.

The term neoclassical is perhaps more applicable to Jordan than to most other neoclassicists. Like Marsalis, Jordan is as endowed a classical artist as he is a jazz artist and frequently concertizes in both arenas. Since 1997 Jordan has been featured in concerts in which a jazz repertoire is

Kent Jordan

presented by orchestral mediums usually employed for classical literature. An example was the 1997 New Orleans Jazz and Heritage Festival,
at which Jordan performed jazz standards with a string orchestra and
harp, but with no rhythm section. The aesthetic result was a subdued
and nuanced presentation that emphasized harmonic and timbral color
without compromising the intrinsic rhythmic elegance of jazz. For the
audience the effect was a pleasant though unexpected shift from the
unrelieved succession of rhythm sections, jazz combos, and big bands
that preceded Jordan's ensemble.

Given Jordan's vast creative endowments it is curious why he is yet to
receive the recognition so generously awarded to artists who are often far
less gifted. Tragically, however, in the world of jazz such asymmetries
have been and are likely to remain a common feature.

The neo-bebop (or neoclassical) movement has produced no scarcity
of talented pianists. One of the most gifted is Donald Brown. Brown's
improvisational style is characterized by a balanced technique, sometimes a deceptively profound simplicity, and often by a haunting and sin-
cere lyricism. The logic of his improvisations reveals great thought and a
nuanced sense of economy, and they are often seamlessly attached to the
themes that precede them. These are qualities common to the great
piano masters of the past.

Brown is also a talented composer whose music, though often rooted
in bebop, shows a broad eclecticism. Brown's "Car Tunes" (Example
10.2), for example, is a singular masterpiece written in a highly rhythmic, nearly atonal style. Its bebop roots are implied by the frequent presence of the bebop motif and by the general rhythmic character of the
work, which is based on the fact there are no adjacent repetitions of
motives—giving the work a Charlie Parker–like quality—and upon the
rhythmic interplay of the bass and the melody.

Some of Brown's music has been inspired by his sensitivity to the
racial inequalities that exist in America and to racism found all over the

Donald Brown

Example 10.2. "Car Tunes" (Donald Brown)

world. One such work, "Cause and Effect," was inspired by the Rodney King incident of Los Angeles, which occurred in 1992. "Capetown Ambush" uses a racial incident in Capetown, South Africa, as a metaphor for black oppression around the world.

Other works by Brown reflect an even deeper, personal sensitivity. "Do We Have to Say Goodbye," for example, derives from a scene in *Roots* where slave children were taken away from their mother. Once again, Brown uses this incident as a metaphor for the general anguish suffered by people who are forcibly separated from their families and friends.

## Third Stream and Eclecticism after 1970

The third stream movement is reflected in several ways in post-1970 jazz and jazz-influenced composition. It is evident, for example, in some of the techniques used by free-jazz artists and in the increased use of the symphony orchestra as a viable and sometimes preferred medium of jazz expression. It is also evident in the classically derived models used by contemporary jazz and eclectic writers: jazz symphonies, jazz cantatas and oratorios, jazz operas, and jazz tone poems, for example.

If we define third stream as a movement aimed at merging Western classical music with jazz, then such a movement clearly started before the 1950s, when the term was coined. In a 1936 essay entitled "Classical Jazz and Modern American Music," Alain Locke spoke optimistically about the future of a movement predicated on the fusion of jazz and classical music that had started decades earlier.

> A most promising sign is that the latest classical jazz is clearly in a style more fused and closer to the original Negro musical idioms. . . . Unlike the first phase of classical jazz, they [the latest classical jazz compositions] are not artificial hybrids, but genuine developments of the intimate native idioms of jazz itself. Thus with these younger generation's efforts, we are considerably nearer to a true union and healthy vigorous fusion of jazz and the classical tradition.[6]

Many such compositions written before 1950 can be used to confirm Locke's observation. Of the better known works are James P. Johnson's "Yamekraw," an orchestral composition orchestrated by William Grant Still; Edmund Jenkins's "Rhapsody no. 2"; and Mary Lou Williams's "Zodiac Suite." We may also cite Duke Ellington's "Black, Brown, and Beige" and "New World a Coming," efforts that helped give birth to the jazz symphonic poem and the jazz concerto, respectively.

Though a substantial literature predicated upon the merging of jazz and classical elements clearly existed before 1950, it must be borne in mind that this literature was sporadic, peripheral, and had little if any impact on the main currents of jazz before 1950. Before such a compositional approach could become a new current in jazz (a third stream) it had to be championed by a personality charismatic enough to recast it into one worthy of serious and consistent attention by contemporary and subsequent jazz and classical artists. Such a personality proved to be composer/conductor/historian Gunther Schuller (b. 1925).

Modern extended compositions reflecting the influence of third stream have been both impressive and diverse. The influence is evident in the early extended works of Alvin Batiste (b. 1932); for example, *Kheri Hebs* and *North American Idiosyncrasies*, written in the late 1960s. *Kheri Hebs* was the name of the Gnostics, or Egyptian priests who kept the knowledge. *North American Idiosyncrasies* was an extended blues composition meant to exemplify, in the composer's words, "certain idiosyncrasies in the American experiences that emanate from the African American experience."[7] The work was originally written for saxophonist Julian "Cannonball" Adderley.

One of Batiste's greatest works in this vein is *Musique D'Afrique Nouvelle Orleans*. This work, composed in the 1970s, is in effect a concerto grosso written for symphony orchestra and a small concertino (solo) unit consisting of clarinet, bass guitarist, vocalist, and percussion. It amalgamates many diverse vernacular elements and quotes, against an African-influenced rhythmic and textural background, the jazz standard "When The Saints Go Marching In" in a surprisingly effective and rhythmically compatible manner. The work was given its New Orleans premiere in 1981 by the New Orleans Philharmonic (now called the Louisiana Philharmonic).

Like Batiste, Houston composer and jazz trumpeter Howard Harris (b. 1940) has made a prodigious contribution to the symphonic third

Alvin Batiste

Howard C. Harris Jr.

stream repertoire. His earlier efforts trace back to the 1960s with works like "March of the Non-Violent," written for symphonic band. The name of this work was later changed to "Elegy to Martin Luther King" (ca. 1968) following the civil rights leader's assassination. The work shows strong jazz influences, uses bitonality to symbolize the conflict of the races, and derives motifs from the patriotic song "Glory, Glory Halleluia."

Other works in a similar vein by Harris include *Folk Songs* (early 1970s) for symphony orchestra, *Blues For The New World* (1975)—a work inspired by the composer asking himself "If Dvořák was me what music would he write?"—also for symphony orchestra, and *Jazz Memorabilia* (1977). All of these efforts exemplify the fusion of jazz and nonjazz elements. Among his latest works are *Song for the Children* (1987, revised 1989), a multimovement work that opens in a gospel style and ends with excerpts from Martin Luther King's "I Have a Dream" speech, and a jazz version of the Twenty-third Psalm (1993) for four-part chorus and jazz orchestra.

Jazz or jazz-influenced extended works for theater proliferated after 1970. Anthony Davis (b. 1951) has been a leading composer of operatic works. Davis's most acclaimed work in this genre is *X, The Life and Times of Malcolm X* (1985), a work that addresses the life of America's foremost black Muslim activist who, like Martin Luther King, was assassinated in the 1960s. An impressive musical that extensively employed jazz and popular styles was *Big Man*, a work based on the life of John Henry. The work was composed by Julian Adderley (1928–1975), recorded in 1975, and was to be his last major opus; he died in the same year.

The arena of vernacular oratorio and cantata is best represented by the works of New York composer/pianist Valerie Capers (b. 1935). Capers is the sister of the late Bobby Capers, noted saxophonist who played with Mongo Santamaria in the 1960s and 1970s. At the behest of her brother,

Valerie Capers

she authored no fewer than four important commercial works for Santamaria during the 1960s: *El Toro* (the Bull); *La Gitana* (the Gypsy); *Ah Ha* (a soul hit); and *Chili Beans*. Her excursion into the world of the vernacular cantata emanates from an invitation extended to her by John Motley to write a Christmas song. She responded with the composition "Sing About Love" (ca. 1971), written in gospel style and scored for chorus, tambourine, piano, electric bass, and drums. The work, and the untimely death of her brother, inspired a cantata by the same name.

*Sing About Love*, the cantata, premiered in 1974. It was scored for strings, acoustic bass, assorted percussion (trap drums, congas, bongos, claves, cow bells, timpani), saxophonists doubling on flutes, bass clarinet, trombones, trumpets, and tuba. Most of the text derives from the Old and New Testaments. The story is essentially that of the Messiah but features the composer's own textual interpolations. The composition uses many vernacular and classical styles. For example, in the section entitled "Herod and the Wise Men," Herod sings in a rhythm and blues style. The blues is used in the interchange between Herod and the wise men. A bossa-nova, featuring a rhythm section and three flutes, underscores the section "No Room at the End." Four years after its premier, *Sing About Love* was performed in 1978 in Carnegie Hall, presented by jazz impresario George Wein.

Capers followed *Sing About Love* with *Sojourner*, a work the composer describes as an "operatorio" (ingeniously combining opera and oratorio). The work deals with the life of Sojourner Truth, and premiered in 1981 at New York's St. Peter's Church during their Jazz Vespers, an ecumenical service founded by John Gensel that features programs performed by jazz artists interspersed with biblical readings. The work was scored for chorus, mezzo-soprano soloist, and chamber jazz ensemble. It was conceived originally as a concert piece but was staged and performed for the first time by Opera Ebony of New York.

The suite is one of the oldest and most frequently accessed forms associated with jazz. We have previously mentioned suites composed by John Lewis and Duke Ellington. Ellington, the most accomplished master of the genre, completed three suites during the last four years of his life (1970–1974), two of which—*The River* and *Three Black Kings*—were written to accompany ballets. More recent composers who have contributed impressively to this repertoire include George Duke (b. 1946) and Hannibal (Marvin Peterson, b. 1948). George Duke's major contribution is the *Muir Woods Suite*. The work is really a combination of a suite and a concerto, despite the name. In its skillful and elegant conjoining of classical and jazz elements, it portrays a more intellectual, romantic, and lyrical side of Duke's musicality, a startling contrast to his typical fusion works. Hannibal's contribution is called *African Portraits*. The work combines indigenous African music, spirituals, blues, gospel music, jazz, and Western classical elements in its chronological depiction of the history of African Americans. It was given its premiere by the Chicago Symphony Orchestra and subsequently recorded by them under the baton of Daniel Barenboim. We may also include as significant contributions to this genre the recent balletic efforts of Wynton Marsalis, particularly his *Jazz: Six Syncopated Movements*.

Modern third stream and eclectic piano literature are beautifully represented by the works of Valerie Capers and Richard Thompson (b. 1954). Thompson's most impressive contribution is called *Six Preludes*, a set of short pieces composed between 1992 and 1993 that draws heavily upon the composer's Western classical and jazz backgrounds.

Capers's most impressive work in this vein is a collection of pieces composed in 1976 entitled *Portraits In Jazz* (Example 10.3). Each of the twelve movements is dedicated to an eminent jazz artist and is composed in a manner stylistically suggestive of the artist to whom it is dedicated.

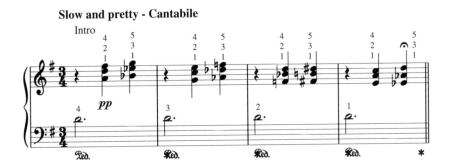

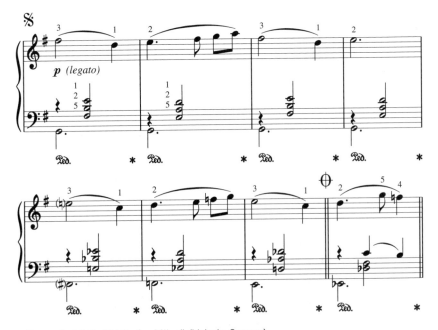

Example 10.3. "Waltz for Miles" (Valerie Capers)

The individual movements are engaging, often challenging, and eminently idiosyncratic.

Of all the traditional models used by jazz and third stream composers, the symphony—in the sense of a multimovement composition—

appears to be the least favored. One exquisite exception is Yusef Lateef's Symphony no. 1, *Tahira*, a work that beautifully displays Lateef's genius for combining Eastern idioms and American jazz idioms. It is striking in its use of ostinati (repeated melodic motifs), choral and instrumental pedals (drone notes), and improvisation.

Another more recent example of third stream symphonicism is Richard Thompson's Symphony no. 1, entitled *Voices* (1996). The work is in traditional four-movement design. The first movement has the quality of a spiritual. The second movement is a mournful jazz ballad, subtitled *Sorrow*. The melody for the ballad was originally written in 1987 while the composer was visiting his home in Aberdeen, Scotland. It derives from a vision the composer had of slaves gathered around a campfire. The third movement is a waltz with a trio, and the finale an African dance in $\frac{12}{8}$ meter.

One of Thompson's most impressive ventures into symphonicism is his *Lemuria Fantasy* for orchestra. The work was composed between 1995 and 1996 and, like previous efforts, combines the many stylistic influences that shape Thompson's background. The lyrical and developmental depth of this composition, however, is transcendent, and is rivaled by few other modern efforts of similar vein.

The Cape Verde islands, in the eastern Atlantic off Africa, were originally a colony of Portugal and have contributed many unique personalities to jazz, including Horace Silvers. Another important Cape Verdan is Ramiro Da Rosa Mendez, who has worked both as a popular and third stream composer. Mendez is best known for his traditional folk compositions like "Coladeras," "Mornas," and "Banderas," and for the work he has done with the internationally renowned Cape Verdan vocalist, Cesaria Evora. Mendez is, however, no stranger to either symphonic settings based upon Cape Verdan folk material or arrangements and orchestrations of Cape Verdan folk songs. Three of Mendez's most engaging efforts in this vein are *Dispidida*, which he composed himself;

Richard Thompson

Ramiro da Rosa Mendez

*Mal D'Amor* composed by Eugenio Raveres and arranged for orchestra by Mendez; and *Partido*, composed by B. Leza and orchestrated by Mendez. These works were all premiered by the Boston Orchestra and Chorale in 1990.

PART **3**

# Popular Styles
# since 1940

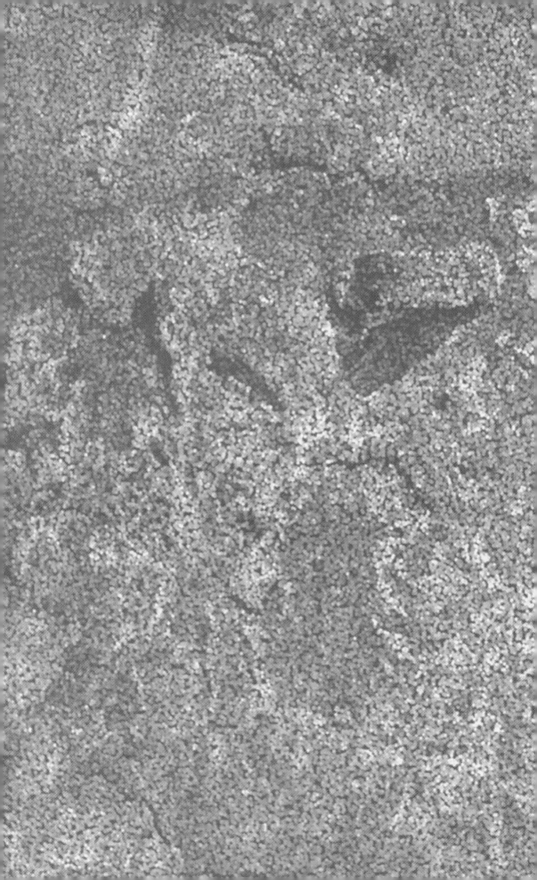

## CHAPTER 11

## RHYTHM AND BLUES: 1940 TO 1960

**R**ECORDING EXECUTIVES have classified music performed by and/or targeted at African Americans in many different ways. The earliest recordings aimed at an African American market were classified as "race" records. Jazz, folk blues, Broadway show tunes, and gospel music were all marketed as "race" records. When *Billboard* began its music charts in the mid-1940s, it picked up the "race" name for African American popular music. On July 25, 1949, *Billboard* changed the name of this chart to *rhythm and blues*. This substitution not only provided a euphemistic alternative to the term *race* (which had taken on a negative tone) but also acknowledged and officially designated a new genre that by then had already appeared.

Rhythm and blues (R&B), in its earliest manifestation, was a popular dance music that developed in the 1940s. It was rooted in the boogie-woogie blues and the jump rhythms of swing bands of the late 1930s. The style was generally performed by a small instrumental combo consisting of a rhythm section (piano, guitar, bass, drums) and horns. It combined boogie-woogie bass patterns, an underlying swing feel, jazz and urban blues electric guitar styles, and gospel-influenced vocality. The blues often served as the formal basis of the style. The lyrics were based on themes reflecting the backgrounds, life styles, and street language of urban blacks.

## Louis Jordan

The father of rhythm and blues was saxophonist/vocalist/showman Louis Jordan (1908–1975). Jordan recorded his first vocal number in 1934 with the Clarence Williams band. He joined the Chick Webb Orchestra in 1936 and remained with Webb until the bandleader's death in 1939. Jordan did some recording and stage work as a vocalist with Webb's band, but the featured artist, and the vocalist on whom all the attention was focused, was Ella Fitzgerald. After Webb's death, Jordan organized his own group. The group consisted ultimately of seven members, though they were known as the Timpani Five.[1] After the Second World War, big bands were struggling to survive; the cost of employing a large group of musicians, both on the road and during down-times, was great and the popularity of the music was waning. This opened the door for small groups like Jordan's to succeed both musically and financially.

Jordan and his Tympani Five scored their first hits in 1942, with "Knock Me a Kiss" and "Outskirts of Town." During the next few years other hits followed. These included most of the historic cuts on which Jordan's reputation rests; for example, "Let the Good Times Roll," "Ain't Nobody Here but Us Chickens," "Choo Choo Ch'boogie," "Caldonia," and "Saturday Night Fish Fry."

With these and other hits Jordan became a forceful and influential presence in popular music. By 1947, his songs were consistently at the top of both the rhythm and blues and pop charts. He had "crossed over" to the pop (white) audience, a major accomplishment for a black artist of his day. His influence was felt by jazz, blues, and pop artists of his time and those of the next decade. Perhaps more important, Jordan and the Timpani Five laid down the stylistic paradigm that would eventually establish the language of rhythm and blues as something quite distinct from any of the styles that constituted it.

Giving an overall description of Jordan's music is difficult, because his arrangements were often startlingly inventive. Among the relatively invariable features were:

1. instrumental introductions, given either by the horn section or a solo instrument;

2. instrumental solos, as contrast to the vocal work in verses and choruses;

3. a swing rhythm (compound duple rhythm);

4. four-to-the-bar bass patterns, often derived from boogie-woogie.

Blues elements were present in the verses or choruses of many of Jordan's hit songs, but not always in a manner consistent with the traditional blues form. In "Let the Good Times Roll," for example, both the instrumental introduction and the verses are based upon near-standard blues harmonic progressions. The phrase structure as rendered by the solo vocalist, however, is not in an AAB format. The same is true of "Choo Choo Ch'Boogie." Conversely, works like "I'm a Good Thing," "I Got the Walkin Blues," and "I'm Gonna Move to the Outskirts of Town" are standard blues, complete with AAB phrase designs. In these latter works, one can easily see how bluesmen like B. B. King were influenced by Jordan. Sometimes the blues feature was evidenced only in part of the composition. In "Ain't Nobody Here but Us Chickens," the blues is present only in the chorus.

Jordan seemed to prefer the modified blues harmonic progression of I-IV-I-ii-V-I, also a favorite of many bebop artists. But even within this design interesting embellishments occurred, for example the use of the flatted seventh ($^\flat$VII) in "Choo Choo Ch'Boogie." The $^\flat$VII also occurred, occasionally, as a passing chord; see for example the end of "I'm a Good Thing." Various chords based upon the $^\flat$VII scale degree, for example, $^\flat$VII, $^\flat$VII$^6$, $^\flat$VII$^7$, $^\flat$VII(+7), would become a standard aspect of the harmonic lexicon of black popular music of the 1960s and beyond.

Some works showed no blues features at all. An example is "Helping Hand." This composition is striking in its use of daring modulations to and from the chorus and in its uplifting lyrics. These are features common to rhythm and blues of the 1960s but quite rare for a 1950s composition.

Another general feature of Jordan's hits were improvisations of the basic melody played on the solo instruments. Often these improvisations were given by Jordan himself on the saxophone; occasionally other instruments were featured, like the piano. Call-and-response patterns between the solo voice and electric guitar, or the saxophone and the electric guitar, were also relatively common.

Jordan's works generally closed with the chorus, often performed by the entire group at full volume to create an exciting send-off. The work "Beans and Cornbread" is noteworthy because it features a half-spoken, sermonizing vocal near the end of the composition just before the final statement of the melody. This gospel-derived feature is strongly reminiscent of lyric improvisation sections found in rhythm and blues and soul compositions of the 1960s and 1970s.

## The Rhythm and Blues Explosion

The growth of rhythm and blues in the 1940s was facilitated by jukeboxes and nickelodeons (jukeboxes that showed brief film clips of singers performing their hits), black recorded music on radios, and the rise of independent record companies. By realizing the import and relevance of the new dance music to black urban and working-class audiences, the newly formed independent labels were able to cultivate new, untapped markets and thereby wrestle much of the power away from the major record companies. The major labels, for the most part, concentrated on an idealized pop music that catered to the taste of the mainstream white audience.

One of the most innovative of the white independent labels was Atlantic Records. The company was cofounded by Ahmet Ertegun, the son of the Turkish ambassador to the United States, and Herb Abramson and his wife Miriam in 1947. Producer Jerry Wexler was brought in later and ultimately became a partner. Ertegun and Abramson started Atlantic with $10,000 and built the company into one of the most successful, influential, and profitable of all the independents. During the first five years of its existence, Atlantic had under contract five of the biggest names in rhythm and blues: Ray Charles, Ruth Brown, Ivory Joe Hunter, Joe Turner, and La Vern Baker.

Ertegun distinguished himself not only as an astute business executive with a deep sensitivity for black music and a keen insight into how it could best be marketed, but also as a respectable songwriter. Many of the early hit songs sung by Atlantic artists were written by Ertegun, including "Fool, Fool, Fool" by the Clovers, "What Cha Gonna Do" by Clyde McPhatter and the Drifters, and "Don't Play That Song" by Ben E. King.

Central to the development of the Atlantic sound were the contributions of a black musician and songwriter name Jesse Stone. During a trip to the deep South by Stone, Ertegun, and Abramson in 1947, Stone observed that the rhythmic vitality of the groups he heard playing in bars and clubs was absent from the music Atlantic was recording. He concluded that what was needed was a more rhythmical bass line. Nelson George notes, very astutely, the relationship between the change in the role of the bass line that Stone's observation sparked and the growth in popularity of the electric bass:

> In the hands of master swing bassists such as Oscar Pettiford or
> Count Basie's Walter Page, the bass line was a gentle stream that
> flowed well under the ensemble brass and reed lines that domi-

nated the big-band style. But when Leo Fender gave Monk Montgomery a prototype for his bass guitar in 1953, he more than improved the basic sound, The electric bass forever altered the relationship between the rhythm section, the horns, and other melodic instruments.[2]

Stone also contributed to Atlantic his arranging and songwriting skills. One of his most influential and controversial works was "Shake, Rattle, and Roll," a blues sung by Joe Turner.[3] The original text to this song was considered so explicit that it had to be rewritten.

The most important of the early black independents was Vee-Jay Records. This company was founded in 1953 by the husband-and-wife team of Vivian Carter and James Bracken ("Vee" and "Jay," respectively). They produced their first record with $500 they borrowed from a pawnshop. The first artists to sign with Vee-Jay were the Spaniels. With their recording of "Baby It's You," Vee-Jay launched its label and also had its first big hit.

From this point on Vee-Jay would sign some of the most talented rhythm and blues artists of the era; among them were groups like the Dells, the El Dorados, the Impressions, the Pips, and individual greats like Jerry Butler, Betty Everett, Priscilla Bowman, and Gene Chandler. They also signed the great bluesmen Jimmy Reed and John Lee Hooker and historic gospel groups like the Five Blind Boys, the Staple Singers, the Highway QC's, the Harmonizing Four, the Sallie Martin Singers, the Swan Silverstones, and the Gospel Harmonettes.

Vee-Jay scored its first million seller in 1961 with the release of "Duke of Earl" by Gene Chandler. The label then moved aggressively into the white pop market, signing the popular Four Seasons and even releasing the Beatles' first LP (*Introducing the Beatles*) in the United States, after Capitol turned it down. From 1963 to 1966 managerial difficulties besieged the organization and caused the company to go bankrupt. However, during its heyday, and before the establishment of

Motown, Vee-Jay was the most important and successful black-owned record company in America.

Rhythm and blues, in its earliest form, had several stylistic hallmarks. Today it is perhaps more nostalgically viewed as an upbeat, blues-derived or blues-influenced, dance music performed by a lead vocalist backed by a small instrumental combo. However, it also existed in a ballad form, rendered in a smooth, soulful vocality—epitomized by the sound of Charles Brown. This ballad form had a great impact on 1950s rhythm and blues artists like Ray Charles, and when merged with stronger gospel influences, played a significant role in the later development of soul music.

## Doo Wop

Rhythm and blues existed as well in a form performed by small vocal ensembles in a style reminiscent of the Ink Spots and the Mills Brothers but with stronger and more conspicuous black influences. The Ink Spots, Mills Brothers and other early black popular groups emulated the smooth vocal styles of white pop quartets and also performed pop standards of their days usually to the same type of creamy accompaniments favored by white popsters. The newer groups, formed on street corners in black urban ghettos, favored a grittier sound, often performing original material or covers of pop songs that were transformed rhythmically and vocally into more black-sounding material. The new style was known as *doo wop*, and became the dominant form of rhythm and blues in the 1950s.

The archetypal doo wop groups before 1950 were the Ravens and the Orioles. The Ravens' first commercially successful recording was a cover of "Ol' Man River," a classic from the Jerome Kern/Oscar Hammerstein musical *Show Boat*. Rhythm and blues historian Arnold Shaw notes that the Ravens' version of "Ol' Man River" "swung in a jazzy, four-beat rhythm reminiscent of the Delta Rhythm Boys [a small combo reminiscent of Jordan's Timpani Five]."[4] Many hits followed between 1947 and 1950, including "Write Me a Letter," written by the black songwriter Howard Biggs.[5] Though also highly influential in the late forties, the

Orioles are best remembered for their 1953 hit "Crying in the Chapel," a cover of a previous country and western hit

Inspired by the success of the Ravens and Orioles, doo wop groups began to proliferate, frequently taking on the names of birds, automobiles, flowers, musical references, and royalty. By the early 1950s a definitive doo wop style had evolved, with several standard features.

Doo wop groups were frequently quartets or quintets. They featured a lead singer who extemporized the melody, accompanimental voices from which the underlying vocal harmony was provided, and a bass voice that counterpointed the melody with a distinctive ostinato or quasi-ostinato bass pattern—one that often emphasized the roots of the underlying harmonies. The accompanimental voices generally provided sustained or homorhythmic backgrounds based either upon text derived from the title, the immediate phrase, nonsense syllables, vowel sounds, or words like *doo wop, do do wop, shoo-doop, shoo-be-do, o-o-o-o, a-a-a-ah,* or *la-la-la*.

A typical doo wop song began with a brief introduction. The introduction was either purely instrumental or featured the accompanimental voices or some combination of both. The song proper opened with a refrain—a verse in which the title and *hook* (a short, catchy melodic phrase usually including the title in its lyric) were clearly expressed. The opening refrain ($R^1$) generally contained either two phrases or four phrases. In refrains with two phrases, the second phrase constituted a musical repetition of the first—aa or aa$^1$. Refrains with four phrases were most often structured in aaaa, aaab, or aabc patterns. The fourth phrase was often shorter than the previous three; in such cases, the accompanying voices filled in the rest of the phrase.

The opening refrain of the doo wop classic "In the Still of the Night," sung by the Five Satins, exemplifies an aa phrase design. It ends with an authentic cadence, that is, the standard dominant (V)–tonic (I) progression (Example 11.1). Conversely, "I See a Star" (Example 11.2), sung by the Roulettes features a four-phrase opening refrain that ends with a half-cadence; that is, it closes on the dominant.

Phrase #1:  In the | still of the | night I | held you, held you | tight. Cause I |
              I          vi      ii               V

Phrase #2:  | love, love you | so. Promise I'll | never let you | go in the still
        I               vi            ii         V

of the | night.     | . . . . . . . |
     I     IV  I

Example 11.1. "In the Still of the Night" (opening refrain = aa$^1$)

Phrase #1:       | I see a | star | in the | sky |
                 i      vi   ii    V

Phrase #2:       | It seems to | say | that you might | care for me |
                 I         vi  ii        V

Phrase #3:       | Shines so | brightly | it re- | minds me of |
                 I      vi      ii   V

Phrase #4:       | you   |   |   |
                 I      vi   ii   V

Example 11.2. "I See a Star" (opening refrain = aa$^1$a$^2$a$^3$)

If the four-phrase opening refrain (R$^1$) ended with a half-cadence, as many did, a second refrain (R$^2$) followed, either with the same or different text. The second refrain generally ended with an authentic cadence. A contrasting section, popularly known as a *bridge,* followed R$^2$ and ended on a half-cadence. A third refrain (R$^3$) then ensued. If the opening refrain (R$^1$) consisted of two phrases, it typically ended with an authentic cadence and progressed directly to the bridge.

Depending on the tempo of the work, or other aesthetic factors, either an instrumental solo based upon the music of the refrain followed or the bridge immediately returned. Whatever the choice, a final refrain ensued or was substituted by closing material. The ending of the work was often marked by some conspicuous change in the structure of the song—either in the underlying harmony, or the text, or both. The ending was sometimes signaled by a temporary halting or slowing of the tempo.

A stereotypical doo wop harmonic progression quickly evolved. It consisted of I|vi|ii|V or I|vi|IV|V repeated either throughout the refrain or underlying its first two phrases. "Goodnight, It's Time to Go" is an example of the latter (Example 11.3). So enduring was this paradigm that it could still be found in doo wop (and doo wop–influenced) works of the early sixties, as evidenced by later classics like "Duke of Earl."

The harmonies used in the contrasting section were no less stereotypical. The subdominant chord more often than not opened the bridge. A typical progression was IV|IV|I|V$^7$|IV, or IV|iv|I|V$^7$|IV. A half-cadence, ii-V or IV-V, generally concluded the last phrase, and the bridge.

So common were these harmonic patterns that when something different occurred it was readily noticeable. But from time to time deviations or alternative patterns did occur. The doo wop song "Are You Sorry," sung by the Whispers, opens with the progression ii|V|I. (The same progression opens "Tears in My Eyes," by the Baltineers.) "To the Aisle" by the Five Satins opens with I|V$^7$|IV|IV|I|IV|I|ii-V|I. "At My Front Door" by the El Dorados and the doo wop classic "Get a Job" by the Silhouettes both employ the standard blues harmonic pattern.

Doo wops of the 1950s existed in both a ballad and an up-tempo form. Although both types were typically written (musically notated) in simple meter, they were most often performed in compound duple meter, like other types of rhythm and blues. Compound meter implies

Example 11.3. "Goodnight, It's Time to Go"

three pulses to the beat, that is, three eighth notes to every dotted quarter note. Such groupings of three eighth notes were often directly expressed in the accompanimental voices, or the guitar or piano, and highlighted by the drummer on the cymbals. They were also expressed as arpeggios played by the piano or guitar.

Doo wop instrumental bass lines generally consisted of one-to-the-bar or two-to-the-bar patterns that emphasized the roots, or roots and fifths, of harmonies. This sometimes contrasted strongly with the more rhythmically animated patterns rendered by the vocal bass (Example 11.4). The instrumental bass line sometimes jumped to an up-tempo walking bass, or boogie-woogie bass, pattern in the bridge, providing an interesting rhythmical and tempo contrast to the patterns underlying the refrains.

Example 11.4. Vocal Bass Doo Wop Patterns

## Rhythm and Blues in the 1950s

Though doo wop was the dominant rhythm and blues trend of the fifties, it did not completely usurp the earlier rhythm and blues styles initiated in the 1940s. The artists that cultivated the forties rhythm and blues styles seeded a new fifties generation of rhythm-and-blues artists. These new artists included blues stylists like Ruth Brown, Willie Mae "Big Mama" Thornton, Ivory Joe Hunter, La Vern Baker, and Joe Turner; and saxophone "honkers" like Earl Bostic and particularly Curtis Ousley (King Curtis). Also among the exceptional rhythm-and-blues artists of the fifties was boogie-influenced pianist/singer Antoine "Fats" Domino (b. 1928) who, along with his partner David Bartholomew, contributed classic recordings like "I'm in Love Again," "I'm Walking," and a successful cover of a 1941 Gene Autry ballad, "Blueberry Hill."[6]

Two rhythm-and-blues artists contributed hugely to the shaping of rock and roll. These men are generally regarded as two of the most innovative and influential artists in the history of modern American popular music. They are Richard Wayne Penniman (Little Richard), and Charles Edward Anderson (Chuck Berry).

Penniman was born in Macon, Georgia, in 1932. His musical career began as a child singing gospel songs with a children's group called the Tiny Tots. He later performed for churches and revivals with the Penniman Singers, a group partly made up of his siblings. Tiring of school, he dropped out in the ninth grade and began traveling with various vaudeville shows, acquiring during this time the stage name Little Richard and many of the outrageous performance idiosyncrasies that characterized his later style.

Though his recording efforts date back to the early fifties, his first recording success came in 1954 with "Tutti Frutti." This was followed by classics like "Long Tall Sally," "Lucille," and "Good Golly Miss Molly." Richard retired from pop music in 1957 to pursue the life of a preacher (the first of several such retreats out of the pop music world). His return to popular music in 1960 was marked by a European tour in which he met the Beatles and other eminent (or soon to be eminent) European pop artists who admired his work. Though Richard was able to make a successful comeback by the early seventies he is remembered principally for the classics he recorded in the middle and late fifties. His often risque and unrestrained stage antics—considered controversial and unprecedented in the fifties—established, as it turns out, a precedent for later entertainers like The Artist Formerly Known As Prince.

Charles Edward Anderson (Chuck Berry) was born in 1926 in San Jose, California, and raised in St. Louis and Wentzville, Missouri. His musical career traces back to a trio he formed with pianist Johnny Johnson in the early 1950s. At the advice of his idol, blues guitarist Muddy Waters, Berry contacted Leonard Chess, owner of Chess Records. Impressed by the professional manner in which Berry had conducted himself, Chess invited Berry to submit a tape of his original material. Among its four original compositions was a "hillbilly tune" called "Ida May." On the strength of these four pieces Chess offered Berry a recording opportunity. On May 25, 1955, Berry and the other members of his trio (with Willie Dixon added as bassist, to fill out the group) recorded "Ida May" (whose name was changed to "Maybellene"), "Wee Hours," "Thirty Days," and "You Can't Catch Me."

"Maybellene" became the first of many great classics by Chuck Berry. Others in the late fifties included "Roll over Beethoven," "School Day," "Sweet Little Rock and Roller," and "Johnny B. Goode." In the sixties such classics included "Nadine" and "No Particular Place To Go." In the early seventies Berry again scored big with "Ding-a-ling." As a performer Berry became particularly noted for his famous "duck walk," which consisted of a comic strut across the stage with bended knees while playing his guitar.

Chuck Berry's music shows diverse influences, a quality that probably aided in its crossover appeal. Works like "Maybellene" and "Thirty Days" show conspicuous country-western influences. It was in fact this quality in "Maybellene" ("Ida May") that attracted Leonard Chess so strongly to the song and prompted Chess to urge Berry and his group to record this work first in their 1955 session. Chess reportedly was astonished at the thought of a black man singing in a "hillbilly" style.[7] "Guitar Boogie," as the name implies, shows the influence of country-boogie of the period. "School Days," "Oh Baby Doll," and "Sweet Little Sixteen" were works that alluded to the peculiarities of adolescence. "Havana Moon" and "Drifting Hearts" were works which bespeak Berry's interest in pop music, particularly the music of crooner Nat King Cole.

The strongest influence in Berry's music is the blues. Indeed, the blues structure factors prominently in many of his classics in various ways, and to various degrees. In some works ("School Days," "Carol"), the blues form governs the verses, and influences strongly the choruses. In "Johnny B. Goode" both the verses and chorus are paradigmatic blues. In "Maybellene" only the chorus features the blues form.

Blues-influenced guitar solos are common. So are call-and-response passages in which Berry answers himself with his guitar. Sometimes the response was given in the same or a similar rhythm as the call, (see, for example, "School Days"). In the same work the guitar response motives are sometimes rendered with a contour (a melodic shape) similar to that of the vocal call and sometimes in a manner that mimics the inflections of the voice.

There were some Berry compositions that were not governed ostensibly by the blues, even though cursory blues elements were occasionally present. One such work was "No Money Down." This work was composed in the mid-1950s and is particularly noteworthy because its verses, all featuring end-rhymes, are mostly spoken rather than sung. Because these nonintoned verses are rhymed and are integral to the structure of the work, this work—like that of Joe Tex in the 1960s—may be viewed as an antecedent of modern rap music (see chapter 13).

In all, Chuck Berry's contribution both to black vernacular music and to American popular music generally is huge. He was clearly one of the early architects of rock and roll. He was also one of rock and roll's great songwriters, contributing to the tradition a sizable number of classics. His compositions were greatly admired by early American and European popular entertainers. Artists like the Beatles, the Beach Boys, the Rolling Stones, and Linda Ronstadt either covered (rerecorded the same work) or recorded works inspired by Berry.

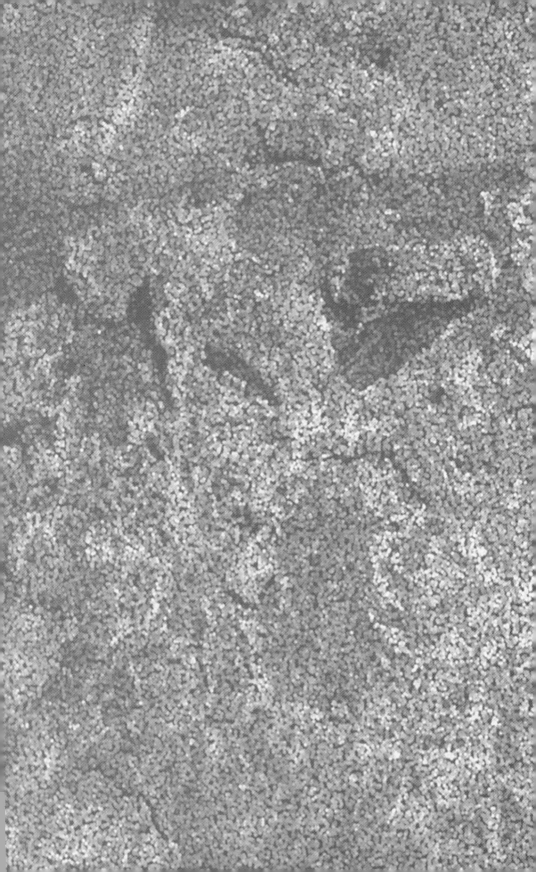

## CHAPTER 12

## SOUL MUSIC: 1960 TO 1980

**A** NEW TYPE OF RHYTHM and blues emerged between 1957 and 1963, which came to be known as *soul* music. Technically, soul music combined some of the features of 1950s rhythm and blues and doo wop with stronger and more conspicuous gospel influences. Hints of the style could be heard as early as 1954 and 1955 in rhythm-and-blues hits like "I Got A Woman" by Ray Charles. But Charles was not alone in shaping the vocal basis of soul music; substantial credit must also be given to Sam Cooke, Jackie Wilson, James Brown, Otis Redding, and Aretha Franklin.

A precise definition of soul music is difficult because many of its prominent features vary. There is, for example, no one type of bass pattern that characterizes soul music, nor is there a standard harmonic scheme on which the verses of most soul compositions are based. Soul music has also not been limited to one specific medium. Because of the diverse nature of soul music, many popular music scholars disagree on what they consider soul music to be. Within the broad parameters of soul music, however, are found enough definitive elements to construct a workable definition. We will consider these features in detail shortly.

As previously stated, soul music combined elements from rhythm and blues and gospel music. From rhythm and blues, including doo wop, were derived the basic song forms used in soul music. The harmonic progressions of doo wop also found their way into soul music, particularly early soul music, but as a part of a much larger harmonic vocabulary. Doo wop and early gospel quartets also influenced the background vocal style that characterized early soul music.

The lead-vocal style of soul music was derived from gospel music. This style was often an intensely emotional expression characterized by an improvised, half-spoken, half-sung quality. Shouts, moans, falsetto, turns, spoken vocality, microtonal inflections (blue notes), and particularly melismas were among the vocal devices frequently and skillfully accessed by soul vocalists (see chapter 1 for a definition of these vocalisms).

Melodies in soul music were frequently based on the pentatonic scale or often showed a strong pentatonic bias. This feature also emanates from gospel music and entered soul music largely by way of the gospel backgrounds of many of its earliest vocalists and composers. From gospel music also came many of the chord progressions, based on the diatonic (major/minor) scales, that became an integral part of the harmonic vocabulary of soul music.

Soul music made some unique contributions of its own. It built upon and expanded the song form structures inherited from rhythm and blues. It built on the harmonic vocabulary of gospel and R&B, extending it beyond the major/minor tonalities of these earlier forms. By the early 1970s, soul music had stretched the timbral boundaries of black popular music to unexpected heights. Also, soul music served as a perfect musical vehicle for the expression of the political and social turbulence that characterized black America in the 1960s and early 1970s. The social commentary songs that grew out of this movement were decidedly outspoken and unapologetic.

## The Innovators of Soul Music

The essence of soul music is largely found in its unique, gospel-based vocality. The paradigm for this vocal style was Ray Charles (b. 1930). Charles' early vocal style was modeled on the pop styles of Nat King Cole and Charles Brown. This is quite understandable, because they were among the most successful and musically influential black male soloists during the late 1940s and early 1950s. In his autobiography, *Brother Ray*, Charles writes:

> I had my Nat Cole/Charles Brown routines down clean by now. Yes, by 1948 and 1949, I had my program together . . . I'd been working on my repertoire for three years—three long years of on-the-job-practice—and you'd be surprised how many people actually confused me for Nat or Charles![1]

Charles's first hit, recorded around 1948, and written by his friend Joe Lee Lawrence, was "I Love You, I Love You." This and subsequent recordings for the next five years continued to reflect, though to a progressively diminishing degree, the influence of Cole and Brown. By 1951, however, Charles was ready to make some changes. He began searching for his own voice.

> Slowly I began to wean myself and come into my own. Still trying to be my own man, but not about to give up what I already had. Matter of fact, even after I changed record companies— from Swingtime to Atlantic in 1952—I was still doing Nat Cole and Charles Brown–type numbers.
>
> But by 1951, I had ever so slowly edged away from what I had been doing for so long. I was trying to be accepted as me.[2]

During the years 1953 to 1955, Charles gradually discovered, or rather rediscovered, his true sound. He turned back to his earliest background, to the gospel songs and harmonies of his youth. It all came together in late 1954 with his recording of "I Got a Woman." According to Charles, this song was a reworked spiritual based on the gospel song, "I Got A Savior." The lyrics were provided by one of his band members, trumpeter Renolds Richards, while Charles was hanging out in New

Orleans. "I Got a Woman" was an enormously influential, and contro-versial, work. Fans of gospel song were not used to hearing an unre-strained, church-like vocality applied to a secular subject, in this case the love of a woman. Many of Charles's subsequent successes were predicated upon the same formula used to construct "I Got a Woman"; that is, refashioning gospel songs into rhythm and blues works.

Charles's first million seller occurred in 1959 with "What I Say"—a blues noted for its church-like call-and-response passages between Charles and his background singers, a female group he dubbed the Raeletts. After nearly single-handedly creating the soul style, Charles made another career change in the early 1960s, recording influential R&B albums drawing on the country music repertoire. He also experimented with contemporary jazz. Charles has remained popular to this day, drawing on an eclectic repertoire while maintaining his unique, gospel-flavored vocal style.

Ray Charles may have established the essential vocal aesthetic for soul music, but it was Sam Cooke more than anyone else who refined it into the form we recognize today as soul singing. Cooke was born in Clarksdale, Mississippi, in 1931 but raised in Chicago; his death in 1964 was tragic and controversial. His life as a musician, however, was highly productive both as a singer in the gospel and rhythm and blues traditions and as a composer.

Cooke's career as a vocalist began at age nine when he joined a group consisting of his two sisters, Mary and Hattie, and his brother Charles. They called themselves the Singing Children. They appeared mainly at their father's church or with the Reverend Cooke at other churches.[3] During his adolescence, Sam Cooke joined a neighborhood quartet called the Highway QC's. This group modeled themselves on the style of one of gospel music's legendary quartets, the Soul Stirrers. Though the group was never able to acquire the status of the Soul Stirrers (in great part because they sounded too much like their idols), Cooke gained a lot of experience touring with them, as both a singer and composer.

In 1950 Cooke left the Highway QC's to join the Soul Stirrers. The experience he acquired with this group allowed him to refine his vocal talent to its highest professional level. Many of the stylistic idiosyncrasies that characterized Cooke's unique vocality in the rhythm and blues world—his distinctive verbalisms and matchless, powerful melismas—were perfected while he was with the Soul Stirrers. His compositional skills were also honed while with the group. Gospel compositions like "Nearer to Thee," "Be with Me Jesus" (Example 12.1), "Jesus Give Me Water," "Touch the Hem of His Garment," and "That's Heaven to Me," were all written for and premiered by the Soul Stirrers.

Example 12.1. "Be With Me Jesus" (Sam Cooke)

A case could be made that Cooke may have been the first great songwriter of soul music, if not rhythm and blues in general. During his lifetime Cooke wrote, by one account, more than 100 compositions, and a sizable portion of them are now recognized as classics. Cooke's interest in composing songs surfaced during his stint with the Highway QC's. His prolificness during this period was motivated greatly by his need to improve the competitiveness of his group by supplying them with new material. In this regard his biographer Daniel Wolff notes:

> It was as a QC that Sam first understood how important it was to have your own songs. If the group couldn't have a totally original sound, it was at least possible to have original material. And it was as a QC that he fixed the habit that would stay with him all his life: writing whenever and wherever he was.[4]

Though Cooke did not have the technical training needed to notate all of his ideas, his innate musicality clearly went beyond the simple conception of a melody with lyrics. His arranger René Hall is quoted as saying:

> Practically all the arrangements we did were Sam's ideas. . . . He'd come up to my office . . . and he'd tell me exactly what he wanted the girls to sing or what he wanted the voices to do. What he wanted the horns to play. Even down to what he wanted the bass to play sometimes! So, he knew, note for note, exactly what his orchestration would sound like before he even went into the studio.[5]

But even had his gift been limited to lyrics, melody, and chord progressions—that is, leadsheets—his contribution to soul music would still have been prodigious; for Sam Cooke wrote truly beautiful, haunting melodies, which often betrayed his gospel background by their strongly pentatonic or quasipentatonic character. When he embellished them with his interpolated verbalisms and billowing melismas—used ever so tastefully to fill in lyrical gaps or finish off phrases—he imbued them with a deeply moving, timeless emotionality.

This quality was evident in Cooke's first hit in 1957, "You Send Me," which soared to the very top of both the rhythm and blues and pop charts. His quality and popularity remained constant through "A Change Is Gonna Come," his final masterpiece recorded in 1964. During this seven-year career Cooke composed a huge canon of rhythm-and-blues masterpieces, now recognized rightfully as early soul (and pop) classics, including: "Chain Gang," "Only Sixteen," "Cupid," "Wonderful World," "Everybody Loves to Cha Cha Cha," "Shake," "Bring It on Home to Me," "Sad Mood," "Another Saturday Night," "Love Will Find a Way," and "Change Is Gonna Come."

## The Rise of Stax and Motown

Rising simultaneously with soul music were two new independent record companies. Both were destined to have a profound impact on the development of soul music, though in different ways. These companies were Stax and Motown records.

Stax Records came into existence originally as Satellite Records. It was founded by Jim Stewart, a white Memphis banker, and his sister Estelle Axton. The name of the company changed from Satellite to Stax when "Last Night," a 1961 rhythm and blues hit released on Stewart's Satellite label, generated a response from a California company who had prior claim to the name. "Last Night" was quickly reissued under a new name derived from the first letters of Stewart's and Axton's last names— St and Ax.[6]

Stax's studio was located in the heart of a black inner city community in Memphis and drew much of its initial talent from this area. Memphis was traditionally one of the major centers of black gospel music in America. Under the supervision of Stewart and his African American vice president, Al Bell, Stax exploited this black natural resource, creating a unique, gospel-influenced soul sound—which came to be known as the Memphis sound—and from 1960 to 1972 brought to light some of the most important cultivators of early soul music. An abbreviated list includes Carla Thomas, Rufus Thomas, William Bell, Johnny Taylor, Isaac Hayes, David Porter, Eddie Floyd, Sam and Dave, Booker T. [Jones] and the MGs, and the white composer/guitarist Steve Cropper.

Stax's greatest gift to the world of soul music was one of the genre's most original performers, Otis Redding (1941–1967). Redding was born in Dawson, Georgia, but was raised in Macon. He was not so much a crooner in the sense of a Nat King Cole as he was a great and original vocal stylist.[7] Central to Redding's unique vocality was the way he used interpolated verbalisms and especially lyric variation. This technique is exemplified beautifully in the composition "Let Me Come on Home," coauthored by Redding (Example 12.2). Lyric variation, as we know, differs from interpolated verbalisms in that its text generally derives from the original lyric (see chapter 1 for a further discussion of this distinction).

As is seen in this example, the opening blues-derived phrase gives the text "Oh ba-by, yeah...babe, wanna come home to ya." This text reduces to "Baby, I wanna come home to ya." From the very beginning, however, Redding enriches the lyric with words that transform it into a plea of great emotional poignancy. In the following phrase Redding provides greater textual enrichment—"Baby, yeah...girl...huh...lawd...said, I got to get home to ya."—thus, intensifying the emotional quality of the music.

In phrases two and three, Redding reduces the textual interpolation considerably. This allows the fifth and final phrase (a restatement of the first phrase) to be given in a way that maximizes the emotionality of the verse. Redding delivers with the greatest amount of textual enrichment: "Oh Baby..yeah, babe...said honey..oh, I wanna come home to ya."

Superposing the first, second, and fifth phrases of the opening verse allows, in each case, the amount of textual enrichment to be seen quite clearly.

1. "Oh baby yeah...babe, wanna come home to ya."

2. "Baby, yeah...girl..huh lawd...said, I gotta get home to ya."

5. "On Baby...Yeah, babe...said honey..Oh, I wanna come home to ya."

Such textual enrichment, and of course the musical embellishments that accompany it, translate to an emotionally intense musical drama.

Example 12.2. "Let Me Come on Home" (Otis Redding, Booker T. Jones, and Al Jackson Jr.)

Redding's first major success was "These Arms of Mine," recorded in 1962 by Stax/Volt. From this point until his death, Redding followed with some of the most emotionally poignant music in the whole canon of 1960s soul. His hits included "Pain in My Heart," "Mr. Pitiful," "Security," "Fa-Fa-Fa Song," "Tramp" (a duet with Carla Thomas),

"Respect" (later covered by Aretha Franklin), and "Sitting on the Dock of the Bay," his final masterpiece coauthored with Steve Cropper.

Motown Records came into existence in 1959, founded by Berry Gordy, Jr., a former prizefight promoter and songwriter. Motown differed from other independents in several important ways: (1) it was completely self-contained; that is, it distributed its own product, published its own music (Jobete Music), recorded in its own studio, groomed and packaged its artists, and cultivated its own songwriters, thereby creating and maintaining a distinctive sound; and (2) its musical offerings betrayed several different stylistic influences, that is, gospel, blues, rhythm and blues, particularly doo wop (earlier on), and white pop music. For this reason Motown was able to construct a style that had a broader appeal than most of the other independent labels.

Motown's contributions to the evolution of soul music are prodigious. Most of the stylistic innovations of 1960s soul began with Motown, from the most advanced harmonic and melodic techniques to the most innovative orchestrational offerings (to be discussed shortly). Also, the lineup of important and influential artists introduced by Motown during this period far exceeds any other independent. It included Smokey Robinson and the Miracles, Mary Wells, Marvin Gaye, Stevie Wonder, the Four Tops, the Temptations, Martha and the Vandellas, Bobby Taylor and the Vancouvers, Brenda Holloway, Diana Ross, the Supremes, Jr. Walker and the All Stars, the Isley Brothers, Jimmy Ruffin, Tammi Terell, Gladys Knight and the Pips (formerly with Vee-Jay), Michael Jackson, the Jackson Five, the Spinners, and many others. So too were the number of soul classics penned by Motown songwriters, many of whom were the artists who introduced them.

Artists from other labels also contributed to the development of soul music in the 1960s and 1970s. First and foremost was Aretha Franklin, the most influential of all female vocalists of the soul tradition. Working with producer Jerry Wexler at the influential Muscle Shoals studios in Georgia, Aretha transformed herself from a pop-jazz singer into one of the most soulful of them all, with hits including "Respect," "Chain of Fools," and "You Make Me Feel Like a Natural Woman." Her commanding presence as a vocalist and choice of material made her an important voice of a new generation of female singers who projected strength and determination.

Other artists renowned for their distinctive styles include Dionne Warwick, Roberta Flack, Donny Hathaway, Wilson Pickett, Bobby Bland, Al Green, Jerry Butler, Curtis Mayfield, Joe Tex, and quintessentially James Brown (to be discussed later), to name a few. Distinguished vocal groups and bands include Sly and the Family Stone, Kool and the Gang, the Ohio Players, the Impressions, the Ojays, the Delphonics, the Stylistics, the Spinners, and Earth, Wind and Fire.

## Characteristics of Soul Music

Soul melodies draw on the same scalar resources as other black popular forms: the major and minor scales, pentatonic and blues scales, and occasionally ecclesiastical modes. Chromatic embellishments in soul melodies are common. One frequent source of chromatic embellishment in melodies based upon major or minor scales are blue notes, particularly the flatted third (Example 12.3).

Many soul melodies are based on or show the influence of the pentatonic scale, including some of the most beautiful and enduring of all soul melodies of the 1960s and 1970s. In some cases, the melodies of the verses and chorus (or verses and bridges) of virtually the entire composition are based on this scale. Soul classics like "My Girl" (written by Smokey Robinson, and sung by the Temptations; Example 12.4), "A Change Is Gonna Come" (written and performed by Sam Cooke), "I'm So Proud" (written by Curtis Mayfield, and sung by Curtis Mayfield and the Impressions), "I've Fallen in Love with You" (written and performed

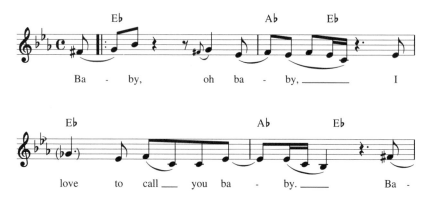

Example 12.3. "B-A-B-Y" (Isaac Hayes and Dave Porter)

by Carla Thomas), and "Baby I Need Your Lovin'" (written by Holland, Dozier, and Holland and sung by the Four Tops) are excellent examples.

In other cases, pentatonic melodies are featured only in the verses (for example, Thom Bell's "La La Means I Love You") or only in the choruses (for example Stevie Wonder's "Don't You Worry 'Bout A Thing").

Example 12.4. "My Girl" (William "Smokey" Robinson)

Sometimes pentatonic melodies are reserved for just the introduction or concluding episodes of a work (for example, Stevie Wonder's "My Cherie Amour" and "Master Blaster," respectively).

Modal influences emanating from scales other than the pentatonic scale are also occasionally suggested in soul melodies, particularly those sung by Motown artists. For example, the melody in the verse of Smokey Robinson's "Get Ready" (as sung by the Temptations) suggests the D dorian mode, despite the absence of E (the second scale degree) from the melody and the underlying harmony (however, E is indicated in the key signature; see Example 12.5). In contrast, the chorus, which modulates to F major, features a pentatonic melody.

The dorian mode is even more strongly suggested in the Norman Whitfield/Barrett Strong classic, "I Heard It Through the Grapevine" (Example 12.6). Every pitch of the E dorian mode is present in the melody of the verse. The dorian mode is also confirmed by the under-lying harmonic structure, which emphasizes the chord A⁷ (IV in dorian) and the progression A⁷ to e (IV-i), a typically dorian progression. (The chord B is the only harmony foreign to the mode; its presence is explained by its V-i relationship to the tonic, which is tonally stronger than what the mode could provide.)

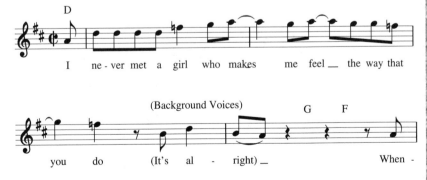

Example 12.5. "Get Ready" (William "Smokey" Robinson)

Example 12.6. "I Heard It Through the Grapevine" (Norman Whitfield and Barrett Strong)

Dorian melodic and harmonic influences are evident in the verses and chorus of Stevie Wonder's "I Wish." They are also found in Clarence Paul's and Henry Cosby's "Fingertips (Part 2)," as performed by Stevie Wonder. The Isaac Hayes masterpiece "Shaft" is unique in that at different points in the composition different modalities are suggested, including the phrygian and the mixolydian modes and the pentatonic scale.

The harmonic language of soul music is similar to that of other forms of popular music, ranging from diatonic root progressions to blues progressions and chords borrowed from the parallel minor. The most commonly used diatonic vernacular root progressions are IV to I, V to IV, V-IV-I (Example 12.7), vi to I, and ii to I; less frequently used are iii to I, iii to V, ii to vi, and vi to iii. Occasionally, other more esoteric chords are used. Triads (standard, three-note chords) are employed more frequently than seventh, ninth, or eleventh chords, but the latter chords are heard as well.

Blues progressions occurring in soul songs based on the twelve-bar blues form are common. Both major and minor key blues progressions

Example 12.7. "These Arms of Mine" (Otis Redding)

are featured in soul music, though the minor key blues occurs less often. "Green Onions," recorded by Booker T. and the MG's, is an excellent example of the latter. Blues progressions in soul music of the 1960s and 1970s, however, are by no means limited to blues contexts. In the opening verse of "Take Me to the River," written by Al Green and Mabon "Tiny" Hodges, $E^7$ constitutes a blues chord, and A to $E^7$ a blues progression (IV to $I^7$), despite the absence of the dominant seventh in the A chord (Example 12.8). The dominant seventh does occur as a melodic pitch in measure fourteen, harmonized by the A chord. Also, an $A^7$ concludes the chorus and resolves consequently to $E^7$, the opening chord of the ensuing verse.)

Though outlining a descending fourth progression—a common occurrence in soul music—the chords underlying this excerpt are all based on roots derived from an incomplete E blues scale, that is, $E^7$, A, D. This is interesting given that the melody is also based upon a hexatonic blues scale on E. In fact, the only pitch missing from the blues-derived melody is A sharp. (In the recorded version of this work, Al Green sings the 5th note of the scale as if it were the sharp fourth; that is, he sings A sharp instead of B.)

Harmonic progressions based upon roots derived from the pentatonic scale were one of soul music's most striking features during the 1960s and 1970s. One of the earliest examples of this technique is found in the

Example 12.8. "Take Me to the River" (Al Green and Mabon Hodge)

chorus of "Baby I Need Your Lovin'" (Example 12.9). A close examination of the chorus reveals that the harmonies are all based upon roots derived from a descending A♭ pentatonic scale.

$$\text{Chorus} = | \, A^\flat \, | \, f \, | \, B^\flat \, | \, c \, \| \, B^\flat \, \ldots .$$

The B♭ harmony completes the descending pentatonic root passage with the progression of the music to the following verse and back to the original key.

Example 12.9: "Baby I Need Your Loving" (Brian Holland, Lamont Dozier, and Eddie Holland)

"Baby I Need Your Lovin'" is by no means singular in its use of harmonic roots derived from the pentatonic scale. Stevie Wonder used the same technique to frame the harmonic structure of "Don't Know Why I Love You" (Example 12.10). In this composition, the verses are repeated over and over, each verse varying only in its text and orchestration. Yet the work remains fresh and interesting, in great measure because of the pentatonically rooted harmonies. The harmonies underlying the bridge of "B-A-B-Y" exemplify yet again the same technique.

Chords derived from the parallel minor—so-called borrowed chords or mutations—are a standard part of the language of soul music. Chords borrowed from the natural minor occur more frequently than chords from any other source. As we have seen in gospel music, these chords were

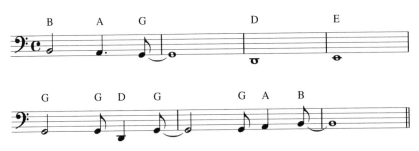

Example 12.10. "Don't Know Why I Love You" (Paul Riser, Don Hunter, Stevie Wonder, and Lula Hardaway)

often drawn from the linear chromatic motion in the inner voices or from the underlying linear logic of the melody. The iv in soul music was often attained in this fashion (Example 12.11).

Sometimes borrowed chords were the result of transposing a previously stated diatonic progression. The flatted seventh ($^{\flat}$VII), occurring in

Example 12.11. "Let's Stay Together" (Willie Mitchell, Al Green, and Al Jackson)

the verses of "B-A-B-Y," resulted in this fashion. The ♭VII was also commonly obtained by way of ascending perfect fourth progressions (see for example the verses of Smokey Robinson's "The Tears of a Clown"). Borrowed chords were also used to embellish preceding or ensuing diatonic progressions. The flatted sixth (♭VI), for example, often preceded the dominant. More often than not, however, borrowed chords simply substituted for their major key counterparts. Sometimes this resulted in imparting a modal color to the work, particularly when the substituted chord was the v (Examples 12.12 and 12.13).

Example 12.12. "I Got a Sure Thing" (Booker T. Jones, William Bell, and Ollie Hoskins)

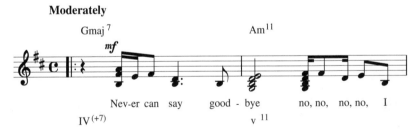

Example 12.13. "Never Can Say Goodbye" (Clifton Davis)

Other borrowed, flatted chords—♭III, ♭III(+7), ♭VII(+7), and the ♭VII⁷—were also frequently used (Example 12.14). The ♭VII⁷ derives from the parallel natural minor, as most of the other borrowed chords do. The ♭VII(+7), however, probably derives from the parallel dorian mode. This later derivation is not surprising given the frequency with which the dorian mode was used during this period.

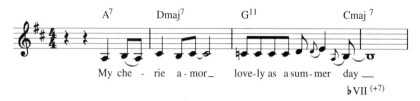

Example 12.14. "My Cherie Amour" (Stevie Wonder, Henry Crosby, and Sylvia Moy)

Diminished chords did not occur frequently in soul compositions of the 1960s or 1970s. When they did they functioned more often than not as unessential or embellishing structures, for example, passing, neighboring, or appoggiatura chords (Example 12.15). Secondary dominants were common to soul music. Extended dominants—dominants resolving to nondiatonic chords—occurred less frequently (Example 12.16).

Soul music used forms inherited from rhythm and blues, the blues, and gospel music, including the AAA or $A^1A^2A^3$ . . . form, the AABA or AABABA form, the twelve bar blues form (with modifications), and the verse/chorus form. From the middle 1960s onward, two new features became apparent, principally in the AABA and verse/chorus designs. The first was the increased use of the *transitional bridge*.[8] This was a section,

Example 12.15. "If I Were Your Woman" (Gloria Jones, Pam Sawyer, and Clay McMurray)

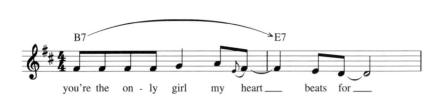

Example 12.16. "My Cherie Amour" (Stevie Wonder, Henry Cosby, and Sylvia Moy)

independent of the verse, which usually preceded the chorus or preceded a repetition of the bridge.

The second, an even more important structural feature, was the use of a gospel-derived device known here as *lyric improvisation*. A lyric improvisation, as the name implies, consisted of a free development of the text or lyric, usually over a musical passage that repeated over and over. As mentioned in chapter 1, it usually constituted a section of its own located at or near the end of the work and was sometimes known colloquially as a *vamp*. The lyric improvisation proper was generally rendered by the lead vocalist. Its effectiveness was judged by how creatively the lead vocalist manipulated the text, how skillfully he or she used a personal repertoire of vocal attributes, and how tastefully he or she interacted with the background singers and with the underlying music. The musical and textual freedom occurring in this section generated an emotional intensity that far exceeded that of any other section. This allowed the lyric improvisation to function as the emotional climax of the work, thereby justifying its placement at the end of the composition.

Textual phrases varied in length, as did verses. Verses of asymmetric length or of lengths asymmetric to previous or ensuing verses in the same song occurred occasionally. An example of both is found in "Baby I Need Your Loving," as sung by the Four Tops. In this song the phrases are short, consisting of only two measures. The opening verse delivers seven phrases before heading into the chorus. The second verse maintains the two-measure phrase length but consists of only five phrases. The final verse surprises the listener by giving eight phrases—an unexpected symmetry. The asymmetrically related verses are balanced by an intervening eight-measure chorus.

Modulations occurred frequently in soul compositions of the 1960s and 1970s. Most modulations took place at the chorus or bridge (when the song began with the verse), at the verse (when the song began with the chorus), and when lyric improvisation occurred. Choruses and verses often featured modulations to related keys—the parallel minor or major (for example, in "Get Ready"), the subdominant (or fourth scale degree; for example, in "Baby I Need Your Loving"), and often the submediant (or sixth scale degree) when the work began in minor (for example, in "Standing in the Shadows of Love").

Modulations to more distant keys were not uncommon, however. In the Holland, Dozier, and Holland Motown hit "Reach Out, I'll Be There" (performed by the Four Tops) the verses are written in G; the chorus, however, begins in B. Such distant modulations grew more common as the 1970s soul movement was ushered in. See, for example, Al Green's "Tired of Being Alone," which opens with the chorus in the key of C, then modulates to D at the beginning of the following verse. When modulations occurred within lyric improvisation sections, they were typically to distant keys, that is, up a minor or major second or down a major second from the original key.

An interesting feature of 1970s soul music—one that was particularly associated with the Philadelphia Sound, a name given to the music produced by Kenneth Gamble and Leon Huff—was the technique of starting the introduction of the work in a distant key, then modulating to the "original" key with the start of the verse. In "Didn't I Blow Your Mind This Time" (written by Thom Bell and William Hart, and performed by the Delphonics) the composition opens in the key of F. The last measure of the introduction (measure four) uses a standard chord progression to introduce a new key for the verse, the key of A. The key remains A until measure seventeen when, by way of softly punctuated brass, a sudden rush of four uninterrupted sixteenth notes followed by two successive eighth notes presents a g⁹/C progression that resolves immediately to F (that is, returning the composition to the key of the introduction).

The Thom Bell/Linda Creed masterpiece "You Are Everything" constitutes a study in the technique of modulation as it applied to soul compositions. The introduction begins in G♭, but modulates to B♭ just before the beginning of the verse. A modulation to A♭ occurs in the middle of the opening verse (measure eleven). A♭ serves as a pivot chord that begins another modulation to E♭. The chorus, consisting of three successive statements of "You are everything, and everything is you" follows the verse, in the same key. Cleverly, the tonic (E♭) is never stated in the chorus.

The same process begins again with the start of the second verse in the key of C. A modulation again occurs in the middle of the verse (measure twenty-nine), this time to B♭. B♭ serves as a pivot chord for yet another modulation to F, and the verse ends in F. The final statement of the chorus starts in the same key, again without ever stating the tonic.

Bass lines varied considerably in type and complexity. Sometimes the bass line consisted of nothing more than a rhythmically animated pedal point (or drone note). Bass lines that outlined the roots and fifths of chords were common as were bass lines that outlined the essential members of the harmony. The manner in which these bass lines were rhythmized, however, varied considerably. Sometimes the rhythmic distinctiveness of the bass pattern constituted one of the composition's most distinguishing features. Isaac Hayes and David Porter were particularly noted for writing intricate, rhythmical bass patterns. Their diversity notwithstanding, most bass patterns shared one thing in common: most were ostinati (consisting of brief, repeated melodic motives). Many ostinato bass patterns comprised more than one motive, but few were longer than two measures.

Early recorded soul compositions were generally written for small combos made up of electric guitar, electric bass, piano, drums, and sometimes horns. Strings were occasionally added. The vocal work was delivered by a lead vocalist, often with background voices. By the mid-to-late 1960s larger recording ensembles became common, reflecting the legacy of the big band tradition as it shifted from jazz to pop. This new application of the medium was legitimized by innovative touring groups like those of Bobby Bland, Joe Tex, and particularly James Brown. Brown's recording and touring group was an expanded unit that featured, in addition to horns, two electric guitars, multiple drummers, electric bass, and sometimes a small complement of amplified violins. Typical late sixties recording ensembles often consisted of studio big bands augmented by strings and sometimes synthesizers.

In the early 1970s, due in large measure to orchestrational innovations introduced by Isaac Hayes and to pre-1970s pop influences, symphonic arrangements of soul music became the vogue. These arrangements differed from earlier arrangements with interpolated strings in that a symphonic unit was integral to the conception and/or orchestration of the work. These arrangements were characterized by the perfunctory use of strings, oboes and English horns, bassoons, full brass, vibraphones, and other instruments, used in conjunction with the standard rhythm section. Varied performance techniques including the use of pizzicato effects became normative for string writing.

Thom Bell continued this symphonic tradition but tempered and in some ways refined it, creating orchestrations that merged perfectly with the expanded chromaticism that characterized his compositional style. Doublings of bassoon and oboe, French horn with the tenor voice, the frequent use of the harp, the use of string tremolos, and the occasional use of added instruments like the baritone horn imparted an unprecedented lushness and timbral elegance to his compositions and arrangements. Bell's orchestrational genius is especially apparent in his work with the Delphonics, the Spinners, and the Stylistics.

## James Brown and the Emergence of the Soul/Funk Tradition

Soul music had barely developed into a style distinct from earlier forms of rhythm and blues when yet a new version began germinating. This new style was rooted in the highly distinctive bass patterns of upbeat soul compositions. Beginning with the attractive, riff-like bass melodies, creative arrangers added other voices—the lead guitar, the horns, the drums, and background voices—to the mix, assigning each its own distinctive, rhythmically interesting part. When all patterns, including that of the voice, blended synchronously the result was *funk*.

The architect of this new, more rhythmically animated type of soul music was James Brown (b. 1933). His musical innovation earned him, quite deservingly, the titles of Soul Brother Number One and The Godfather of Soul. Brown scored his first success with "Please, Please, Please" recorded in 1956. In the following year he recorded "Try Me," a work that became number one on the rhythm-and-blues charts. Both these works show the influence of doo wop, particularly in their form, background vocality, and use of the doo-wop harmonic pattern. However, both songs showcased Brown's highly emotive, gospel-based vocality in a manner far less tempered than what was usually given in contemporary doo wop pieces. In subsequent hits recorded through the early 1960s, Brown continued to develop his vocal skills while also working on developing a new accompaniment style.

By 1965, Brown had worked out the rhythmic formula that would establish his future artistic direction and would alter substantially the direction of uptempo black popular music. This new formula was unveiled in his blues masterpiece "Papa's Got a Brand New Bag." In this work each aspect of the arrangement constitutes a distinct melodic idea; that is, the patterns played by the drums, the horns, the bass, the guitar, and of course the lead vocal (the only invariable element) were distinct, with their own melodic and rhythmic character. Yet all the ideas blended with each other symbiotically, creating a higher rhythmical unity—an effect greater than the sum of its parts. This is the very definition of rhythmic concrescence in the strict African sense (see chapter 1).

The consequence of this new rhythmically oriented music, however, was a progressively diminishing emphasis on melodic and harmonic elegance. Harmonic rhythm consequently grew slower, ultimately to the point where one or two harmonies governed the entire work. And melody in the traditional lyrical sense virtually disappeared. Perpetual, interactive rhythms and the ambiance they created became the primary means of determining the aesthetic efficacy of the composition. Brown would continue to develop and refine this new idiom in works like "Cold Sweat," "Black and Proud," and "Make It Funky."

The influence James Brown exerted on his contemporaries and on black artists of subsequent generations was enormous. Virtually no black popular artist has been untouched by Brown's musical innovation, regardless of the artist's stylistic orientation. The legacy of James Brown passed directly to soul/funk artists like Sly and the Family Stone, the Ohio Players, Kool and the Gang, Earth, Wind and Fire, George Clinton, P-Funk, and scores of other groups and individual artists extending well into the 1980s and 1990s Rap movement.[9] Beginning with Sly and the Family Stone, these groups gradually brought back somewhat the lyrical grace and interesting harmonies that characterized earlier black rhythm-and-blues styles but without compromising the interactive rhythmical subtlety mandated by the funk aesthetic.

## Jimi Hendrix and Sly and the Family Stone

James Brown was unquestionably the dominant force in soul/funk music in the 1960s. He was not, however, the only great innovative force to rise during this period. There were several other artists whose contributions were also singular, two of whom were Jimi Hendrix and Sylvester Stewart.

Jimi Hendrix (1942–1970) was born Johnny Allen Hendrix in Seattle, Washington. His musical career began at twelve when his father bought him a guitar. He taught himself to play from blues recordings, principally of B. B. King and Muddy Waters. By his adolescence he was playing with his own band called the Rocking Kings. While in the military he met a jazz and R&B bassist named Billy Cox. The two men formed a quintet that entertained troops in the area. Upon their discharge they organized a new band called the King Kasuals, performing around Memphis. From this period in Memphis through his stint on the 'Chitlin Circuit' during the next few years (around 1960–1964) Hendrix would meet and perform with a number of artists who would influence his development in various ways. These artists included Curtis Mayfield, Little Richard, the Isley Brothers, and King Curtis.

Hendrix's break occurred in the mid-1960s when, at the behest of Chas Chandler, bassist for the Animals, a noted British group, Hendrix was encouraged to go to London. He arrived there in 1966 and with Chandler immediately put together the trio that would begin the innovative Jimi Hendrix Experience. In addition to Hendrix, the trio consisted of Noel Redding on guitar and drummer John Mitchell.

Their first album was *Are You Experienced*. They were followed by *Axis: Bold as Love* and *Electric Ladyland*. These three album established Hendrix as a powerfully innovative guitarist and songwriter. After the third album the original trio broke up and Hendrix created a new trio called Band of Gypsys.

The Woodstock festival in New York in 1969 provided Hendrix with the venue for his most important sociopolitical statement. During his perfomance he gave a psychedelic, surrealistic rendering of the national anthem ("The Star-spangled Banner") that resonated strongly with the anti-Vietnam sentiments of the day. From this moment onward Hendrix would be regarded as a superstar.

Hendrix began a fourth album titled *First Rays of the New Rising Sun*, but he died of a drug overdose in 1970 before completing the project. He is remembered today mainly as a gifted songwriter and for the blues-based, psychedelic performance techniques he innovated on the guitar.

His influence on subsequent vernacular guitarists, particularly rock guitarists, to this day remains enormous.

One of the contemporary black groups who incorporated the psychedelic aesthetic that Hendrix helped crystallize into their funk-based style was Sly and the Family Stone. This group originally consisted of leader/guitarist/songwriter Sylvester Stewart, singer/guitarist Freddie Stone, singer/bass guitarist Larry Graham Jr., trumpeter Cynthia Robinson, drummer Greg Errico, pianist Rose Stone, and saxophonist Jerry Martini.

The group was established in 1967 and was a multiracial group. Their uniqueness lay in their ability to successfully merge black funk with the loud, psychedelic idioms of contemporary rock music. The singles recorded from 1967 to 1970 introduced many of the works that reflected this new synthesis, and these works became the classics on which their later reputation rested. They included pyschedelic/funk statements like "Dance to the Music" and social commentary songs like "Everyday People" and "Stand." Also included in this canon were "Hot Fun in the Summertime" and "Thank You (Falettinme Be Mice Elf Agin)."

After 1970 Sylvester Stewart (Sly) individually contributed "Family Affair" and "Fresh." Like Hendrix, Stewart was also catapulted to superstardom as a result of his performance at the 1969 Woodstock festival. The success of Sly and the Family Stone, however, withered in the seventies. Nonetheless, their powerful influence was absorbed and carried forward by groups like Kool and the Gang, Earth, Wind and Fire, the Ohio Players, and, very noticeably, Parliament/Funkadelic.

## Disco

By the late 1970s it was evident to most Americans that a new musical style had surfaced. This style was dubbed disco. From all appearances it looked like a mainstream thrust with multicultural leanings but one in which whites were a solid part of its epicenter. This perception was facilitated by a 1977 movie called *Saturday Night Fever* that starred John Travolta and featured an attractive film score by the Bee Gees. In truth, by the late 1970s disco was indeed a multicultural reality, one shared more less equally by blacks, whites, Latinos, and gays; but it did not start out that way.

The roots of the discotheque in America trace back to the 1960s with the establishment of private clubs in which disk jockeys supplied live entertainment. These private clubs frequently catered to a gay clientele. By the late 1960s and early 1970s similar establishments (though no longer private) were common to black communities, as club owners found it more economical to hire disk jockeys than to hire expensive bands. This trend was just as evident in black night clubs in major cities in the deep South as it was in the North.

Disco music differed from earlier funk music in that it was often orchestral, not combo driven; that is, it was frequently performed by large ensembles like jazz orchestras or ensembles featuring sections of strings, woodwinds, and/or brass, which often overshadowed the rhythm section. As we have seen, these ensembles proliferated in the late sixties and early seventies, providing the instrumentation underscoring soul music. These orchestral groups were common to the music of Isaac Hayes and particularly the bands that represented the Philadelphia International sound—a sound created and cultivated by producers Leon Huff and Kenneth Gamble and composer Thom Bell. The groups and individuals they promoted dominated soul music in the early seventies and included the Ojays, the Spinners, the Delphonics, and the Stylistics.

Given the prevalence of these lush ensembles in the early seventies it is not surprising that the work considered to be the first truly disco "tune" showed this influence. This work was called "The Hustle." It was written by Van McCoy in 1974, and performed by Van McCoy and the Soul City Orchestra. According to music historian Arnold Shaw "The Hustle" became the "biggest-selling dance disk of the 1970s" and "the basic dance of disco."[10] This was a fitting tribute to its composer, who died in 1979.

What differentiated disco from orchestral soul was its rhythmic pulse, which centered on a four-to-the-bar bass drum pattern, manipulation of the high hat cymbal in a manner that often complemented the bass drum, electronic effects and synthesized sounds, an anemic or escapist lyrical content, and the lengths of the songs (which were often longer than soul compositions). Disco was not just a dance music, it motivated the egoistic, sexual, and adonis-like preoccupations of its dancers. Despite its stylistic frailities, however, disco fingerprints an important era in American musical and social history. It provided a measure of escape from the lingering anxieties of the Vietnam War. Disco also promoted multiculturalism and tolerance, as evidenced by the success of multiracial groups like the Village People, and the benign manner in which gays were depicted in disco contexts.

Disco also brought to light many new creative talents. Among this cadre was its reigning queen Donna Summer (b. 1950), who contributed hits like "Last Dance" and "Hot Stuff." She was sometimes rivaled by artists like Gloria Gaynor (b. 1949), whose hits included "I Will Survive." Important black or multiracial groups of the late 1970s included The Village People, whose greatest contribution was the classic "Macho Man;" Kool and the Gang, whose hits included "Funky Stuff" and "Celebration;" Chic, whose works included "Dance, Dance, Dance;" Sister Sledge, who contributed "We Are Family"; and A Taste of Honey, with their "Boogie Oogie Oogie."

## CHAPTER 13

## RAP AND BEYOND: 1980 TO THE PRESENT

**T**HE TRADITION of soul/funk music continued through the 1980s and into the present but without the preeminence it commanded in the previous two decades. New, distinctive soul talents have continued to emerge but, because of their tremendous crossover appeal, are often classified as pop artists rather than as soul artists. Their gospel-style vocality, however, links most of them irrefutably with the soul tradition of the past. Such individual artists and groups of distinction include Peabo Bryson, Whitney Houston, Lionel Ritchie, Regina Bell, Luther Vandross, Anita Baker, Stephanie Mills, Janet Jackson, Tony Braxton, Cameo, The Gap Band, Atlantic Star, and scores of others. Lionel Ritchie, Prince Rogers Nelson (formerly known as Prince), and Kenneth "Babyface" Edmonds, are also three of the great songwriters to have emerged since 1980, and as such join a distinguished pantheon of great black songwriters and songwriting teams that includes Sam Cooke, Chuck Berry, Curtis Mayfield, Jimi Hendrix, Holland/Dozier/Holland, Ashford and Simpson, Smokey Robinson, Joe Tex, Isaac Hayes and David Porter, and Stevie Wonder.

The new artists coexist with their forerunners from the 1960s and 1970s—artists like Ray Charles, Stevie Wonder, Aretha Franklin, Wilson Pickett, Roberta Flack, James Brown, Teddy Pendergrass, The Temptations, The Four Tops, Kool and the Gang, Gladys Knight, Michael Jackson, and others. With the exception of Michael Jackson, these older artists are valued more for their contributions of the past than for their ability to fit in with modern trends or their ability to cultivate new trends.

## The Roots of Rap

*Hip hop* is the newest cultural and artistic development in black America since 1980. The visual arts and dance expressions of hip hop culture are graffiti and break dancing, respectively. Hip hop's musical manifestation is called *rap music*. Rap music may be defined loosely as a musical style in which a nonintoned (that is, spoken), usually poetic or quasipoetic narrative is delivered in a highly rhythmized fashion. Rap may be considered poetic to the extent that as a perfunctory aspect of its style it employs poetical devices like rhyme and figurative language, often in highly creative ways.

Like other popular styles before it, rap music seemed to have emerged spontaneously, without earlier rumbling. The evidence, however, suggests that the musical trends leading directly to the development of rap music were logical and well-precedented, and extend back at least to the 1950s. The indirect stylistic and philosophical roots of rap music go back much further, into African oral traditions. Rap is the most recent manifestation of the African-derived technique of vocal rhythmization—the rhythmization of a spoken (and sometimes a sung) text. This technique has had many manifestations in the past, as musicologist Ronald Jemal Stephens notes:

> Over a period of nearly four hundred years, the artful use of words has evolved into a variety of speech genres within the African American community. These genres include the creation of plantation tales, work songs, and unique preaching styles; the telling of rhyming jokes, riddles, singing games, and jump-rope rhymes; woofing, jiving, signifying, rapping, playing the dozens, telling toasts, boasting, and bebop talk.[1]

As a style that combines the communicative property of language and the musical properties of rhythm and tonality, rap relates to other black musical styles. In the nineteenth century, African Americans developed many ways to communicate with each other without directly using speech. These forms are called "speech surrogates" because they substituted or stood in for direct speech but served many of the same communication functions. These include field hollers—that is, cries rendered in a free rhythmic, atonal style—and the use of speaking instruments. Field hollers, according to Eileen Southern, varied from a "call for water, food, or help, [to] a call to let others know where he [the field hollerer] was working, or simply a cry of loneliness, sorrow, or happiness. One cry might be answered by another from a place far distant."[2] Speaking instruments simulated the tonal nuances of a language. For example, the African talking drums were instruments that mimicked speech patterns in their tonalities and rhythms; blues players would often let "the guitar speak," substituting an instrumental passage for one that would normally be sung.[3]

Call and response, when used a communicative device, also functioned as a speech surrogate in the nineteenth and twentieth centuries. For example, it was sometimes used by slave masters to affect the pace of work activities. In such forced labor situations (for example, labor tasks during slavery, and in labor activities of postslavery prison gangs) call and response was used in a manner similar to the way speech would have been employed in the same context.

The relationship between black speech and African American music is evidenced on an even more fundamental level when we consider how speech is represented in black music. Many of the techniques used in black vocal and instrumental music are literally speech-derived. One obvious example is the recitative-like nature of African American vocality, a technique that has engendered frequent commentary by collectors and scholars for the past 130 years. For example, in the foreword to her anthology of spirituals published in 1930 entitled *The Negro Sings a New Heaven*, Mary Allen Grissom states:

> [T]he Negro song frequently opens with the chorus, sung in unison by the group. A sort of recitative by the leader follows as the verse, and then the chorus by the group is again taken up."[4]

In her discussion of the rural music of antebellum slaves, Eileen Southern is even more specific:

> A song might move from speechlike sounds (described as "recitative" or "shrill monotone," for example) through ranges of the musical compass to screaming and yelling, all within the confines of a single performance.[5]

Some scholars consider many of the aesthetic attributes of African-derived music as either emanating from black speech or reflecting the properties of certain black languages. Rudi Blesh observed how improvisation in jazz and blues mimicked conversational patterns:

> The American Negro has vastly extended musical expression through tone. Not only has he based his phrasing on the rhythms of human speech . . . but he makes an intelligible, highly articulate and communicative language of his music by introducing the infinite variety and nuances of the speaking voice into music tone. The meaning of his music . . . becomes clear when it is heard as a conversation. . . . Listen to the blues and real jazz not for the familiar harmonized music, but for a conversation of people, all talking about the same thing, with statements and answers, questions, comments, exclamations, interjections, and even asides. . . . This has its inner logic when we understand the language and know what is being talked about. It is participative and creative, as true conversation . . . always is.[6]

Thus, given the multidimensional relationship that has existed and continues to exist between black speech and black music, the emergence of rap music should not at all be surprising.

Identifying the immediate musical lineage of rap music is, to some, debatable but not overly difficult. Many, if not most, contemporary scholars of rap music trace its direct musical roots to the late 1960s and early 1970s.[7] However, if we define rap music as a musical narrative effected by the skillful conjoining of rhythm, rhyme, and speech, then the musical roots of rap are evidenced in black music of the early 1950s and 1960s (if not earlier) as well, to the extent that aspects of the rap style are already present in the music of this period and function as integral components of the structure of the music.[8]

From the 1950s we may cite the Chuck Berry composition "No Money Down." This work was one of three written for a 1955 music session. In the verses of this work Berry repeatedly provides a nonintoned vocal response to a guitar riff. These spoken verses also feature end-rhymes.

An even better example occurs in the 1960s with the music of Joe Tex (1933–1982), specifically his hit song, recorded in 1964, entitled "Hold On to What You Got." The song opens with the chorus sung by Joe Tex. Because the same music is consistent throughout, we may distinguish the verse from the chorus principally by the fact the latter is sung and the former is spoken. The sung portion of the music functions as other traditional choruses do in that its text, though truncated, is repeated word for word and contains the hook and title of the song in its first appearance. In the ensuing verse (based upon the same music underlying the chorus), Tex delivers the story in a sermonistically spoken narrative; this type of delivery is not surprising given that Joe Tex had once been a minister in the 1950s. A truncated version of the chorus follows the conclusion of the first narrative. The second narrative then ensues and is again answered by the truncated chorus.

In this song neither rhyme nor a distinctive rhythm underlie the narrative, but the narrative is unquestionably an integral aspect of the song's structure.

Joe Tex employs this formula again in several subsequent hits, including "One Monkey Don't Stop No Show," "Buying a Book," "Don't Make Your Children Pay," and his first million seller "Skinny Legs and All," recorded in 1967. "Skinny Legs and All" opens with the verse rather than the chorus. Again no rhyme nor distinctive rhythm characterizes the narrative. In his hit "I Gotcha," recorded in 1972, Tex reverses the formula, using spoken text in the chorus rather than in the verses. In this instance, however, the spoken chorus is delivered with a distinctive rhythm.

In the early 1970s, Isaac Hayes used the same technique in a series of six romantic monologues, each prefacing a musical composition inspired by the monologue's theme. These monologues were often underscored by elegant symphonic orchestrations and were dubbed by the composer in each case as *Ike's rap*.[9] Hayes's raps do not employ rhymes and are delivered in an arrhythmic manner. However, in the Isaac Hayes/Mickey Gregory composition entitled Good Love 6-9969 (on the *Black Moses* album), Hayes opens the work with a brief spoken monologue in which the phrases end with rhymes. Portions of the spoken phrases are cast in distinctive, deliberate rhythms, though the soliloquy as a whole comes across as arrhythmic.

Even closer to modern rap is James Brown's 1968 masterpiece "Say It Loud, I'm Black and I'm Proud". It opens with a call-and-response section in which a plea (the call) is issued by the lead singer and is answered (the response) by background vocalists. Both the call and the response are based upon distinctive rhythmic patterns (Example 13.1). A spoken narrative follows. Though rhymes occur at the ends of phrases, the phrases of the narrative proper are not delivered by way of distinctive rhythmic patterns.

Example 13.1. "Say It Loud, I'm Black and I'm Proud" (James Brown)

Call and response:   (*twice*) Say it loud. I'm black and I'm proud.

Narrative:   Some people say we got a lot of malice, some say its a lot of nerves.

But I say we won't quit movin' until we get what we deserve.

We've been 'buked, and we've been scorned.

We've been treated bad, talked about, as sure as you born.

But just as sure as it takes two eyes to make a pair,

Brother we can't quit until we get our share.

Call and response:   (*three times*) Say it loud. I'm black and I'm proud.

Narrative:   I've worked on jobs with my feet and my hands

But all the work I did was for the other man.

And now we demand a chance to do things for ourselves.

We're tired of beating our head against the wall and working for someone else.

Call and response:   (*four times*) Say it loud. I'm black and I'm proud.

Brown's narrative is insistent, poignant, defiant, direct, and unapologetic. These are attributes typical of much of today's rap music, but atypical and unprecedented at the time "Say It Loud" was first released.[10]

The work is striking in the asymmetric construction of its text. The opening call and response is given twice before the narrative begins. The first part of the narrative proper consists of six lines. The ensuing call and response is stated three times, and is followed by a four line narrative before progressing to the bridge.

The underlying music of "Say It Loud" is also noteworthy. Musically, the verse constitutes, in effect, an extended ostinato composed of five distinct riff-like phrases, most discernible in the horns. This five-phrase ostinato consistently maintains an asymmetric relationship with the call-and-response "chorus" and the narrative proper. Thus the feeling of frustration and agitation, of not being allowed to fit into the society on one's own terms, communicated by the text, is corroborated by the asymmetry of the music and the asymmetry existing between the music and the text.

The only attribute that distinguishes Brown's "Say It Loud" from a modern rap piece is the rhythmically free manner in which each phrase of the narrative proper is delivered. In its theme, its stanzaic construction, its use of rhyme, and in other ways it qualifies as a rap composition.

Similar observations can be made of other works from the same period, for example, Pig Meat Markham's "Heah Comes de Judge," Rudy Ray Moore's "Dolemite" narratives, and the works of the Last Poets and Gil Scott Heron. Scott Heron's compositions "The Revolution Will Not Be Televised," "Brother," and "Whitey On The Moon," written between 1970 and 1972, are particularly interesting in this regard.

The next and most definitive trend leading to the development of rap music began in the mid-1970s, initially in the Bronx, New York. It was started by disc jockeys (DJs) who hosted parties for large numbers of black and Hispanic youths at parks, neighborhood community centers, and playgrounds. To inspire the crowd, these DJs (or MCs as they came to be known[11]) often spoke over the recording at its beginning and ultimately during the breaks in the song—sections where all voices and melodic instrumentation dropped out, leaving only the bass and percussion. The break was also the place in the music where the break dancing began.[12] Clive Campbell (Kool Herc), Joseph Saddler (Grandmaster Flash), and Afrika Bambaataa were three of the most innovative MCs of the era.

As the early MCs began to develop distinctive styles and large individual followings, they began delivering their monologues in the form of original stories and ultimately rhymed narratives. These narratives were often boastful and self-glorifying, but, along with break dancing, did much to intensify the excitement of these events, thus enhancing their popularity. These parties (or *jams* as they were sometimes called) soon spread to Brooklyn and Harlem, then beyond New York to cities with substantial black populations.

With the recording of "Rapper's Delight" by the Sugar Hill Gang in 1979, rap music began its ascension from a subcultural, underground expression to a new black musical genre of international import. Despite its commercial success, "Rapper's Delight" has often been criticized for being unauthentic, for not being consistent with the type of rap emanating from the ghettos of New York. However true this criticism may be, the work is nevertheless important in that it brought rap music to the attention of the world and inspired subsequent rappers to record their material. Other seminal recordings followed, notably Kurtis Blow's "The Breaks," and Grandmaster Flash and the Furious Five's "The Message." Unlike earlier rap recordings, "The Message" provided a poignantly realistic mirror of the horrors of black inner-city existence. In doing so, it influenced substantially the artistic and sociopolitical paths that many later rappers were to traverse.

## Rap Music from 1979 to 1984

The earlier forms of recorded raps were essentially narratives performed over preexisting popular hits, typically funk and disco songs of the era. Working from 45-rpm singles played on turntables, skillful DJs could

Grandmaster Flash

manipulate the background sound by dropping the needle at different parts of the recording, "backturning" the turntable to repeat a phrase, rapidly moving the turntable back and forth to create a percussive, "scratching" sound, and other unique techniques. Eventually, original musical scores were written to accompany raps, while sampling—digitally recording small sections of existing recordings—enabled arrangers to creatively "lift" riffs from popular recordings and add them to the musical texture.

Harmony and melody in the conventional sense were deemphasized in favor of rhythm. Consequently, early rap recordings featuring only two or three harmonies were common. Added special effects and brief countermelodic passages appeared frequently. Colorful harmonies became more common as the period progressed, though they were still presented in the form of harmonic ostinatos, that is, reiterated harmonic phrases. The bass and snare drums and bass guitar were accentuated, the latter frequently performing a syncopated ostinato.

End rhymes predominated; internal rhymes occurred sporadically. Lengths of lines and stanzas varied, as did the types of poetic rhythms found within and between lines. The natural rhythm of the poetry was generally usurped by the musical rhythm of the narrative. For example, the rhythm governing the following lines in "Rapper's Delight" is basically iambic, but the syncopated musical rhythm underlying the lines contradicts the poetic rhythm (Example 13.2).

*Poetic rhythm:*

Now | what you |      hear is     |   not a   | test. I'm | rappin' |   to the    | beat ‖
And |   me, the   | groove, and my | friends are |   gonna   |   try to   | move your | feet ‖

*Musical rhythm:*

Example 13.2. "Rapper's Delight" (Sugarhill Gang)

The types of subjects addressed by rappers varied. The tradition of boasting, inherited from the early MCs, continued but took on strange and sometimes comic forms ("Rappin' Duke"—Shawn Brown). Sometimes a single recording would inspire many answer records (most notably, the record "Roxanne, Roxanne" inspired dozens of parodies, including "Roxanne's Revenge"), and verbal dueling among rappers was common. Rappers also addressed topics dealing with social conditions ("The Message"—Grandmaster Flash), stolen rhymes ("Bite This"—Roxanne Shante), sports ("Basketball"—Kurtis Blow), food ("All You Can Eat"—Fats Boys), and sexuality.

Rap recordings during this period were produced and distributed principally by independent record companies. (New musical styles were typically "discovered" by the smaller independents, and the major labels would then jump on the bandwagon after they realized there was money to be made.) The Sugarhill Gang were named for their record label, Sugarhill (a neighborhood of Harlem). Other eminent early rappers include Kurtis Blow, Grandmaster Flash and the Furious Five, Dana Dane, Roxanne Shante, Run DMC, Fat Boys, Doug E. Fresh and M. C. Ricky D, Whodini, and the Boogie Boys.

## Rap Music: 1985 to the Present

Rap music during the later half of the 1980s witnessed some major changes. For example, the genre began to expand geographically as areas outside of New York became centers of rap activity, including Philadelphia, Chicago, Oakland, and South Central Los Angeles. These areas were well-represented by their own artists. Regional styles ultimately developed, and along with them, regional rivalries.

Another conspicuous change in rap music during this period was the increasing quantity and quality of rap's female performers. Though female rappers were present in the early 1980s, the role they played and the types of themes they addressed weren't radically different from that of their male counterparts. The general view of the female, as espoused by male rappers, was decidedly sexist. Roxanne Shante was one of the first female rappers to confront this image before 1984. Such efforts, however, were generally isolated and unthreatening (for example, "The Real Roxanne").

After 1984 the male dominance of rap music began to be viably challenged, as talented female rappers proliferated and asserted greater autonomy. Among the most influential female rappers to rise during this period were Dana Owens (Queen Latifah), Salt-N-Pepa—a trio consisting of Cheryl James, Sandy Denton, and Dee Dee Roper—and later BWP (Bytches with Problems), a hardcore feminist group. This new cadre of feminist rappers injected themes that emphasized empowerment, self-worth, equality, and a challenge to the prevailing sexual stereotypes espoused by male rappers. Feminist reactions to the prevailing sexist views males espoused sometimes took on angry forms, such as those expressed in Roxanne Shante's "Brothers Ain't Sh∗∗."

All female rappers were not feminists, and those generally known for their feminism did not always adhere strictly to feminist themes. Female rap artists, like their male counterparts, addressed a broad array of topics and matched on every front the creativity of the men.

Rap texts grew more rhymically syncopated. They also featured a greater use of internal rhymes. These rhymes initially occurred in the middle and ending of lines, dividing the lines symmetrically and accelerating their pace. As the period progressed, internal rhymes began occurring more at asymmetrical points within the line—sometimes next to each other. For example, note the rhymes in Queen Latifah's "The Evil that Men Do" (emphasis added):

> *This* rhyme *doesn't require* prime time
> *I'm just sharin' thoughts in* mind

This asymmetry often imparted a disjointed feeling to the lines, a quality that sometimes served the controversial subjects entertained by the rapper. This disjunctedness was often corroborated by the underlying syncopated rhythms of the narrative.

Scratching and other turntable techniques and special vocal effects (for example, beat box) continued to be used in background tracks. Preexisting material also continued to be drawn on to add to the texture of the musical accompaniment, but it took on the new form of (1) sampling, that is, using interpolated excerpts derived literally from previous recordings, and (2) looping, the use of preexisting elements constantly repeated. In some cases other elements, like bass lines and harmonic patterns, were also borrowed from or inspired by preexistent material; see for example Salt-N-Pepa's "Shake Your Thang," which samples and derives material from the Isley Brothers' "It's Your Thang."

Refrain lines often concluded stanzas or sections. Rapped or sung choruses frequently occurred between the narratives. Though refrains sometimes occurred in early recorded rap, these early narratives were nevertheless often freer and more experimental in their use of form. The increased use of refrains and choruses from the later half of the 1980s onward suggests movement back to the formative paradigms that characterized black popular music of the 1950s through the 1970s. Eminent rap artists between 1985 and 1990 included De La Soul, M. C. Hammer, Big Daddy Cane, Heavy D, Salt-N-Pepa, MC Lyte, Jungle Brothers, Roxanne Shante, Slick Rick, Public Enemy, NWA, Queen Latifah, Boogie Down Productions, and L. L. Cool J. Since 1990 other successful artists have come into commercial prominence: Shawn "Puff Daddy" Combs, Mase, Coolio, Missy Elliot, Foxy Brown, The Firm, and Jr. Mafia.

Still further changes occurred in rap music from the late 1980s onward. New genres of rap began to emerge, including *gospel rap*. Gospel rap, according to Jon Michael Spencer, is a form of Christian hip-hop that started around 1989. It differs from its stylistic precursors in that it speaks in the language of the black inner-city youth. It also rejects the traditional depiction of Jesus as white, as Spencer notes:

While the Jesus of old-styled gospel clearly is the "white Jesus"—the ideological icon with lily-white complexion, long, flowing blond or brunette hair, and Nordic facial features—the Jesus of gospel hip-hop is black, owing to the tradition of black Christian nationalism.[13]

Among the artists Spencer identifies as representing the tradition of Christian hip-hop are Preachers in Disguise (PID), End Time Warriors (ETW), Soldiers for Christ (SFC), DC Talk, Witness, D-Boy Rodriguez, Helen Baylor, Michael Peace, and Fresh Fish.[14] Other artists who have joined the ranks of the gospel rappers are MC Hammer and, sporadically, Kirk Franklin.

Another genre that emerged around the same time as gospel rap was *gangsta rap*. This genre is by far the most controversial and frequently criticized of all rap genres. Defining gangsta rap, and consequently the gangsta rapper, is not easy. To some of its detractors, gangsta raps are narratives presented in a profane, degenerate, and unjustifiably insulting manner. They are particularly vulgar and demeaning in their reference to women, and topics dealing with violence and sex are common.

In defense of gangsta rap, however, we must note that not every artist considered to be a gangsta rapper extols degenerate sexual values or violence. Some alleged gangsta rappers are more concerned with what they perceive to be the inequities and social contradictions of the system. Profanity in such raps is often used to accentuate the rage engendered by such contradictions; a good example is Ice T's "Freedom of Speech."

Some gangsta rappers concern themselves simply with reporting, uncensored, the negative realities of the inner-city, for example, crime or such consequences of a criminal existence as life in prison (Example 13.3). The profuse use of profanity to accentuate or embellish these narratives is often unnecessary, because the lifestyles described by these rappers are intrinsically poignant and frightening and need little embellishment.

Within such raps, however, are often found important messages.

> *Bein' incarcerated isn't no joke*
> *The strong survive and the weak get broke*
> *Just like a bone if they can't hold their own*
> *And stand strong, they won't last long*
> *In jail because a cell is hell*
> *The system smells and the food tastes stale*
> *So don't be dumb and come, motherf\*\*k crime*
> *Cause once you cross that line, you're gonna do time*
> *Until they give you a date*
> *But 'til then, you belong to the state[15]*

Example 13.3. "The Real Deal" (Lifer's Group)

Gangsta rappers have spoken frequently and vehemently about police brutality in the black community, as in NWA's notorious "F\*\*k the Police":

> *F\*\*k the police comin' straight from the underground*
> *A young nigger got it bad 'cause I'm brown*
> *And not the other color*
> *Some police think*
> *They have the authority to kill a minority[16]*

Example 13.4. "F\*\*k the Police" (NWA)

The rise in gangsta rap after 1989 occurred at the same time as an increased interest in rap music on the part of major record companies. This interest was no doubt a consequence of rap music's growing appeal to white audiences and has led to the usurpation of many independent companies. It has also led, inadvertently, to a proliferation of rap narratives reflecting the distorted views that many nonblacks have of black inner-city culture.

A genre that has become more widespread since the late 1980s may be called *nationalist rap*. This type of rap continues the musical strain that started with James Brown, the Last Poets, and Gil Scott Heron in the late 1960s and early 1970s. According to Jefferson Morley, the nationalism espoused by contemporary rappers differs from 1960s nationalism in that it emphasizes "an agenda that is cultural, not political, promoting Afro-centrism and the preservation of Black culture rather than demands for territory or reparations."[17] Prominent artists of this genre include De La Soul, Black Sheep, Paris (Example 13.5), Public Enemy, X-Clan, and Jungle Brothers (Example 13.6), Arrested Development, Brand Nubian, Outkast, and Gangstar.

> *With a raised fist, I resist*
> *I don't burn, so don't ya dare riff*
> *Or step to me, I'm strong and Black and proud*
> *And for the bulls**t, I ain't down*[18]

Example 13.5. "Break the Grip of Shame" (Paris)

> *In America today*
> *I have to regret to say*
> *Somethin', somethin' is not right*
> *And it deals with black and white*
> *Tell me Michee, is it me*
> *Naw, it's just society*
> *Filled with propaganda, huh?*
> *But why do we meander, huh?*
> *In a zone with hate for peace*
> *All of their b.s. must cease*
> *All I am is one black man*
> *In a mighty big white hand*

> *Brother brother sister sister*
> *If you're miss or if you're mister*
> *Listen please to this fact*
> *Black is black is black is black*[19]

Example 13.6. "Black Is Black" (Jungle Brothers)

Contemporary rap continues to use many of the musical techniques introduced by earlier performers. Internal rhymes, both symmetrically and asymmetrically placed, are common (see "The Real Deal" by Lifer's Group), as are multisyllabic rhymes. Refrain lines and rap choruses are also common and are quickly imparting a standard structure to modern rap compositions. Jazz influences in rap have become common, as evidenced in the increasing number of contemporary rap compositions that are written in an upbeat compound meter and that often feature jazz-influenced drumming and other jazz elements. Other uses of rap are presently under experimentation, for example, rap music used as an educational device and the use of rap elements by black jazz and classical composers.

## Jazz Rap

Jazz has been used in conjunction with rap narratives since the beginning of rap music in the mid-seventies, although such accompaniments were sporadic. However, the emergence of a distinct genre predicated on the fusion of jazz with rap and hip hop did not become apparent until the early 1990s. A rap composition can be considered jazz influenced to the extent that it employs jazz elements. In some instances the jazz influences are limited to an occasional jazz riff in the horns or perhaps a few references to jazz in the text. If in addition to jazz-style horn riffs the composition employs an underlying compound rhythmic pattern, the perception of jazz will be stronger.

Such patterns are common to the music of the Solsonics and Jazzmatazz. In the Solsonics's "Jazz in the Present Tense," an instrumental, the compound metric pattern contributes greatly to both the jazz and hip-hop character of the work, despite the absence of a narrative. The dual aspect of this pattern is possible because similar patterns are common to raps that are not generally regarded as jazz. They also occur often in contemporary rhythm and blues. In this case, however, the pattern underscores a theme that is followed by a piano improvisation, a contrasting section in which a swing-style walking bass underscores a horn chorus, a recapitulation embellished by a multiphonic vocalise, and a flute solo. With so many jazz features present, the "jazzness" of this work is unequivocal.

The music of Jazzmatazz is no less convincing in this regard. Their composition "Down the Backstreets" is striking in its use of a jazzy horn riff that accompanies the vocal riff separating the verses from the piano improvisation. These features, employed in conjunction with a rhythmic pattern in compound meter, anchor the narrative solidly into a jazz aesthetic.

Even when such strong jazz features are not present, jazzness can still sometimes be communicated. In Us3's "Tumka Yoot's Riddim," for example, a quasi-improvisation on saxophone helps the work's modest jazz effect to be heard. In Jazzmatazz's "Loungin'" it is the exquisitely delivered multiple trumpet solos of Donald Byrd counterpointing the narrative that deliver the jazz effect.

Although jazz-rap narratives are sometimes explicit, profanity is employed only sporadically and seldom to dramatize the content of the lyric. The narratives of the more sophisticated jazz rappers are often proactive and are thus consistent with their pre-rap antecedents. The structure of jazz narratives, however, is consistent with those of other rap styles, particularly in their employment of rhyming techniques. As yet no distinctly rhythmic style characterizes jazz narratives.

Jazz rap is an embryonic genre, but as we have seen, its roots are particularly deep and complex. Jazz rap represents a promising vehicle for artists capable of understanding its creative potential. Its important cultivators at present include Digable Planets, the Solsonics, Us3, the Roots, and Jazzmatazz.

# PART 4

## Theatrical and Classical Traditions

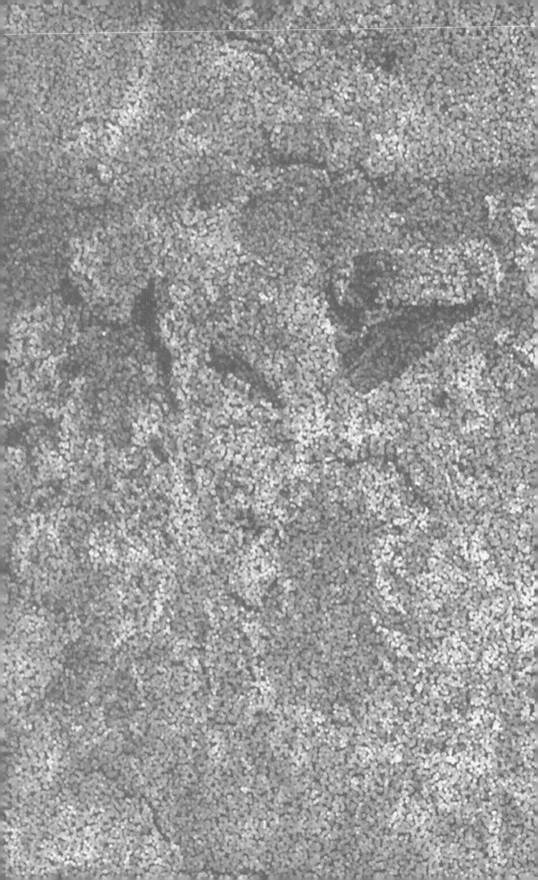

## CHAPTER 14

## THEATRICAL AND EARLY CLASSICAL MUSIC

**A**LTHOUGH THIS BOOK primarily focuses on popular musical styles, African Americans have also contributed to many other musical traditions, most notably theatrical music and the classical repertoire. Many of these compositions drew on the gospel, blues, jazz, and popular styles already described in this book. This chapter offers a brief overview of these two further areas of musical accomplishment.

### Musical Theater

Though minstrelsy began to decline in the last quarter of the nineteenth century, it left a powerful legacy that anchored itself in medicine shows, gillies (small traveling fairs), and carnivals. The value of minstrelsy with respect to the tradition of African American music is best seen in the contributions it brought to black musical theater. The minstrel show provided much of the training for black performers interested in theatrical careers. Minstrelsy also greatly influenced the structure of early African American musicals.

The legacy of minstrelsy was felt in American musical theater principally by way of a new species of popular song called the *coon song*. The first successful composition in this new style was written in 1890 by an African American songwriter named Ernest Hogan (1865–1908), and titled "All Coons Look Alike To Me." Along with the novel subject matter, the song introduced lightly syncopated rhythms to popular music, paving the way for the ragtime explosion that was to come within the following decade (see Chapter 4). Although enormously successful, the popularity of the song was predicated more on the title than the lyric or the music. The song's success inspired subsequent efforts; but unlike Hogan's amorous text, these latter efforts featured lyrics that were typically obscene, demeaning, and racist. These songs were nevertheless embraced by the general public.

Because of their popularity, coon songs soon found their way into Broadway shows.[1] However denigrating and distorted the view coon songs projected of African Americans generally, they did foreshadow the actual presence of black performers in American musical theater. This presence was first witnessed in an 1890 musical called *The Creole Show*. The show was conceived by Sam T. Jack, a theater owner and manager, as one that would "glorify the coloured girl."[2] Though relying heavily on conventions born from minstrelsy, the show was nevertheless novel in several ways. For example, it featured a female chorus. In addition, the conventional rural plantation background was replaced by an urban setting. The first act also featured a minstrel interlocutor but used a female instead of a male, again breaking with tradition.

*The Creole Show* was followed by other black musicals in the 1890s. In 1895, for example, *The Octoroons*, which featured burlesque sketches and emphasized song and dance, appeared. A year later, *Oriental America* was staged, a work which among its other features interpolated operatic selections into its score. Both *The Octoroons* and *Oriental America* were produced by John W. Isham, an agent for *The Creole Show*. *Black Patti's Troubadours* also appeared in 1896. It played for several seasons and featured Sissieretta Jones, one the leading black operatic singers of the day who was known by the stage name of Black Patti.

The first musical comedy written, directed, performed, and produced by blacks was *A Trip to Coontown*.[3] It premiered on April 4, 1898, and featured the writing and production talents of Bob Cole (1868–1911), one of the most important figures in the development of early African American musical theater. Earlier Cole had been enlisted by Sissieretta Jones's managers, Voelckel and Nolan of New York, to write music to highlight Jones's operatic talents, resulting in the score for *Black Patti's Troubadours*. A subsequent salary disagreement between Cole and Jones's managers caused Cole to gather his music and walk out (subsequent court action forced Cole to return the music to Voelckel and Nolan). This action inspired Cole to begin working on a play of his own. The result was *A Trip to Coontown*, an effort destined to mark a new direction for black musical theater. James Weldon Johnson, a contemporary observer and coparticipant in the development of early black musical theater, noted:

> In the season of 1898–1899 he [Cole] came out with *A Trip to Coontown*, the first Negro show to make a complete break from the minstrel pattern, the first that was not a mere potpourri, the first to be written with continuity and to have a cast of characters working out the story of a plot from beginning to end; and, therefore, the first Negro musical comedy.[4]

Two months later, on June 28, 1898, another important black musical premiered. This was *Clorindy; The Origin of the Cakewalk*. The libretto for the musical was originally written by the noted African American poet Paul Lawrence Dunbar (though by the premiere of the musical Dunbar's libretto was eliminated). The score was written by Will Marion Cook (1869–1944), a former student of Dvořák and one of the most successful and prolific composers of black musicals between 1898 and 1908. *Clorindy* was followed by other impressive musicals scored by Cook, including *Just Lak White Folks*, *Dahomey*, *The Southerners*, *Abyssinia*, and *Bandanna Land*.

During the period 1910 to 1920 the black musical receded from Broadway and took refuge in Harlem, leaving white audiences perhaps with the impression that the age of the black musical had come to an end. This retreat made possible the development of what James Weldon Johnson called "a real Negro theatre . . . ; that is, a theatre in which Negro performers played to audiences made up almost wholly of people of their own race."[5] While the cessation of black musicals on Broadway robbed them of the critical acclaim and economic support they needed eventually to compete with nonblack musicals, there were nevertheless some ways in which black musicals and black theater generally benefited by the move to Harlem. One of the most important and valued of the benefits was that black performers were no longer circumscribed by conventions rooted in white supremacy—taboos as Johnson called them—which white managers allegedly representing the taste of white society had imposed upon black performers over the previous forty years. For example, serious romantic scenes involving blacks, strictly forbidden in previous black musicals written for white audiences, occurred commonly in Harlem's "real Negro theater" during this period. Also, black producers no longer felt limited in the types of dramas they could produce. This resulted in stylistically diverse offerings covering a range that "ran all the way from crude Negro burlesque to Broadway drama."[6]

The black musical returned to Broadway in 1921 with *Shuffle Along*. This musical, said by some scholars to have ushered in the Harlem Renaissance, brought critical acclaim to its librettists Flournoy Miller and Aubrey Lyles, its lyricist Noble Sissle, and its composer Eubie Blake. It also launched the international careers of Florence Price, Josephine Baker, and Paul Robeson. It has often been credited as the first book musical written, produced, and performed by African Americans, although it was really just a revue. The musical ran for over a year at the Sixty-third Street Theatre in New York and for several years afterwards as a touring musical. Revivals of *Shuffle Along* continued into the 1930s. Its success inspired countless imitators, including the series of successful *Blackbirds* revues produced in the late 1920s through the early 1930s.

Two classics of the Broadway theater that were not written by African American composers, but greatly influenced by the traditional and popular black musical styles, were Oscar Hammerstein and Jerome Kern's *Show Boat* (1927) and George and Ira Gershwin's "jazz opera," *Porgy and Bess* (1935). *Show Boat* featured the classic ballad "Ol' Man River" and presented its "colored" characters in less-stereotyped and much more sympathetic manner than previous revues. *Porgy and Bess* was a real breakthrough, with its realistic portrayal of life on the Georgia Sea Islands. Gershwin borrowed heavily from jazz and blues in the score, producing many standards including the classic "Summertime." Both musicals offered black actors, singers, and musicians a chance to appear in serious shows in the "legitimate" Broadway setting as the equal of their white counterparts.

The African American presence on Broadway from the 1940s on has been somewhat spotty. There have been few entirely original shows; most have been revues or adaptations of operettas or other musicals for a black cast. The successful *Hot Mikado*, originally produced in 1939, is a case in point. An adaptation of Gilbert and Sullivan's classical operetta, it featured dancer Bill "Bojangles" Robinson in a leading role. Just as ragtime composers liked to "rag the classics," the original Sullivan score was "jazzed up" (with the lyrics adapted to reflect current black slang). In the same vein, nearly forty years later, *The Wiz* opened in 1975 on Broadway. A soulful adaptation of the popular film musical, it introduced pop singer Stephanie Mills to a wide audience and featured the lyrics and music of composer Charlie Small (notably the pop hit song, "Ease on Down the Road") and the choreography of Geoffrey Holder. It later was made into a feature film with pop singers Diana Ross and Michael Jackson in the cast.

In the 1970s, 1980s, and 1990s a slew of revue-type shows featuring the work of noted African American popular composers appeared on Broadway. Shows based on the life and careers of Duke Ellington

(*Sophisticated Ladies*), Eubie Blake (*Eubie!*), and more general song-and-dance revues (*Black and Blue*) were enormously successful. While their popularity is to be applauded, it also must be noted that there was a dearth of original, new work by African Americans appearing on the Broadway stage at this time. Of course, new musicals in general have become more costly to produce and therefore are less likely to appear. But still the lack of new composing talent for the popular stage is disturbing.

## The Roots of African American Classical Music

African Americans did not achieve great success in the classical arena prior to the twentieth century. However, developments in the classical art music tradition of the eighteenth and nineteenth centuries predicated upon the efforts of both black and white composers, were forerunners of this later achievement. During this same period, the rumblings of an independent, black classical musical thrust, however faint, began to be heard.

In his book entitled *Notes on the State of Virginia* Thomas Jefferson noted the penchant of many blacks (mainly slaves) for music, but went on to note that the innate musicality of blacks was yet to manifest itself creatively in advanced forms of music. Jefferson was undoubtedly speaking about the American blacks he knew. Jefferson could not have been aware of the musical contributions blacks from other parts of the world had already made in the arena of European classical music or of the contributions they were currently making. These achievements were not limited to specific areas of music. Blacks distinguished themselves as virtuosi of various instruments as well as music critics, authors about music, recital artists, operatic divas, and notably as composers.

Among the important music theorists of the eighteenth century was Ignatius Sancho (1729–1780). Sancho was born allegedly aboard a slave ship en route to the Spanish West Indies from Vienna. He was eventually taken to Greenwich, England, and placed in the care of three women who were friends of the Duke of Montague. Montague encouraged and supported Sancho's intellectual and musical development. Sancho ultimately became a noted music critic and the author of an important textbook on music theory.

Another important figure from the eighteenth and nineteenth centuries was George Bridgetower (1789–1860). Bridgetower was a highly distinguished violin virtuoso born in Biala, Poland. His mother was Polish and his father was an African who was an accomplished musician. Bridgetower's career as a violin virtuoso began in Paris at the age of nine with a recital that was said to have surpassed all expectations. With the success of this concert, the young prodigy was frequently extended invitations by the royal courts and aristocracies of several European countries, including King George III of England. Bridgetower is principally known as the violinist who premiered Ludwig van Beethoven's most famous violin sonata, the *Kreutzer*.

Several noted performers of the eighteenth and nineteenth centuries were also noted composers. Among the more accomplished composers from this period were Joseph Boulogne, Joseph Nunes Garcia, Jose White, and Samuel Coleridge-Taylor.

Joseph Boulogne was born in 1739 on the Caribbean island of Guadeloupe. He was the offspring of a romance between the general controller of the island, Jean de Boulogne, and an extraordinarily beautiful native girl named Nanon. Joseph Boulogne was christened the Chevalier Saint George, after a ship anchored in the harbor at that time. Sometime during his early adolescence he allegedly went to Paris, where he received an extensive education in music, literature, science, fencing, riding, and other disciplines.

It was as a fencer that Boulogne first came into public prominence, competing impressively with some of the most eminent swashbucklers of the day. He was destined, however, to make a much deeper mark in music. Boulogne distinquished himself as both a violin virtuoso and a composer. Violin concerti, sonatas for violin, and string trios, including François Joseph Gossec's six string trios (Opus 9), were dedicated to him. Other dedications were given by Antonio Lolli and J. Avolio. Boulogne's career as a composer began with the publication of his first opus in 1765, his six quartets for strings, said to be among the first of the French school. To this Boulogne later added twelve violin concertos, thirteen symphony concertantes, a concerto for bassoon, a concerto for clarinet, two symphonies, and several comic operas.

The most distinctive characteristic of Boulogne's music is his lyricism, which has often been compared to Mozart's. Nowhere is this lyricism better exemplified than in Boulogne's first symphony, written in G major. The work, composed in 1780, is in three movements (Allegro, Andante, Allegro assai), a movement scheme typical of the Italian overture that was very popular in France at the time. The symphony derives from the overture to Boulogne's comic opera *L'Amant anonyme.*

In general, the movements of Boulogne's first symphony paint a lighter, somewhat galant portrait of the sonata principle as it was practiced in late eighteenth-century Europe. Though polished, balanced, and superlatively crafted, its emotionally restrained, perfunctory character prevents this symphony from being placed on a par with the works of Boulogne's contemporary and friend Simon Le Duc, or the contemporary German masters of the genre, Mozart and Haydn. The second symphony of Boulogne opens with a more auspicious theme, but the promise of a deeper, more emotionally engaging musical treatment is thwarted by the absence of a sound development of the thematic material.

Some of the superficiality of Boulogne's symphonies can be explained by the fact that they were derived from his overtures, which were typically lighter in their construction and emotional depth. A more plausible reason for the perfunctory nature of his symphonies, however, owes to the galant nature of the composer's style generally.

Though the term *galant* was applied to a rather broad array of composers during the eighteenth century, it generally alluded to music that featured light, symmetrical melodies, form characterized by elegance and balance, homophonic texture, a circumscribed use of counterpoint, and a clear harmonic vocabulary that moved in harmonic rhythms slower than those featured in baroque music. Barry S. Brook notes, appropriately:

> If one were to attempt to name the composer of the 1770s and 1780s who best typifies the galant aspect of French instrumental style, Le Chevalier de Saint-Georges would be an ideal choice. With the exception of the adagio in F minor . . . (and one operatic aria) all of his known music is sunny, melodic, and pleasant—uncomplicated by sombre tonalities or harmonic surprises. His treatment of form is as regular as can be. His orchestration is simple, his phraseology square. Nevertheless his melodic gift is sufficiently strong to make his works attractive.[7]

In his symphony concertantes and violin concertos we see a more adventurous composer, at least with respect to the virtuosic treatment of his orchestral and solo material. His eleventh concerto is especially noteworthy. Its first movement shows a conspicuously stronger development of the material generally. A slightly deeper emotionalism is evident in the second movement, despite its brevity and simplicity. The same may be said for the more lyrical moments of the third. In its harmonic invention and form, however, the work remains conservative.

It is futile to look for conspicuous or unequivocal black idioms in the works of Boulogne. Such idioms are simply not present. However, allusions to his racial identity may be inferred by his lyricism, which has been described as exemplifying a "touch of creole melancholy."[8] Because such terminology was seldom if ever used to describe the lyricism of any of Boulogne's better-known contemporaries, we may assume that critics and scholars heard something in his music that wasn't present in the music of others, something that relates in some way to his mixed racial background.

Reflecting more the spirit of late classicism is the music of Jose Mauricio Nunes Garcia. Garcia was born in Rio de Janeiro in 1767. Professor Dominique Rene de Lerma notes that as a child Garcia began singing popular songs in cabarets and performed in local ensembles as a violinist and pianist. He helped subsidized his musical study with the money he earned from such ventures. Garcia wrote mostly religious music. This stylistic penchant, de Lerma further notes, was a reflection of his affiliation with religious organizations after 1791.

Romanticism is beautifully exemplified in the works of three composers: Jose White, Louis Moreau Gottschalk, and Samuel Coleridge-Taylor. Jose White was born in Matanzas, Cuba, in 1839. He was educated initially by his father, who was an amateur violinist. After his debut in 1855, White was accepted into the Paris Conservatory.

White was an accomplished violinist who concertized frequently in Cuba, Mexico, South America, and the United States. His compositional output was small by the standards of nineteenth century composers, but it was substantive. White wrote works for solo violin and piano, chamber ensembles, and orchestra. Representative of his larger-scale compositions is his Violin Concerto in F♯ minor, written in 1864. The work is a typical three-movement format of the traditional concerto. In its harmonic content and in the lyrical quality of its themes, it is romantic; in its form, however, it reflects more the design of the late classical concerto. The first movement, for example, opens with a lengthy orchestral exposition in which the two themes of the concerto are eloquently presented. The solo exposition follows in which the themes are restated and expanded. The ensuing closing material is so strongly predicated upon the opening theme that the entire exposition suggests a cyclic structure.

The development section is dominated by solo material, with little creative interchange between the soloist and orchestra. Therefore, when the recapitulation opens with an orchestral statement of the principal theme, there is an eminent sense of appropriateness. The first movement connects, by way of a brief episode, with the second in a manner reminiscent of Mendelssohn's Violin Concerto in E minor. The second movement is slow and in a three-part design. The finale reflects an abab design in which the themes are bridged by transitions and retransitions in a manner falsely suggestive of a rondo. The themes are strongly contrasted, both in their character and modality. Closing material follows the final theme and brings the movement to a satisfying conclusion.

Because of their brevity in comparison with the first movement, the second and third movements do not impart a satisfying formal balance to the piece. This fault robs the work of the grandeur promised by the architectonic prodigality of the opening movement. This structural frailty, however, is compensated (or at least diverted) somewhat by the presence of beautiful themes, sound craftsmanship, and often intriguing and challenging solo writing.

It is debatable whether Gottschalk can (any longer) be classified as a black composer. The previous justification for doing so was based upon his alleged creole background. By way of the Louisiana Legislative Code no. 111, the presence of an African ancestry to any degree justified a "Negro" classification. Recent research, however, has begun to cast doubt upon the claim that Gottschalk possessed any black blood at all. This debate notwithstanding, Gottschalk was raised as a creole, was treated as a creole while in America, and from all available evidence believed himself to be so. To this extent we may continue to classify him as a creole American composer.

Louis Moreau Gottschalk was born in New Orleans, Louisiana, in 1829. His father was English and his mother Haitian. Gottschalk was sent to France for his education in 1842, and during his ten-year residency in

Europe, he dazzled audiences and composers with his piano virtuosity and his compositions. His piano technique was regarded as brilliant and formidable, and his works were regarded as among the best of exotic products then being written. As a result, Gottschalk earned the praise and support of some of the most acclaimed art music composers in Europe, including Frederic Chopin, Hector Berlioz, and Théophile Gautier.

The role he played in the development of a school of African American classical composers and in later Afro-vernacular composition is immensely important and frequently overlooked. Gottschalk pioneered much of the aesthetic terrain that later Pan-Africanists and black nationalist composers were to travel. He was, for example, one of the earliest American composers to incorporate black and creole idioms into an art music context. He was also one of the earliest American composers to use preexisting African-derived or black-influenced folk material in his compositions. His early piano compositions like "La Bananier," "Le Savane," and "Bamboula" show quite noticeably the African-derived influences he absorbed in his youth. "Bamboula" is subtitled "Danse de Negres" and uses a creole melody often sung with the bamboula (a popular dance form). "La Bananier" is subtitled "Chanson Negre" and is also based upon a creole melody. "La Savane" is subtitled "Ballade Creole" and is again based upon a folk melody common in New Orleans during Gottschalk's day.[8]

Influences of the African diaspora are seen in later piano works like "Danza," "La Gallina," and particularly the second movement of his symphony *A Night in the Tropics*. These works show quite admirably Gottschalk's skill in handling habanera and tango rhythms, influences he acquired as a result of his visits to Cuba, Puerto Rico, Haiti, and Guadeloupe. Spanish influences are seen in compositions like "La Jota Aragonesa," "Caprice Espagnol," and "Minuet a Seville, Caprice."

Some of Gottschalk's late piano music, "La Gallina" for example, have rhythmic structures that are at times strongly reminiscent of ragtime. Conversely, we find tango rhythms in Joplin's ragtime masterpiece,

"Solace." We find West Indian influences, common in the works of Gottschalk, occurring later in jazz. Gottschalk's use of harmony in his late piano pieces was occasionally reminiscent of harmonies later found in jazz. The notion of the "black dance" (*danse Negre*) generally, and the bamboula specifically, taken up by Gottschalk early in his career, was to be revisited by Afro-European and African American composers only a few decades later.

Gottschalk's often fast-paced life-style, accentuated by the massive concerts he organized, damaged his health. He died in Rio de Janeiro in 1869 at the age of forty. Six years later another figure of great importance to the development of the African American school of classical composition was born. Like Gottschalk, he would cultivate an African diaspora musical agenda but would anchor it more solidly on an African American aesthetic, cultural, and musical foundation. In so doing he would lay more definitively than any earlier composer the seeds on which the present school of African American composition was to be based. His name was Samuel Coleridge-Taylor.

Born in Croydon, England, in 1875, Coleridge-Taylor's circumstances were not very favorable as a young child. His father, Daniel Hughes Taylor, abandoned his family during the child's infancy, a departure that was prompted by his inability to build an independent medical practice because of his race. Under the supervision of a white Croydon doctor with whom he was employed soon after the birth of his son, his career took a turn for the better. When his supervisor left Croydon, however, the clients who had patronized both men refused to patronize Daniel Taylor as an independent doctor.

Coleridge-Taylor's musical development began at the age of five when he was given a small violin. Rudimentary instructions on the instrument followed. His musical career, however, officially began a few years later, and in a most curious way. He was about seven years old when a prominent musician in Croydon, Joseph Beckwith, then the conductor of the orchestra at the Croydon Theater, observed the child on his hands and knees playing marbles on the pavement in front of Beckwith's house while Beckwith was giving a music lesson. Struck by the youth's odd appearance—he was shooting marbles with one hand while holding his small violin in the other—Beckwith invited the boy in and placed in front of him some simple violin duets. The child's rendering of the duets and his social circumstances impressed Beckwith so deeply that he offered free lessons to the boy. These lessons continued for the next seven years.

With the support of Colonel Herbert A. Walters, Coleridge-Taylor entered the Royal College of Music in 1890. Under the tutelage of Sir Charles Stanford, Coleridge-Taylor began to distinguish himself as a budding composer. Compositions written during this period were promising and attracted the attention of music critics. His Nonet in F minor, Opus 2, written for a chamber ensemble of piano, winds, and strings, and *Zara's Ear-rings*, Opus 7, a Rhapsody for Voice and Orchestra, were among his early works.

In 1895 and 1896 Coleridge-Taylor won the coveted Lesley Alexander Prize for composition. Winning this award brought him to the attention of England's leading composer, Edward Elgar, who provided Coleridge-Taylor with his definitive break. When commissioned by Sir Herbert Brewster to write a composition for the Three Choirs Festival in 1898, Elgar responded:

> I have received a request from the secretary to write a short orchestral thing for the evening concert. I am sorry I am too busy to do so. I wish, wish, wish you would ask Coleridge-Taylor to do it. He still wants recognition, and he is far and away the cleverst fellow going amongst the young men.[9]

On the strength of Elgar's recommendation Coleridge-Taylor was extended the commission. The result was his *Ballade in A Minor*, a symphonic score that brought national recognition to the composer.

Coleridge-Taylor followed his *Ballade* with *Hiawatha's Wedding Feast*, a cantata scored for chorus, baritone soloist, and orchestra. The text of the cantata was derived from Henry Wadsworth Longfellow's poetic masterpiece, *The Song of Hiawatha*. It was conducted in 1898 by Sir Charles Stanford at the Royal College of Music. Though the reviews of the work varied, they were generally favorable. The response of audiences to the work, however, was consistently favorable and remains so to this day.

*Hiawatha's Wedding Feast* is a beautifully scored choral and orchestral tone painting of the setting and the guests attending Hiawatha's wedding. The music is spiced with infectious rhythms and haunting melodies throughout. This work was not Coleridge-Taylor's first creative investment in the Hiawatha legend. Nor was he the first composer to undertake a project based on Longfellow's poem. Dvořák several years earlier contemplated its use as the basis for a tone poem; however, no such work resulted. But the influence of the Hiawatha legend is felt in Dvořák's ninth symphony, *Symphony from the New World*.

Coleridge-Taylor's first venture with the Hiawatha legend resulted in an earlier work for violin and piano entitled *Hiawatha Sketches*. He would follow the *Wedding Feast* with *The Death of Minnehaha* in 1899—a cantata sharply contrasting with the first by its lugubrious mood and its deeply felt pathos—and *Hiawatha's Departure*, written in 1900. Together the three cantatas form a trilogy and for a number of years after the composer's death were frequently performed as such. Coleridge-Taylor also wrote an overture to the trilogy that was based upon a black spiritual as well as a set of balletic sketches inspired by the Hiawatha legend.

Coleridge-Taylor's connection with African American culture was felt in several ways, through: (1) his works inspired by poetry written by black and nonblack poets; (2) his works inspired by African American folk material, particularly spirituals; and (3) his visits to America, which brought the composer into contact with African American performers, composers, and eminent intellectuals. The African American poet who influenced Coleridge-Taylor more than any other was Paul Lawrence Dunbar. They met when Dunbar visited England in 1896. By this time Coleridge-Taylor's fame had already spread to the United States and had attracted the attention of eminent African American intellectuals and artists.

Coleridge-Taylor's meeting with Dunbar resulted in several early settings of Dunbar's poems, including "The Corn Song," "At Candle Lighting," and "African Romances." One of Coleridge-Taylor's earliest symphonic scores was also inspired by a Dunbar poem, "Danse Negre," a work which, by its rhythmic and melodic character, showed beautifully Coleridge-Taylor's ability to musically depict blackness. "Danse Negre" ultimately became the fourth movement of his *African Suite*, Opus 35. Though "Danse Negre" specifically, and the *African Suite* generally, did not employ authentic African-derived elements, the manner in which the suite suggested the Africanicity suggested by the titles of the works did not escape critical notice. The music critic of the *Times*, a local newspaper, remarked:

> An African Suite, with its deeply poetical "Negro Love Song," is worth a good many New World symphonies, for it has the genuine national or racial ring about it.[10]

A later collaboration with Dunbar resulted in *Dream Lovers*, an operetta. In addition, it is likely that Dunbar's "Ethiopia Saluting the Colors" was probably the inspiration behind Coleridge-Taylor's concert march of the same name.

Coleridge-Taylor drew the text for his *Five Choral Ballads* from Henry Wadsworth Longfellow's poems on slavery. The *Ballads* were written to fulfill a request by the Samuel Coleridge-Taylor Choral Society for original material to be presented at the Washington Festival in 1904. The festival was a three-day event featuring the works of Coleridge-Taylor to celebrate his first visit to the United States. Three of the five *Ballads* were premiered by the Choral Society on the second concert of the festival. Additionally, Coleridge-Taylor composed vocal works inspired by African American spirituals (see Chapter 2).

Coleridge-Taylor's fame stimulated the interest of many important African American and non–African American luminaries. Some, like the poet Paul Lawrence Dunbar and the philanthropist Carl Stoeckle, met with Coleridge-Taylor during their trips to England. Most others, however, came into contact with him by way of the three visits he made to America in 1904, 1906, and 1910.

These visits were of great importance to Coleridge-Taylor. They validated the composer's mission to do for black music "what Brahms has done for Hungarian folk music, Dvořák for the Bohemian, and Grieg for the Nowegian."[11] They connected him with some of the most important black and nonblack personalities in America and assured his position as the most important black musical personality in the world at that time. They placed at his disposal important musical organizations, such as the Samuel Coleridge-Taylor Choral Society, an organization established in 1901 composed entirely of black singers; the Litchfield County Choral Society; and the Philharmonic Society of New York (now known as the New York Philharmonic), which premiered Coleridge-Taylor's *Bamboula* under the composer's baton.

The visits were also important to artistic-minded black Americans. The regard by which many black (and nonblack) Americans held Coleridge-Taylor and his music was phenomenal, as may be evidenced from the following excerpt of a letter sent to the composer on April 26, 1908, by Andrew F. Hilyer, honorary treasurer of the Samuel Coleridge-Taylor Society:

In composing *Hiawatha* you have done the coloured people of the U. S. a service which, I am sure, you never dreamed of when composing it. It acts as a source of inspiration for us, not only musically but in other lines of endeavors. When we are going to have a *Hiawatha* concert here, for at least one month we seem, as it were, to be lifted above the clouds of American colour prejudice, and to live there wholly oblivious of its disadvantages, and indeed of most of our other troubles.

I suppose, of course, that you have heard of the many Samuel Coleridge-Taylor societies being organised all over the country. Your compositions are often rendered by prominent white orchestras and musicians. Last week the *African Dances* were rendered at a fine concert by some white artiste—a lady, by the way. Mr. C. C. [Clarence Cameron] White is planning a big concert with the daughter of B. T. Washington, Mrs. Pittman, as the star.[12]

That Coleridge-Taylor was a disciple of Antonin Dvořák did not hurt his credibility with Dvořák's students and adherents. Harry T. Burleigh, Clarence C. White, Horatio Parker, and many other American artists befriended and supported him. President Theodore Roosevelt received him in the White House after one of his concerts. Booker T. Washington praised him for his accomplishments and, in the preface of his *Twenty-four Negro Melodies* dubbed him the greatest black composer of the race. Members of the New York Philharmonic called him the "African Mahler" in response to the originality of his composition *Bamboula* and the excellent manner in which he conducted the orchestra.[13] Coleridge-Taylor's engagement by the Philharmonic marked the first time they had been conducted by a black. In the eyes of his African American contemporaries, his success was a fortuitous event in the evolution of their nationalism and could do nothing less than confirm the possibility of their own success.

## CHAPTER 15

# CLASSICAL MUSIC: 1850 TO THE PRESENT

## White Composers Working with Black Idioms

While it is true that few black classical composers exerted any lasting influence on the main current of European musical development, the same fate has not befallen African-derived musical idioms. European composers since the nineteenth century have shown a strong interest in musical influences emanating from outside of European cultural environs. Influences from Africa and aspects of the African diaspora were part of their interest. During the nineteenth century, black influences were viewed as exotic and composers drew on them just as they did other folk and national traditions to add "color" to their works.

The experimentation with African-derived idioms or nigrescent (black) references produced a rather large body of literature during the nineteenth and twentieth centuries. In the world of opera, for example, *L'Africaine*, written by Giacomo Meyerbeer, which premiered in 1865, drew on "African" elements. Though the principal characters of this composition were not African, the backdrop of Africa was an important element in the work and contributed to its exoticism. Both *Aida* and *Otello*, written by Giuseppe Verdi and premiered in 1871 and 1887, respectively, featured black characters in leading roles. The character Aida is an Ethiopian slave girl, and Otello, based on the Shakespearean drama *Othello*, a great military general who was formerly a slave. *Aida* goes further in that it is set in Egypt, addresses a conflict between two ancient African nations, and contains music which, though not African-derived, is clearly meant to represent "Egypt-ness" in its exotic appeal. Carlos Antonio Gomes, a minor but important Brazilian protege of Verdi, composed an opera entitled *Lo Schiavo* (The Slave),[1] which during its time was hailed as "the opera of emanicipation par excellence" by its contemporaries.

Many other romantic and preromantic operatic works not based on African-derived themes nevertheless featured black characters in prominent roles. Often these works bespeak a Moorish connection. The last operas of Mozart and Tchaikovsky are two prominent examples: Monostatos the Moor in Mozart's *Magic Flute,* and Ibn Hakia the Moorish doctor in Tchaikovsky's *Yolanda.*

Romantic and postromantic ballets containing nigrescent references are no less numerous. One of the better-known incidental references is the famous "Pas des Ethiopeans" in the second act of Léo Delibes' *Sylvia,* which premiered in 1876. Nigrescent elements are more strongly exemplified in two early-twentieth-century ballets written by Darius Milhaud: *Le Boeuf sur le Toit* (The Bull on the Roof), based on a scenario by Jean Cocteau, and *Le Création du Monde,* based on a scenario by Blaise Cendrars. *Le Boeuf sur le Toit* features a black character in a prominent role (the black dwarf) and a score by Milhaud that is strongly predicated on Brazilian and Afro-Brazilian influences.

Cendrars derived his subject for *Le Création du Monde* from African folklore. The conspicuous nigrescent musical influences in *Le Création du Monde* are derived from the blues, and feature simulated blue notes in several sections of the score, particularly the fugue. There is also a curious relationship between an interior motive within the countersubject of this fugue and the principal motive of William C. Handy's "St. Louis Blues." The blues influences in *Le Création* probably emanated from a collection of 78 rpm records the composer brought back to Paris from his trip to New York in 1922. They may also have derived from the black jazz musicians Milhaud heard in Harlem nightclubs during the same trip.

There are many examples of romantic and postromantic instrumental music that referenced nigrescent elements. In some instances these references were obtained directly from black sources. Gottschalk's "Le Bananier," popular in both Europe and America, was transcribed for cello by Jacques Offenbach. It was in fact Offenbach who assigned the subtitle "Chanson Negre" to the composition. Camille Saint-Saëns's fifth piano concerto, Opus 103, known popularly as the *Egyptian* concerto, features a Nubian song in its second movement. The composer heard this song while cruising down the Nile and notated it on his shirt sleve.

An earlier work by the same composer is even more illustrative of his interest in African idioms. This work, a fantasy for piano and orchestra, is appropriately titled *Africa*. An examination of the opening melody (Example 15.1) reveals that the composer's ability to handle African rhythm is unusually convincing. Saint-Saëns was a young classmate of Gottschalk during his time at the Paris Conservatoire. As a young music student in Paris, Saint-Saëns would have heard many of Gottschalk's popular compositions for piano.

Perhaps the most famous "borrowing" of all was Dvořák's ninth symphony, *From the New World*, based as it was on the spirit of African American spirituals (see chapter 2). We have already discussed how

Example 15.1. *Africa* (Camille Saint-Saëns)

Dvořák's championing of black music led to a new interest in this musical style among "serious," white scholars if not white composers.

Other important romantic, postromantic, and neoclassical instrumental compositions employing black idioms include (1) Claude Debussy's *Golliwogg's Cakewalk*, for piano, which shows a definitive ragtime influence; (2) Igor Stravinsky's *The Soldier's Tale* and *Ebony Concerto* for clarinet and swing band, which show jazz influences; (3) George Gershwin's *Rhapsody in Blue, Piano Preludes, Piano Concerto in F*, which show jazz and blues influences; (4) Darius Milhaud's *Saudades do Brasil*, completed in 1921 and inspired by South American rhythms; (5) Maurice Ravel's *Concerto in G major*, first performed in 1932, which in its first and third movements makes sporadic references to contemporaneous blues and jazz idioms; (6) Ralph Vaughan Williams's *Symphony no. 6*, the first movement of which makes rhythmical references to jazz; and (7) Leonard Bernstein's *Prelude, Fugue, and Riffs*.

These works are but a few of such compositions written between the mid-nineteenth and mid-twentieth centuries. They testify to the broader European and European-American interest in African derived idioms, an interest that by 1950 was already more than one hundred years old. Though the efforts of twentieth-century African American composers were predicated upon incentives much deeper than exotic curiosity, there is little doubt that the previously mentioned compositions of their white counterparts had no small impact.

## Twentieth-Century Black Classical Music

The roots of African American achievement in classical music were laid in the nineteenth century. Thanks to growing access to musical education, performance opportunities, and the success of some pioneering composers and performers—and an increased interest in African American musical expression among a broad audience—new opportunities blossomed for those interested in pursuing a classical music career.

Much of this early activity initially took place in New Orleans, Louisiana. New Orleans afforded free blacks and creoles opportunities for classical musical training much earlier and more prodigiously than what was generally available to blacks in other American cities. This was due in part to New Orleans's operatic tradition—the most important one in America in the nineteenth century—which served as a magnet for European musicians in search of opportunities as performers and teachers. Many of these musicians were not opposed to teaching blacks. Blacks who could afford it were also educated abroad, mainly in France. Such blacks became noted music educators, concert artists, and composers.

The objection of many free blacks to sitting in segregated areas of the theaters led to the establishment of their own theaters, though most such establishments were short-lived. The earliest black theaters trace back to the late 1830s and include the Marigny Theater, which opened in 1838, and the Theatre de la Renaissance, which opened in 1840. These theaters offered, among other things, opera-comiques and vaudeville programs to their black clientele. The early 1830s also witnessed the establishment of the Negro Philharmonic Society, which contained over 100 members. A second black orchestra in New Orleans emerged in 1877, organized by Louis Martin.

Out of the rich musical enviroment of New Orleans emerged a number of talented blacks who distinguished themselves as concert artists, educators, and composers. They included Arthur P. Williams, Charles Veque, Victor Eugene Macarty, and Samuel Snaer.[2] Of this group, Macarty and Snaer were particularly celebrated as composers. Cities such as Philadelphia and Boston also produced black composers in the nineteenth century, but the output of most of these artists consisted mainly of lighter efforts (songs and marches). The most noted in this category are Francis (Frank) Johnson (1792–1844) and the gifted piano prodigy Thomas Green Bethune, popularly known as Blind Tom.

## The Nationalists

The proliferation of music schools and conservatories in the latter half of the nineteenth century (mainly in the northeastern part of the United States), along with educational opportunities abroad and the patronage of eminent visiting European composers and performers, greatly increased the opportunities for African American composers to receive high-quality training in composition. However, opportunities to have their works performed by symphony orchestras and opera companies were, unfortunately, not so numerous, given the segregationist policies prevalent in most of these musical organizations. Nevertheless, by the turn of the century a cadre of African American composers was trained and poised to continue the tradition started by their earlier black counterparts. Unlike these earlier pioneers, however, their attention would be fixed more upon the use of African American themes and idioms. By way of this focus, they would usher in a new era in African American composition. Eileen Southern has dubbed this group of composers "nationalists." Among the most celebrated were Harry T. Burleigh (1866–1949), Clarence Cameron White (1880–1960), Robert Nathaniel Dett (1882–1943), William Levi Dawson (1899–1991), Hall Johnson (1888–1970), John Rosamond Johnson (1873–1954), and William Grant Still (1895–1978). This group included most of the composers previously mentioned in Chapter 2 for the roles they played in the development of spirituals.

Several interrelated factors inspired and supported the nationalist composers. As we noted in Chapter 2, Antonin Dvořák was impressed by the indigenous, African American music he heard during his visit to America between 1892 and 1895. He admonished American composers to consider seriously African American folk music as the basis of a unique American school of composition. However, with the exception of a few minor European-American composers whose efforts were largely insignificant, Dvořák's call was ignored—except by black composers.

Another influential factor in the development of nationalism among African American composers was the success of Samuel Coleridge-Taylor (see Chapter 14). As we have seen, Coleridge-Taylor's own agenda was Afrocentric and Pan-Africanistic. Much of his music was based on the use of folk materials of the African diaspora. With these resources he obtained a greater fame than any black composer before him. By way of the approbation showered on Coleridge-Taylor by African American leaders, black America cemented its claim on him as the musical emissary chosen to champion their loftiest artistic aspirations, particularly those represented by the use of African American musical resources. Numerous African Americans were inspired to pursue musical careers by Coleridge-Taylor's success.

The use of black idioms and themes did not begin with black American concert composers. Their employment is well precedented in the poetry, novels, narratives, essays, and journalism of black and white writers at least a half-century earlier. Longfellow's poems on slavery and Harriet Beecher Stowe's *Uncle Tom's Cabin* are important examples of European-American literature drawing on this tradition. The novels of Frederick Douglass, Williams Wells Brown, and Harriet E. Wilson exemplify beautifully and poignantly the contributions of African American writers in this vein. These works set the stage for the more intense efforts of late nineteenth-century black writers like Frances E. W. Harper, Charles Chesnutt, and Paul Lawrence Dunbar. Thus, if we define artistic nationalism as the addition of African-derived idioms into an art work and/or basing an art work on these themes, then the nationalism shown by black composers at the turn of the century was a part of a broader nationalistic thrust that had already begun in other black art forms.

By the late teens, the interaction among black artists and intellectuals had given rise to a collective black arts movement. Though national in scope, the movement was based in Harlem and became known as the Harlem Renaissance. James Weldon Johnson and Alain Locke were its most articulate spokesmen. Other participants included Arthur A. Schomburg, Joel A. Rogers, Claude McKay, Aaron Douglas, Langston Hughes, and Zora Neale Hurston. This movement became the final and perhaps most important factor in the development of the school of nationalist composers. Though the Renaissance was mainly a literary one, it nevertheless gave to the nationalist composers a cultural, aesthetic, and ideological legitimacy and anchor they had never before enjoyed.

H. T. Burleigh was the first of the African American nationalist composers to rise to national prominence. He was born in Erie, Pennsylvania, and attended the National Conservatory of Music in New York on a scholarship. Burleigh studied voice with Christian Fritsch and counterpoint with John White and also played double bass and timpani in the consevatory orchestra.

In 1894 Burleigh was employed as baritone soloist for the St. George's Episcopal Church, a position he held for fifty-two years. Six years later, in 1900, he took a second position as soloist with the Temple Emanu-El, where he remained for twenty-five years. Burleigh became a good friend of Coleridge-Taylor and participated in his productions of *Hiawatha* as baritone soloist during Coleridge-Taylor's visits to the United States. Their friendship was probably enhanced by the connection both shared with Dvořák (see Chapter 2).

Burleigh's reputation today lies principally on his arrangements of spirituals and his compositions influenced by spirituals. His arrangements were typically written in the style of art songs. His harmonic language was, like most of his African American contemporaries, direct, clear, and essentially romantic. Occasionally, however, these arrangements offered harmonic surprises that generally emanated from his use of passing chromatic structures, borrowed chords, chords featuring the free use of the seventh, and unusual combinations like minor-major seventh chords.

Clarence Cameron White, violinist and composer, was born in Clarksville, Tennessee. He was educated at Oberlin College. He studied violin with the Russian violinist Michael Zacharewitsch. White's compositional style was postromantic but strongly based upon the use of African-derived folk idioms. As stated in Chapter 2, he also arranged spirituals, which helped to popularize the form among a middle-class audience. Another important work by White is his opera *Quanga*, which won the distinguished David Bispham medal. *Quanga* employs Caribbean rhythms and is based on a Haitian theme. White also wrote several violin concertos and a symphony in D minor.

The reputations of Hall Johnson, Robert Nathaniel Dett, J. Rosamond Johnson, and William L. Dawson today rest principally on their frequent and imaginative settings of spirituals, particularly those arranged for choruses. Hall Johnson was born in Athens, Georgia. His education was quite extensive, having attended the Knox Institute, Allen University, Atlanta University, the University of Pennsylvania, and the New York Institute of Musical Art. Johnson also enrolled in graduate courses at the University of Southern California. His work with choruses (many of which carried his name) is legendary. Choruses under his direction performed in theaters, movies, on radio programs, and on recordings. Johnson's compositional approach was generally simple, direct, and predicated on a romantic harmonic vocabulary. In addition to his arrangements of spirituals, Johnson scored the Broadway show *Run Little Chilun* and composed a cantata, *Son of Man*.

Robert Nathaniel Dett was born in Drummondsville, Canada. He received his undergraduate degree in composition and piano at Oberlin. Dett's piano compositions *In the Bottoms* and *Magnolia* are early works that have remained modestly popular to this day. In addition, he published two major collections of spirituals (see Chapter 2). Dett's more formidable choral efforts include the motet, *The Chariot Jubilee* (1919) and particularly his oratorio, *The Ordering of Moses* (1937).

J. Rosamond Johnson was educated at the New England Conservatory in Boston, Massachusetts. His greatest contribution to the musical literature of this period may very well be his arrangements of the spirituals contained in *The Book of American Negro Spirituals*, books one and two, initially published in 1925 and 1926, respectively, which he coedited with his brother, James Weldon Johnson. Also of note is Rosamond Johnson's arrangement of *Sixteen Negro Spirituals* (1939).

To some, Hall Johnson was the most masterful arranger of the concert spiritual; to others, this honor properly goes to William Levi Dawson. Dawson was born in Anniston, Alabama. He received his bachelor of music degree from the Horner Institute of Fine Arts in Missouri and his master's in theory, orchestration, and composition from the American Conservatory of Music in Chicago. Dawson became the director of music at the Tuskegee Institute in 1930. During his tenure of twenty-five years, he raised the Tuskegee Choir to international renown. Like Johnson, Dawson established himself as an imaginative choral conductor and as a result received many invitations to conduct choruses at prestigious venues, including Carnegie Hall, Radio City Music Hall, the White House, and various sites in Europe.

Dawson wrote music for chamber group, piano, symphonic, and choral mediums. It is, however, in the latter category that he made his greatest contribution to black concert literature. His arrangements of spirituals, most of which were arranged for the Tuskegee choir, are beautifully crafted, elegantly harmonized, and often challenging to perform. For these reasons his arrangements have remained popular with modern choruses who include spirituals as part of their repertory.

Though his greatest body of literature consisted of arrangements of spirituals, his most ambitious effort may very well have been his monumental *Negro Folk Symphony*. This composition was completed in 1932 and premiered in 1934 under the baton of Leopold Stokowski. A symphony in three movements, it is characterized by a motto motif introduced at the beginning of the first movement that returns in the second. This motto theme is described by the composer as representing a "link . . . taken out of a human chain when the first African was taken from the shores of his native land."[3]

After a trip to Africa in which the composer turned his sights to the study of African music, Dawson revised the score to his symphony, freely allowing the newly absorbed African rhythms to influence it. Upon the completion of the revision Dawson contacted Leopold Stokowski, and the work was subsequently reintroduced by the conductor, again to critical acclaim.

The *Negro Folk Symphony* is written in a postromantic style and showcases both the composer's strong contrapuntal skills and his ability to develop ideas in an imaginative and structurally satisfying manner. The work is also imaginative in its use of orchestral colors. An example is the opening of the second movement, in which the melody is taken by a solo English horn and supported by the harp and muted strings softly enunciating the underlying harmony on each beat.

The movements are subtitled "The Bond of Africa," "Hope in the Night," and "O Le' Me Shine." As is evident in the subtitles, the world of the spiritual is not very far away. The composer used two spirituals (he preferred the term "Negro folk songs")—"O Le' Me Shine" and "Hallelujah, Lord, I Been Down into the Sea"—as a basis for the themes in the third movement of the symphony.

The most important of all of the African American composers to emerge before 1950 was William Grant Still. Still was born in Woodville, Mississippi, and received his education at Wilberforce University, Oberlin College, and the New England Conservatory. Still was the first African American to conduct a major symphony orchestra in the deep South, when in 1955 he led the New Orleans Philharmonic (now known as the Louisiana Philharmonic Orchestra). Though Still wrote numerous works based on or influenced by spirituals, he also wrote works that reflected the blues, including his *Afro-American Symphony*, written in 1930. This composition is in four movements, with each movement prefaced by excerpts from poems written by Paul Lawrence Dunbar. The excerpts were placed after the symphony was written.

Of all the movements of the symphony, the first is by far the most interesting, and unorthodox. It can be shown schematically as:

| Exposition | Development | Recapitulation |
|---|---|---|
| Introduction—A—transition—B \| Development \| B—retransition—A—Intro. | | |
| Ab | G | Ab |

The movement opens with an introduction taken by the solo English horn. The introductory melody is derived exclusively from the hexatonic blues scale. This introduction forecasts the main theme, which starts six measures later, and consists of a twelve-bar blues, the melody of which is carried by the solo trumpet. Its accompaniment, shared by the strings, woodwinds, and harp, creates the effect of a strumming banjo. The theme is repeated with the melody taken over by the solo clarinet, accompanied by spiccato strings. The opening *call* of the clarinet is followed by a colorful *response* delivered by the flutes, piccolo, oboes, and clarinets. The ending of the theme, which dissolves into a transition carried by interracting sections of the orchestra, is based largely upon material derived from the blues theme. The transition cadences on the dominant of G major, the key of the secondary theme.

The composer described his secondary theme as being "in the style of a spiritual and bears sort of a relationship to the Blues theme."[4] His intent is illustrated by the melancholic nature of the theme and even more so the pentatonic prominence of its first five measures. The "blues-ness" of the theme is suggested by the flat seventh and flat third in the melody. The first statement of the secondary theme—consisting of eight bars—is mournfully delivered by a solo oboe over a moderato accompaniment of flute, harp, and strings. The first violins follow this phrase with a contrasting four-measure motive, usurped in the ensuing four measures by the solo flute, which concludes the statement. The initial statement returns in the cellos, but only for four measures. The remainder of the phrase dissolves into material which prepares for the development.

The development introduces a new, faster tempo and is based on material derived from the blues theme, but substantially transmuted. The development is brief, consisting of only thirty-six measures. It is, however, beautifully crafted and orchestrated and provides an effective dramatic contrast to the preceding material. It ends, like most of the previous sections, with a brief retard. The recapitulation begins with the secondary theme stated in the original key of A♭ major.

Only the first phrase of the secondary theme returns, and in a rhythmically altered form. It is carried by the first violins, harmonized homorhythmically by the second violins. The accompaniment is rendered by the lower strings, harp, French horns, and woodwinds, and is therefore much fuller than it was in its initial statement. The B theme is followed by a brief retransition. The principal theme follows four measure later, carried by the trumpet, and accompanied by pizzicato strings and responsory woodwinds. It too is abbreviated, consisting of only one complete statement of the blues, and is followed by a four-measure bridge that prepares for the restatement of the opening introductory material, still in the key of A♭, but this time carried by the bass clarinet. The completion of the introductory material is immediately followed by a brief two-measure conclusion.

Thus the opening movement outlines a sonata-allegro design, but one with an unorthodox shape. The exposition is different only in the key chosen for the secondary theme, which is not the expected dominant or for that matter even a related key. Otherwise, it follows the standard format of principal theme followed by secondary theme. The development, though brief, offers no structural problems either. The recapitulation, however, reverses the usual order of the themes.

The second movement is a mournful adagio. The third movement is an upbeat, rhythmically animated frolic that provides a brief relief from the lugubrious melancholy of the second movement. The countermelody to the opening theme of the third movement is strongly reminiscent of George Gershwin's "I Got Rhythm." The third movement is also given distinction by its use of the tenor banjo. Though the instrument is used incidentally to supply harmonies on the offbeats, Still's *Afro-American Symphony* may have been the first symphonic score in which the banjo was employed.

The fourth movement opens with a beautiful legato melody, striking in its dignity and optimism despite its opening in a minor modality. It is followed by much thematic and dramatic contrast before returning. New material of a more rhythmically exuberant character is then performed, bringing the movement and the symphony to a close.

Though the movements of the symphony are brief, they are nevertheless proportionate. In all, the symphony is elegantly crafted, imaginatively orchestrated, accessible in its harmonic language, and direct in its appeal. These qualities have no doubt contributed to the enduring popularity of the work.

Other acclaimed symphonic efforts by Still include *Black Bottom* (1922), *Darker America* (1924), *Africa* (1928), Symphony no. 2 (1937), Symphony no. 3 (1958), Symphony no. 4 (1947), Symphony no. 5 (1945), *Poem for Orchestra* (1944), *Festive Overture* (1944), and *Threnody: In Memory of Jan Sibelius* (1965). Still also wrote scores for ballet, operas, vocal works based on spirituals (see Chapter 2), and numerous chamber works. William Grant Still's contributions to African American music literature earned for him sometime ago the sobriquet Dean of African American composers. It is an appellation which, much like his music, has effortlessly withstood the test of time.

Within the cadre of important black nationalist composers were no small number of female composers, including Florence Price (1888–

1953), Margaret Bonds (1913–1972), and Undine Moore (1904–1989). Of the three, the contributions of Florence Price were ground breaking and yet to this day remain, curiously, the least celebrated. Price was born in Little Rock, Arkansas and was educated at the New England Conservatory of Music and the American Conservatory, among other places. After winning first prize in 1932 for the Wanamaker Music Competition, Price's Symphony in E minor was performed by the Chicago Symphony Orchestra in 1933, marking the first time that a symphony composed by an African American woman was premiered by a major symphony orchestra.[5]

Price wrote eloquently for diverse mediums but was particularly imaginative in her piano compositions and art songs. The most noted of her piano compositions is her Sonata in E minor. This composition, romantic in its structure and harmonic language, illustrates Price's skill and inventiveness in the treatment of the themes and showcases elegantly her sensitivity for harmonic nuance and color. The work is highly expressive and technically engaging.

## Classical Music: 1950–1970

The period between 1950 and 1970 witnessed many changes in Western art music. Mainstream classical music showed two primary, contradictory trends. One trend was predicated upon an *ultrarationalist* approach to composition, in which all aspects of a musical composition are subject to the control of the composer—for example, *multiserialism*. Another was its opposite, *antirationalism*, an approach that endorsed the abandonment of composer controls—for example, *improvisation, chance music*. *Electronic music* (composing with electronic instruments and computers) also came to the fore during this period, in addition to *minimalism* (compositions based on short, repeated melodic motives and simple harmonies and rhythms) and *third stream* (the wedding of jazz and classical music).

Few African American composers whose styles matured during this period embraced any of the mainstream trends wholly, but the impact of these trends was sufficient to induce black composers to consider expanding the stylistic resources that governed their writing. The result was not an abandonment of black elements, but when black elements were employed, they were not always aurally conspicuous.

Numerous black composers obtained national distinction during this period. Among the most celebrated were Howard Swanson (b. 1909), Thomas Kerr (1915–1988), Noah Ryder (1914–1964), Mark Fax (1911–1974), Ulysses Kay (1917–1996), George Walker (b. 1922), and Olly Wilson (b. 1937). Swanson is generally known for his art songs and for his *Short Symphony*, written in 1948. His style is essentially postromantic, though some works (for example, *Night Music*) show an expanded, sometimes dissonant chromaticism. Like Swanson, the styles of Fax and Ryder also range from post-romantism to an expanded, nearly atonal chromaticism. Both wrote competently for diverse media.

Of all the black composers to rise between 1950 and 1970, Ulysses Kay, George Walker, and the younger Olly Wilson were among the most acclaimed. Ulysses Kay was educated at the University of Arizona and the Eastman School of Music, among other places. He was a student of German-born composer Paul Hindemith. Kay's compositions have earned him many awards, including a Fulbright, a Guggenheim Fellowship, and the prestigious Prix de Rome.

His works show a broad eclecticism, both in their employment of diverse stylistic languages and their use of black elements, particularly jazz. That jazz elements are occasionally found in his music (for example, in the third movement of his *Four Inventions for Piano*) is not surprising. He is the nephew of Joseph "King" Oliver, mentor of Louis Armstrong (see Chapter 6).

Kay's music readily betrays a strong sense of line, which manifests itself both in lyrical melodies and strongly woven polyphonic textures. His harmonic language, particularly in his later works, shows his penchant for dissonance, although not to the point of inaccessibility. Kay wrote effectively for many different mediums, ranging from piano works to choral works, operatic works, and symphonic scores. Of his better known works are the operas *Jubilee* and *The Boor* and the orchestral scores *A Short Overture, Six Dances for String Orchestra, Markings,* and *Portrait Suite.*

George Walker studied at Oberlin College, the Curtis Institute of Music in Philadelphia, the American Academy in Fontainebleau, France, and the Eastman School of Music. His teachers in composition included Rudolph Serkin and Nadia Boulanger. Walker is also an accomplished pianist, and because of this his works for piano are particularly noteworthy. His earlier works, like *Lyric for Strings*, show his mastery of tonal idioms. In subsequent works, like his first Piano Sonata, his Concerto for Trombone and Orchestra, and ultimately his Concerto for Piano and Orchestra, we witness a stylistic evolution that moved through neoclassical efforts to atonal works based largely on twelve-tone procedures. George Walker was awarded the Pulitzer Prize in 1996 for his composition, *Lilacs.* This work, a symphonic score based upon a poem by Walt Whitman, creatively incorporated vernacular elements that imbued it with a decidedly American quality.

Olly Wilson, one of the foremost contemporary composers of our time, was born in St. Louis, Missouri. He received his undergraduate degree from Washington University in St. Louis, his masters of music degree from the University of Illinois, and his doctorate from the University of Iowa. Since 1968, with his award-winning composition *Cetus,* Wilson has distinguished himself in both electronic and acoustic genres with works like *Reflections* for orchestra, *Akwan* for piano and orchestra (influenced by West African idioms), and *In Memoriam: Martin Luthur King, Jr.* for chorus and electronic sounds. Wilson's music has been performed by some of the most prestigious orchestras in the United States.

Many of these modern composers used black elements in their compositions in a relatively tempered way. Often the black idioms were not very conspicuous. There were, conversely, African American composers whose use of black idioms, particularly jazz idioms, was far more thoroughgoing. Among these composers are Hale Smith (b. 1925), Thomas J. Anderson (b. 1928), David Baker (b. 1931), Coleridge-Taylor Perkinson (b. 1932), and Arthur Cunningham (b. 1934).

Hale Smith received his education at the Cleveland Institute of Music. His compositional experience runs the gamut from art music, to third stream, to popular music, to jazz. As a jazz arranger he has written for Oliver Hamilton, Chico Hamilton, Eric Dolphy, and Quincy Jones. He has also written music for television and documentary films. Much of his music is atonal, often based on serial techniques; *Contours for Orchestra*, one of his most noted compositions, is one example. Among his other well known works are *Comes Tomorrow* (a jazz cantata), *Music for Harp and Orchestra*, *Faces of Jazz* for piano, *Evocation* for piano, and *Meditations in Passage* for soprano, tenor, and piano.

Like Smith, the music of Thomas J. Anderson showcases the composer's ability to blend Afro-vernacular influences and modern Western classical elements into an expression uniquely his own. Anderson was educated at West Virginia State College, Pennsylvania State University, the Cincinnati Conservatory, and the University of Iowa. Hildred Roach quotes Anderson's description of his own compositional technique:

> The works are organized around motific sets or small patterns of notes which function in many types of musical environment associations. Emphasis is on the use of effects which relate directly to the musical ideas. Melodies tend to be predominantly disjuncted and show a preference for symmetrical rhythm. These ideas are expanded by use of numerical proportionalism, multirhythmic values and metric modulation. . . . Harmony

functions from a linear context and tends to be identified with free atonalism.[6]

Among Anderson's well-known works are *Squares, Swing Set,* and *Variations on a Theme by M. B. Tolson.*

David Baker and Arthur Cunningham are particularly known for their association with jazz and for the strong jazz and blues qualities that pervade many of their works. Cunningham was educated at the Metropolitan Music School, Fisk University, and the Juilliard School of Music, and has studied with John Work, among other noted teachers. He has written ballets, chamber operas, and literally hundreds of songs. He is at home in both tonal and atonal styles, and art music and popular styles. Some of his compositions, like *Lullaby for a Jazz Baby,* show readily the unapologetic manner in which he deals with jazz and other Afro-vernacular materials. Other noted compositions by Cunningham include *Engrams,* written for piano, and *Concentrics* written for orchestra.

David Baker was educated at Indiana University. He has studied with such jazz luminaries as John Lewis, J. J. Johnson, Gunther Schuller, and George Russell, among others. Like Cunningham, much of his music readily betrays his strong jazz background. Representative works by Baker include his Sonata for Cello and Piano, *Levels* for flutes, horns, strings, solo contrabass, and jazz band, and his more recent Jazz Suite for Clarinet and Symphony Orchestra. Baker has also distinguished himself as a major modern jazz theorist. His most acclaimed publications in this area include a multivolume treatise called *Jazz Improvisation,* and *Developing Improvisational Technique based on the Lydian Concept.*

Coleridge-Taylor Perkinson received his education at New York University and the Manhattan School of Music. He has distinguished himself in many areas of music, ranging from ballet scores, to solo, chamber, choral, and orchestral compositions, to compositions for films. One of the most beautiful of his film scores was written for *A Warm December,* a touching movie that starred Sidney Poitier. Among his noted scores are Sinfonietta for Strings, Concerto for Viola and Orchestra, and *Thirteen Love Songs in Jazz Settings*.

To the list of important black composers who rose to distinction between 1950 and 1970 could be added many more names, such as Julia Perry (1924–1979), Noel Da Costa (b. 1930), Carmen Moore (b. 1935), Roger Dickerson (b. 1934), Wendell Logan (b. 1940), Adolphus Hailstork (b. 1941), Talib Hakim (1940–1988), William Fischer (b. 1935), and Frank Tillis (b. 1930). Tillis studied at Wiley College and the University of Iowa. His works show diverse stylistic influences and are based on both tonal and atonal approaches. His noted efforts include *Militant Mood for Brass Quintet, Spiritual Cycle* for soprano and orchestra, and *Ring Shout Concerto*.

Talib Hakim (born Stephen Chambers) was educated at the Manhattan School of Music and the New York College of Music, among other institutions. His teachers included Margaret Bonds and Ornette Coleman. Hakim's style is typically atonal. His noted works include *Visions of Ishwara* for orchestra, and *Shapes* for chamber orchestra.

Roger Dickerson studied at Dillard University in New Orleans, Lousiana, and Indiana University. Like Hakim, Dickerson's style is principally atonal but highly expressive. His works have been frequently performed by the Louisiana Philharmonic (formerly the New Orleans Symphony). Dickerson's noted efforts include Sonatina for piano, *A Musical Service for Louis* for orchestra, Concert Overture for orchestra, Psalm 49 for choir and tympani, *African American Celebration* for choir, *Orpheus an' his Slide Trombone* for orchestra and narrator, *Beyond Silence* for brass and organ with soprano and baritone soloists, and *New Orleans Concerto*.

William Fischer received his education at Xavier University and Colorado College in Colorado Springs. Fischer has been and remains actively involved with jazz and blues artists, and this affiliation is often manifested in his works. He has toured with Muddy Waters and Ray Charles, has produced music for McCoy Tyner, and has written music for Edward "Kidd" Jordan. His noted compositions include *A Quiet Movement* for orchestra, *Experience in E* for jazz quintet, *Circles*, and *Tchoupitoulas Tales*.

Wendell Logan was educated at Florida A&M University, Southern Illinois University, and the University of Iowa. His works are often strongly influenced by jazz. Logan has written for diverse media, including electronic music. Among his noted works are *Dance of the Moors* for jazz group, drummers, and chorus, and *Song of Our Time* for choir and instrumental ensemble.

## Classical Music: 1970 to the Present

The past three decades have witnessed the rise of a new generation of African American composers along with the birth of a type of neonationalism that can be seen in a return to the overt use of African-derived musical resources and increased references to black subjects and themes. The trend became pronounced after 1980. As jazz and classical music began to mingle more and more, and as vernacular influences of the African diaspora (particularly African elements) became more accessible, differentiating the stylistic orientation of African American composers became increasingly difficult, and in the eyes of some, unnecessary.

This merging of jazz and classical elements was a by-product of the experimentation of both jazz and classical artists. As we have seen, the experimentalist jazz artists of the 1960s and 1970s contributed greatly to the reconciliation of jazz and Western classical music (see Chapters 9 and 10). Their experiments with form, color, rhythm, notation, and improvisation brought them much closer to the mainstream of the classical avant-garde than to their African American classical counterparts. This is evident in the music of Cecil Taylor, Ornette Coleman, Anthony Braxton, Kidd Jordan, and Oliver Lake, among others. Conversely, aspects of the classical avant-garde—like the postromanticists and neo-classicists before them—were by no means insensitive to the influence of jazz. In this regard, Eric Salzman notes:

> Not all of the composers involved in the new performance practice were veterans of twelve-tone serialism, aleatory, or electronic music; the presence of an active, younger generation of American performers, a certain currency of ideas and personalities, and a more unbroken tradition of new-musical and experimental activity and performance gave a certain distinct "third stream" character (to use in a wider sense Gunther Schuller's term for the jazz/non-jazz merger) to much new musical activity in the United States.[7]

Compositions like Milton Babbitt's *All Set* (1957) for jazz ensemble, Stefan Wolpe's *Battles Sonata* for Piano, *Quartet* for trumpet, tenor saxophone, percussion, and piano, and *Enactments* for three pianos, and Gunther Schuller's *Abstraction* for jazz group and orchestra, and many other works composed by classically trained third-stream disciples of Schuller, all attest to the influence of jazz. By such efforts aspects of the classical avant-garde also contributed to the reconciliation of jazz and classical music, though their motivations were different from those of jazz experimentalists.

Thus African American composers were never without incentives for incorporating jazz into their works. But the African-derived elements they used in their works, particularly after 1980, were by no means limited to jazz. Many compositions written during the last twenty years show an increasing interest in merging African and African-derived idioms with African American idioms. They also show a greater tolerance for contemporary American popular, blues, and rhythm and blues idioms. This trend toward the use of African vernacular idioms was first seen in classical works such as Olly Wilson's *Akwan* and third-stream works like Alvin Batiste's *Musique D'Afrique Nouvelle*; both works were written in the mid-1970s. The trend toward the use of blues, rhythm and blues, and other popular idioms is, as we have previously noted, precedented in works like Valerie Capers's *Sing about Love*, also written in the 1970s. Both trends are evidenced today in theatrical works like *X: The Life and Times of Malcolm X* by Anthony Davis, oratorios (operatorio) like Valerie Capers's *Sojourner*, and the author's *Al-Inkishafi* for chorus, corps de ballet, soprano soloist, orchestra, and Kiswahili and English narrators, and symphonic scores like Hannibal's *African Portrait.*

Noted composers who have come into national prominence since 1970 include Alvin Singleton (b. 1940), Primous Fountain (b. 1949), and Anthony Davis (b. 1951). Fountain was the youngest person ever to receive the Guggenheim Fellowship, having won this award a year after winning the BMI composition competition. Among Fountain's noted works are his *Duet for Flute and Bassoon*, Concerto for Cello and Orchestra, and Caprice for Orchestra. Alvin Singleton received his B.A. degree from New York University and his master of music from Yale. His noted orchestral works include *After Fallen Crumbs, Shadows, Even Tomorrow*, and *Cara Mia Gwen*. Anthony Davis is distinguished both as an eminent contemporary jazz pianist and as a composer. His music shows readily the influence of the jazz experimentalists of the 1960s and 1970s, some of whom he worked with over these decades.

## Summary

What has made the black composer a distinctive entity is the creative referencing of nigrescence. The first occurrence of this may have manifested itself not in the use of distinct African-derived idioms but in the peculiar way standard materials were accessed. The lyricism of Joseph Boulogne, for example, was to his contemporaries something that could not be separated from his racial background. In the nineteenth and twentieth centuries the interest of white composers in the use of black idioms, the growing interest of scholars in the study of African American idioms as well as those derived from the African diaspora, and the literary efforts of white and black creative writers, artists, and intellectuals encouraged African American composers to engage in the unqualified cultivation of black idioms and themes. Though the intensity of this engagement has varied from time to time, the process has continued to the present, bringing forth highly creative efforts, the latest of which have often blurred the lines between Western classical and vernacular expression. What constitutes the future of African American classical composers is not certain. What is certain, however, is that it is promising.

# N O T E S

**Part One**

## Chapter 2

1.  Lerone Bennett Jr., *Before the Mayflower: A History of the Negro in America* (New York: Penguin Books, 1975), p. 221.

2.  Edward Thorpe, *Black Dance* (Woodstock, N.Y.: Overlook Press, 1990), p. 45.

3.  Ibid., p. 45.

4.  James Weldon Johnson and J. Rosamond Johnson, *The American Negro Spirituals: Books One and Two* (New York: Da Capo Press, 1973).

5.  Though this version of "Go Down Moses" is a notated arrangement, it is consistent with recorded performances of the work.

6.  Natalie Curtis-Burlin, *Negro Folk-Songs: Book II* (New York: G. Schirmer, 1918), p. 5.

7.  Henry Edward Krehbiel, *Afro-American Folk Songs: A Study in Racial and National Music* (New York: Frederick Ungar Publishing Co., 1962; originally published: New York: G. Schirmer, 1914), p. 73.

8.  For a more in-depth explication of black dialect in the spirituals, see Johnson and Johnson, *American Negro Spirutuals*, pp. 42–46.

9.  Curtis-Burlin, *Book II*, p. 7.

10. Arnold Shaw, *Black Popular Music in America* (New York: Schirmer Books, 1986), pp. 7–15.

11. Ibid., p. 11.

12. Ibid.

13. John W. Work, *American Negro Songs and Spirituals* (New York: Bonanza Books, 1940), pp. 19–20.

14. Ibid.

15. Ibid., p. 19.

16. Ibid.

17. W. E. B. Du Bois, "Sorrow Songs," in *The Souls of Black Folk* (New York: New American Library, 1982), pp. 264–78.

18. Ibid., pp. 269–70.

19. Work, *American Negro Songs and Spirituals*, pp. 14–16.

20. Ibid., p. 16.

21. Joseph Horowitz, "Dvořák and the New World: A Concentrated Moment," in *Dvořák and His World*, ed. Michael Berkerman (Princeton, N. J.: Princeton University Press, 1993), p. 96. See also album notes by John Michel on *Dvořák Symphony no. 9, "From the New World."* Czech Philharmonic, Vaclav Neuman, SR Pro-Arte Digital, PAD-157.

22. Horowitz, *Dvořák*, p. 96.

23. W. C. Berwick Sayers, *Samuel Coleridge-Taylor, Musician: His Life and Letters*, 2nd ed. (London: Augener, 1927), p. 256.

24. Ibid., p. 264.

25. Coleridge-Taylor believed that two of the African American melodies were of Irish derivation.

26. Berwick Sayers, *Samuel Coleridge-Taylor*, p. 268.

27. The friendship between Coleridge-Taylor and Burleigh probably began with their first professional contact on November 16, 1904, when Burleigh functioned as one of the principals—the baritone soloist—during the opening concert of a three-day Coleridge-Taylor Festival held in Washington, D.C., and dedicated to the performance of *Hiawatha*.

28. Eileen Southern, *The Music of Black Americans*, 2nd ed.(New York: Norton, 1983), p. 268.

29. For additional information refer to John Lovell Jr., *Black Song: The Forge and the Flame* (New York: Macmillan, 1972), pp. 450–51.

## Chapter 3

1. Bessie Smith, "Backwater Blues," Columbia Records. Lyrics in *Afro-American Writing: An Anthology of Prose and Poetry*, 2nd ed. (University Park, Pa.: Pennsylvania State University Press, 1992), p. 284.

2. See such notated blues compositions as Joe McCoy's "Love Me" (copyright 1941), and Ollie Shepard's "It's a Low Down Dirty Shame" (copyright 1938).

3. It is an oversimplification to speak of a single "blues scale." Blues singers may vary scale notes from performance to performance. However, for the purposes of this study, a typical "blues scale" can be described.

4. Abbe Niles, "The Story of the Blues," foreword to the 1949 edition of *Blues: An Anthology*, edited by W. C. Handy (New York: Da Capo Press).

5. Some of these harmonies could have been derived from nonblues sources, but given the degree to which the blues has influenced virtually all other jazz-derived vernacular styles in America in the twentieth century, another source is unlikely.

6. Though a prototypical version of the substitute dominant is found in the works of Scott Joplin, the infrequency of its use makes classic ragtime an unlikely source for the introduction and widespread use of this structure in subsequent African American vernacular styles.

7. William Christopher Handy, *Father of the Blues* (New York: Da Capo Press, 1941), p. 142.

8. Ibid., p. 74.

9. Ibid.

10. Ibid., p. 75.

11. Jeff Todd Titon, *Early Downhome Blues* (Urbana: University of Illinois Press, 1994), p. xv.

12. Jimmie Giuffre, "Two Kinds of Blues," *The Blues in Modern Jazz*, Atlantic 1337.

13. Quincy Jones, "Blues at Twilight," *The Blues in Modern Jazz*, Atlantic, 1337.

## Chapter 4

1. Charles Albert Tindley, "Stand By Me," in *Gospel Pearls*, rev. ed., no. 144 (Nashville, Tenn.: Townsend Press of the Sunday School Publishing Board, National Baptist Convention, USA, Inc., 1994).

2. Jon Michael Spencer, *Black Hymnody: A Hymnological History of the African-American Church* (Knoxville, Tenn.: University of Tennessee Press, 1992), p. 36.

3. Tilford Brooks, *America's Black Musical Heritage* (Englewood Cliffs, N.J.: Prentice-Hall, 1984), p. 157.

4. Michael W. Harris, *The Rise of Gospel Blues* (New York: Oxford University Press, 1992), pp. 67–75.

5. Ibid., p. 209.

6. Some quartets, like the Highway QC's and the Soul Stirrers, featured two lead vocalists.

7. Harris, *The Rise of Gospel Blues*, pp. 210–13.

8. However, it may have been written two years earlier, because the published version of the work bears a dedication to her mother, dated 1919.

9. Southern, *Music of Black Americans*, p. 454.

10. William H. Brewster, *How Far Am I from Canaan: The Story behind the Song* (Chicago: Martin and Morris Studio, 1946), p. 2.

11. Daniel Wolff, with S. R. Crain, Clifton White, and G. David Tenenbaum, *You Send Me: The Life and Times of Sam Cooke* (New York: William Morrow, 1995), p. 58.

12. Ibid., p. 65.

## Part Two
### Chapter 5

1. Other paradigms, such as ABCDC and ABCD, also occurred, but less frequently.

2. Neither the repetition of a section nor the statement of certain sections in contrasting keys were requirements in early twentieth century ragtime. See, for example, Tom Turpin's *A Ragtime Nightmare* (1900).

3. Harmonic motion refers to the rhythmic motion within a harmony. Harmonic rhythm however, refers to the rate at which harmonies change.

4. This style of writing, common in rag literature, is probably the basis of more complex manifestations of similar effects found later in swing literature.

5. Scott Joplin, *The Collected Works of Scott Joplin*, vol. 2, ed. Vera Brodsky Lawrence (New York: New York Public Library, 1971), p. 7.

## Chapter 6

1. Four-beat strumming is common in recordings of classic jazz in the twenties. The absence of recordings prevents us from knowing how often four-to-the-bar strumming occurred in the earlier New Orleans style.

2. This legislation—Section 1 of Ordinance 13,032 C. S.—was conceived by Alderman Sidney Story in response to a virtual prostitution industry that had grown out of control in the city from 1857 to the time the ordinance was implemented (October 1, 1897).

3. Jack V. Buerkle and Danny Barker, *Bourbon Street Black* (New York: Oxford University Press, 1973), pp. 7–9.

4. The influence of this music had already been heard in the piano literature of Louis Moreau Gottschalk.

5. Buerkle and Barker, *Bourbon Street Black*, p. 13.

6. See Frank Tirro, *Jazz: A History*, 2nd ed. (New York: Norton, 1993), p. 202.

## Chapter 7

1. Louis Armstrong, *Swing That Music* (New York: Da Capo Press, 1993; reprint of 1936 edition), pp. 30–34.

2. James Weldon Johnson and J. Rosamond Johnson, *American Negro Spirituals*, vol. 1 (New York: Da Capo Press, 1969), pp. 28–30. This work was originally published in two volumes by Viking Press in 1925 and 1926.

3. Rudi Blesh and Harriet Janis, *They All Played Ragtime*, 4th ed. (New York: Oak Publications, 1971), pp. 24–25.

4. Albert McCarthy, *Big Band Jazz* (New York: Berkley Publishing Corporation, 1974), p. 10.

5. Ibid., p. 12.

6. Douglas Daniels, "History, Racism, and Jazz: The Case of Lester Young," *Jazz Forschung* 16 (1985): p. 87.

7. See Douglas Daniels, "Lester Young: Master of Jive," *American Music* 3, no. 3 (1985): pp. 313–28.

8. Ibid., p. 314.

## Chapter 8

1. Dizzy Gillespie, *To Be, or Not . . . to Bop: Memoirs* (New York: Doubleday, 1979).

2. Quoted in Gillespie, *To Be or Not . . . to Bop*, pp. 149–51.

3. Ibid., pp. 119–20.

4. Ibid., p. 134.

5. Ibid., pp. 225–26.

6. Ibid., p. 258.

7. Ibid., p. 260.

8. Borrowed chords in jazz derived vernacular harmony are chords derived from a parallel scale or mode.

9. Gillespie, *To Be or Not . . . To Bop*, p. 92.

10. Ibid., p. 92.

## Chapter 9

1. Quincy Jones, "The Quintessence," Quincy Jones and His Orchestra, Impulse Records, A-11 AS11.

2. John Lewis, *European Windows*, RCA, APM1-1069. Quote taken from the album notes written by Robert Palmer.

3. Eileen Southern, *The Music of Black Americans: A History*, 3rd ed. (New York: Norton, 1997), p. 479.

4. See Ramsey Lewis, *Up Pops Ramsey Lewis*. Cadet, Mono LP-799, Stereo LPS-799.

5. LeRoi Jones (Amiri Baraka), *Dutchman*, in *Dutchman and the Slave* (New York: William Morrow, 1969), pp. 34–35.

6. See Archie Shepp, *Junebug Graduates Tonight*, in *Black Drama Anthology*, edited by Woodie King and Ron Milner (New York: Signet, New American Library, 1971), p. 33.

7. Rob Backus, *Fire Music: A Political History of Jazz* (New York: Vanguard Books, 1976), pp. 66–83.

8. Interview with Oliver Lake, July 26, 1996.

9. Ibid.

## Chapter 10

1. Ronald M. Radano, *New Musical Figurations: Anthony Braxton's Cultural Critique* (Chicago: University of Chicago Press, 1993), p. 5.

2. Interview with Douglas Ewart, August 1, 1996.

3. Ibid.

4. Ibid.

5. Interview with George Lewis, August 2, 1996.

6. Alain Locke, "Classical Jazz and Modern American Music" in *The Negro and His Music* (New York: Arno Press and the New York Times, 1969) p. 106.

7. Interview with Alvin Batiste, November 1996.

## Part Three

### Chapter 11

1. Nelson George, *The Death of Rhythm and Blues* (New York: E. P. Dutton, 1989), p. 19.

2. Ibid., p. 38.

3. The song has been published under the name of Charles Calhoun, one of the pseudonyms Stone used for his music publications.

4. Arnold Shaw, *Honkers and Shouters: The Golden Years of Rhythm and Blues* (New York: Macmillan, 1978), p. 134.

5. Ibid., p. 135.

6. See Arnold Shaw, *Black Popular Music in America* (New York: Schirmer Books, 1986), p. 264.

7. Chuck Berry, *Chuck Berry: The Autobiography* (New York: Harmony Books, 1987), p. 100.

## Chapter 12

1. Ray Charles and David Ritz, *Brother Ray: Ray Charles' Own Story* (New York: Warner Books, 1978), p. 114.

2. Ibid., p. 143.

3. Daniel Wolff et al., *You Send Me: The Life and Times of Sam Cooke* (Morrow, 1995), p. 28.

4. Ibid., p. 60.

5. Ibid., p. 193.

6. Rob Bowman, liner notes to *The Complete Stax/Volt Singles: 1950–1968* (The Atlantic Group, Atlantic Recording Corporation, 1991), 82212-2, p. 1.

7. For a more detailed biographical sketch of Otis Redding, see Peter Guralnick, *Sweet Soul Music: Rhythm and Blues and the Southern Dream of Freedom* (New York: Harper and Row, 1986), pp. 133–51.

8. Pat Pattison, professor of songwriting at the Berklee College of Music, defines a transitional bridge as "a section between a verse and a Chorus that introduces a new idea (different from the verse idea) whose purpose is to prepare us for the statement of the Chorus or the title." Sheila Davis, according to Pattison, refers to this device as a "lift." See Pat Pattison, *Lyric Structure: How It Works*, book one in the series, *Song Lyrics* (Boston: Berklee College of Music), p. 92.

9. Rickey Vincent has provided, to date, the most in-depth critique of funk yet written. See Rickey Vincent, *Funk: The Music, the People, and the Rhythm of the One* (New York: St. Martin's, 1996).

10. Arnold Shaw, *Black Popular Music in America* (New York: Schirmer Books, 1986), p. 250.

## Chapter 13

1. Ronald Jemal Stephens, "The Three Waves of Contemporary Rap Music," in *Black Sacred Music: A Journal of Theomusicology* 5, no. 1 (Spring, 1991), p. 25.

2.  Eileen Southern, *The Music of Black Americans,* p. 156.

3.  In his book, *The Music of Africa,* Kwabena Nketia discusses the nature and function of speaking instruments in West African music. John Storm Roberts offers a brief but similar discussion. See J. W. Kwabena, *The Music of Africa* (New York: Norton, 1974), pp. 178, 228.

4.  Mary Allen Grissom, *The Negro Sings a New Heaven* (New York: Dover, 1969; originally published by the University of North Carolina Press, 1930).

5.  Eileen Southern, *The Music of Black Americans,* p. 201.

6.  Rudi Blesh, *Shining Trumpets: A History of Jazz,* 2nd ed. (New York: Da Capo Press, 1976), p. 105.

7.  This is consistent with the fact that the term *rap* was a common part of 1960s and 1970s street language. The term was used commonly as a verb ("Let me rap to you, brother") and as a noun ("Check out this guy's rap.").

8.  Non-intoned vocality occurred sporadically in rhythm and blues of the 1940s. See for example Louis Jordan's "Caldonia," specifically, a section where Jordan exclaims in deliberate, distinctive rhythms the words "Caldonia? Caldonia? What makes your big head so hard?" Later, a subsequent unrhythmized text (arrhythmic prose) is interpolated in which Jordan—after letting everyone know that his Caldonia weighs in excess of 300 pounds—insists, comically, that he "can't put her down. I can't pick her up!"

9.  To the author's knowledge this is the first time the word *rap* was used to designate a musical work, in whole or in part. However, it was not the first time the word *rap* was ever used, even within a musical context. The term occurs, for example, in the Temptations' rendition of "Ball of Confusion," recorded in 1970 ("Rap on brother, rap on").

10. Because of its highly controversial nature, "Say It Loud" was not played by most white radio stations in the deep South.

11. Writers on rap music do not agree on the meaning of the acronym MC. Some consider MC to mean "Master of Ceremonies," others claim that the acronym MC means "Mic Controller."

12. This practice is said to have derived from a similar practice common in Jamaica in the 1960s called toasting.

13. Jon Michael Spencer, "The Emergency of Black and the Emergence of Rap." *Journal of Theomusicology* 5, no. 1 (Spring 1991): 1–11.

14. Ibid., p. 8.

15. Lifer's Group, "The Real Deal," in *Rap: The Lyrics*, edited by Lawrence A. Stanley (New York: Penguin Books, 1992), p. 200.

16. NWA, "Fuck the Police," ibid., p 234.

17. Jefferson Morley, introduction to *Rap: The Lyrics*, p. xxviii.

18. Paris, "Break the Grip of Shame," ibid., p. 245.

19. Jungle Brothers, "Black Is Black," ibid., p. 176.

## Part Four

### Chapter 14

1. For a more in-depth explanation of this phenomenon, see chapter 1 of Allen Woll, *Black Musical Theatre: From Coontown to Dreamgirls* (Baton Rouge: Louisiana State University Press, 1989).

2. James Weldon Johnson, *Black Manhattan* (New York: Arno Press, 1968), p. 95.

3. Allen Woll, *Black Musical Theatre*, p. 12

4. James Weldon Johnson, *Black Manhattan*, p. 102.

5. Ibid., p. 170.

6. Ibid., p. 172.

7. Barry S. Brook, ed., "The Symphonic Music of Saint George," in *The Symphony: 1820–1840* (New York: Garland, 1983), p. xxviii.

8. Joel-Marie Fauquet, liner notes to *Six Quatuors a deux violins, alto et violoncelle*, translated by Charles Whitfield, Arion, ARN 38365.

9. See Richard Jackson, "Gottschalk of Louisiana: Introduction," in *Piano Music of Louis Moreau Gottschalk* (New York: Dover Publications, 1972), pp. v-xiv.

10. The contents of a postcard written by Sir Edward Elgar to Herbert Brewster, quoted by W. C. Berwick Sayers in his biography of Samuel Coleridge-Taylor, *Samuel Coleridge-Taylor, Musician: His Life and Letters* (London: Cassell and Company, Ltd., 1915), pp. 51–52.

11. Ibid., p. 258.

12. Ibid., p. 258.

13. W. C. Berwick Sayers, *Samuel Coleridge-Taylor, Musician: His Life and Letters*, p. 219.


## Chapter 15

1. Carlos Antonio Gomes has been claimed by some scholars to be of black or part black ancestry. The author has found little evidence to support such a claim.

2. John W. Blassingame, *Black New Orleans, 1860–1880* (Chicago: University of Chicago Press, 1973), p. 141.

3. George Jellinek, *William Dawson: Negro Folk Symphony*, from liner notes, VC 81056.

4. Robert Bartlett Haas, ed., *William Grant Still and the Fusion of Cultures in American Music* (Los Angeles: Black Sparrow Press, 1975), p. 19.

5. Rae Linda Brown, "William Grant Still, Florence Price, and William Dawson: Echoes of the Harlem Renaissance" in *Black Music in the Harlem Renaissance*, edited by Samuel Floyd, Jr. (Knoxville, Tenn.: University of Tennessee Press, 1993), p. 79.

6. Hildred Roach, *Black American Music: Past and Present* (Boston: Crescendo Publishing Company, 1976), p. 160.

7. Eric Salzman, *Twentieth-Century Music: An Introduction*, 2nd ed. (Englewood Cliffs, N.J.: Prentice-Hall, 1974), p. 161.

# G L O S S A R Y

**Abstract rhythm**  A rhythmic pattern that, because of its context or the manner in which it is accentuated, lends itself to more than one metrical interpretation.

**Ad libitum**  An indication to the performer that the strictness of the tempo may be varied.

**Antiphony**  A texture characterized by alternating choruses or alternating instrumental sections. In Afro-vernacular music the term *antiphony* is often used as a synonym for call and response.

**Attributes of African vocality**  Repertory of vocal devices used to emotionalize the music.

**Augmented triad**  A three-note chord made up of superposed major thirds.

**Binary**  Consisting of two parts.

**Binary form**  A form made up of two distinct sections.

**Blue notes**  **1.** Microtonal inflections of pitches; bent notes. **2.** The flatted third, flatted seventh, and sometimes the flatted fifth sounded (usually in the melody) against the natural versions of the pitches.

**Blues paradigm**  A stereotypical model consisting of an AAB (or AA¹B) phrase structure, a twelve-bar metric structure, and a I–IV–I–V–IV–I (or I–IV–I–V–I) harmonic pattern.

**Borrowed chord**  **1.** (in Afro-vernacular music) A chord borrowed from any parallel scale or mode. **2.** (in traditional Western music theory) Generally chords borrowed from the parallel minor, if the starting key is major (for example, an f-minor triad used in the key of C major).

**Chord scale** A scale made of the members of chords, the pitches contextually compatible against or within the chord (extensions), and the pitches contextually incompatible with the chord (non-chord tones).

**Chorus** 1. A choir. 2. A specific section of a musical composition containing the hook of the song.

**Chromatic** Derived from outside of the key.

**Compound rhythm** A single rhythmic pattern which gives the impression of two patterns.

**Diatonic** Derived from within the key.

**Eleventh chord** A chord containing the interval of a seventh and an eleventh against the tonic.

**Extemporization** Variation of a melodic idea, but not beyond the point where the original melody is no longer recognizable.

**Extended dominant** In vernacular music, a chromatic dominant emanating outside of the key and resolving normatively to a chord outside of the key; technically an extended dominant is a chromatic dominant that contains extensions which do not implicate the key governing the work.

**Extension** A contextually compatible pitch that is not a member of a chord but nevertheless occurs within or against it.

**Gutteral sounds** 1. Moans, groans, shouts, and other vocal sounds that emanate from the throat. 2. Part of the attributes of African vocality.

**Harmony** (abstract concept) The blending or concordance of specific elements.

**Harmony, blues** 1. Harmonies containing blue notes. 2. Harmonies of the blues scale or derived from the blues scale. 3. Harmonies whose function is influenced by blues idioms or blues conventions.

**Harmony, as chords** Aggregates of pitches heard as a unit.

**Harmony, diatonic** Harmony derived from the key.

**Harmony, traditional** Harmonic conventions underlying European classical music from about 1600 to 1900.

**Harmony, vernacular** Harmonic conventions underlying most African American styles from about 1875 to the present.

**Heterophony** A texture in which the same melody is given simultaneously by two or more performers, but each in a varied version.

**Hexatonic blues scales** **1.** A six-note scale containing the intervallic pattern m3, M2, m2, m2, m3, M2 (for example, C, E♭, F, F♯, G, B♭, C):

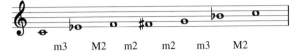

**2.** A parasitic scale containing the lowered third, seventh, and sometimes the fifth when used against a major scale based on the same tonic (starting pitch).

**Homophony** A texture in which one melody is the main event, with chords often constituting the accompanimental element.

**Homorhythm** A texture in which a melody and its harmony are expressed simultaneously with the same rhythm. Synonyms: melodic harmony, harmonic melody.

**Improvisation** A spontaneously delivered, on the spot development of a musical idea.

**Intervallic pattern** The specific arrangements of half steps and whole steps.

**Inversion (chord inversion)** The repositioning of the notes of a chord in such a way that the root of the chord is not the bass.

**Melodic contour** Graphic shape of the melody.

*melodic contour*

**Melody** A succession of musical tones.

*melody*

**Meter** A grouping of pulses defined by a characteristic accent pattern.

**Meter, asymmetric** A meter in which the beats are not strictly divisible by two or three; for example, $\frac{5}{4}$ or $\frac{7}{4}$.

**Meter, compound duple**  Meters featuring two groupings of three pulses. In $\frac{6}{8}$ meter, for example, six eighth-notes are often musically interpreted as two groups of three eighth-notes.

**Meter, compound triple**  Meters featuring three groupings of three pulses; for example, $\frac{9}{8}$.

**Meter, free**  A meter in which only the pulse unit is present; for example, $\frac{X}{8}$. Compositions governed by such time signatures usually do not employ bar lines, though the presence of accent patterns may sometimes be contextually inferred.

**Meter, simple duple**  Meters containing two beats with the first beat accented.

**Meter, simple triple**  Meters containing three beats with the first beat accented.

**Meters, changing**  The presence of several different meters in all or part of a composition.

**Meters, compound**  Meters divisible by three.

**Meters, simple**  Meters divisible by two.

**Mode**  1. One of the ecclesiastical, or church modes. 2. A term used to distinguish the qualities of scales; for example, something said to be in a "major mode" in contrast to a "minor mode."

**Modes, ecclesiastical**  1. A system of scales from which Western musical compositions were constructed up to about 1650. 2. A system of scales each having its own characteristic intervallic pattern; known also as church modes. The system consists specifically of the dorian mode, the phrygian mode, the lydian mode, the mixolydian mode, the aeolian mode, the locrian mode (seldom used), and the ionian mode.

**Motif**  A stereotypical motivic pattern or idiom that characterizes a style.

**Motive**  A distinct melodic or rhythmic pattern that creates phrases when they are juxtaposed with other motives.

**Mutation**  *See borrowed chords.*

**Nigrescence**  The presence of African-derived idioms, or the implication or suggestion of Africanity.

**Ninth chord**  A chord containing the interval of the ninth above its root; usually the seventh is also present or implied.

**Pentatonic scale**  A scale containing five pitches.

**Polyphony** A texture characterized by the simultaneous statement of two or more melodies, often of equal or near equal significance.

**Polyphonic front line unit** Part of a classic jazz ensemble that usually consists of a trumpet, a clarinet, and a trombone.

**Primary progression 1.** In traditional harmony, primary chords are the tonic, subdominant or supertonic, and dominant chords. **2.** When applied to vernacular harmony, primary chords are the harmonies diatonic to the key.

**Progression 1.** A chord. **2.** Two or more chords occurring successively.

**Rhythmic concrescence 1.** A rhythmic symbiosis that takes place when two or more rhythmic patterns, or rhythmically oriented melodies, are blended into a higher unity creating an effect greater than the sum of their parts. **2.** Rhythmic consonance.

**Rhythmic contention 1.** The effect that results when two or more musical events do not blend into a higher unity. **2.** Rhythmic dissonance.

**Rhythmic harmony** The blending of rhythms into a higher unity. *See rhythmic concrescence.*

**Riff** A highly distinctive rhythmic pattern, or a distinctively rhythmized motive or melody.

**Rondo form 1.** An ABACA design, known as a five-part rondo. **2.** An ABACABA design, known as a seven-part rondo.

**Root (chord root)** The note upon which the chord is built (for example, in a C major chord, C is the root).

**Scale** Diatonic or stepwise ordering of the pitches governing a musical composition or some part thereof.

**Scale, augmented (whole tone scale)** A scale consisting of whole steps; for example, C, D, E, F♯, G♯, A♯, C.

**Scale, diminished (symmetrical eight-tone scale) 1.** A scale consisting of the intervallic pattern M2, m2, M2, m2, M2, m2, M2, m2; for example, D♭, E♭, E, F♯, G, A, B♭, C, D♭. **2.** A scale pattern consisting of the successive statements of m2 and M2. **3.** A scale composed of interlocking diminished seventh chords.

**Scale, major** A scale containing the intervallic pattern M2, M2, m2, M2, M2, M2, m2. In a C major scale, this intervallic pattern gives C, D, E, F, G, A, B, C.

**Scale, minor** 1. *natural minor* A scale containing the intervallic pattern M2, m2, M2, M2, m2, M2, M2. In a natural minor this intervallic pattern gives A, B, C, D, E, F, G, A. **2.** *harmonic minor* A scale containing the intervallic pattern M2, m2, M2, M2, m2, A2, m2. In a harmonic minor this intervallic pattern gives A, B, C, D, E, F, G♯, A. **3.** *melodic minor* A scale containing the ascending intervallic pattern M2, m2, M2, M2, M2, M2, m2. (The descending pattern of the melodic minor is the same as that of the natural minor.) In a melodic minor this intervallic pattern gives A, B, C, D, E, F♯, G♯, A.

**Secondary dominant** In vernacular music, a dominant chord emanating outside of the key that resolves normatively to a chord in the key; for example, $A^7$ to e in the key of C major. Technically, a secondary dominant is a chromatic dominant that contains extensions diatonic to the key to which it is expected to resolve.

**Secondary progressions** Secondary dominants and leading tone chords.

**Sixth chord** A major triad with the added interval of a major sixth above the root of the chord.

**Sonata allegro form** A form containing an exposition, a development, and a recapitulation. The exposition introduces a principal theme (PT) which is followed by a contrasting secondary theme (ST), and sometimes a closing theme (CT), before progressing onward to the material that closes out the section. A transition generally bridges the PT and ST and effects a modulation from the opening key to a closely related key. The development features the creative reworking and unfolding of previously stated or new material. The recapitulation brings back the essential material of the exposition in its original key and maintains it in this key.

**Substitute dominant (tritone substitution)** A dominant seventh chord whose root is located a tritone away from the dominant for which it substitutes and shares with this dominant interchangeably its third and seventh. That is, the third and seventh of the substitute dominant is the seventh and third of the dominant located a tritone away.

**Syncopation** The feeling of displacement of the beat; technically, the accentuation of a pulse that is normally unaccented.

**Syncopic stratification, horizontal** Diverse syncopations in a single melody line.

**Syncopic stratification, vertical** Diverse syncopations in the lines of several melodies occurring simultaneously.

**Ternary (tripartite)** Three parts.

**Texture** The fabric of the music. *See homophony, antiphony,* and *polyphony.*

**Thirteenth chord** A chord containing or implying the presence of the interval of the eleventh and the thirteenth against the root of the chord.

**Time signature** A fraction-like figure placed at the beginning of a musical composition. The lower number identifies the pitch that gets one count, the upper number identifies the number of pulses per measure. For example, if given the time signature $\frac{3}{4}$, the 4 states that the quarter note is the pulse unit, the note that receives one count; the 3 states that there must be three quarter notes—or the rhythmical equivalent of three quarter notes—in each measure governed by this time signature.

**Tonic** The note upon which the scale is based; for example, C is the tonic of a C major scale.

**Transmutation** The metamorphosis of a recognizable musical idea to another.

# SELECT BIBLIOGRAPHY

## Part One: General Reference Works

Allen, William Francis, Charles Pickard Ware, and Lucy McKim Garrison. *Slave Songs of the United States*. New York: Peter Smith, 1929; originally published: New York: A. Simpson, 1867.

Armstrong, Louis. *Swing That Music*. New York: Da Capo Press, 1993.

Backus, Rob. *Fire Music: A Political History of Jazz*. Vanguard Books, 1976.

Badger, Reid. *A Life in Ragtime: A Biography of James Reese Europe*. New York: Oxford University Press, 1995.

Berendt, Joachim E., and Gunther Huesmann. *The Jazz Book: From Ragtime to Fusion and Beyond*, 6th ed. Chicago: Lawrence Hill & Co., 1992.

Berlin, Edward A. *Ragtime: A Musical and Cultural History*. Berkeley, Cal.: University of California Press, 1980.

———. *Reflections and Research on Ragtime*. New York: Institute for Studies in American Music (Brooklyn College of the City University of New York), 1987.

———. *King of Ragtime: Scott Joplin and His Era*. New York: Oxford University Press, 1994.

Blesh, Rudi, and Harriet Janis. *They All Played Ragtime*. 4th ed. New York: Oak Publications, 1971.

Blesh, Rudi. *Shining Trumpets: A History Of Jazz*. 2nd ed. New York: Da Capo Press, 1976.

Bogle, Donald. *Brown Sugar: Eighty Years of America's Black Female Superstars*. New York: Da Capo Press, 1980.

Bowman, Rob. *Soulsville USA: The Story of Stax Records.* New York: Schirmer Books, 1997.

Brooks, Tilford. *America's Black Musical Heritage.* Englewood Cliffs, N.J.: Prentice-Hall, Inc. 1984.

Broven, John. *Walking to New Orleans: The Story of New Orleans Rhythm and Blues.* Sussex, England: Blues Unlimited, 1974.

Buerkle, Jack V., and Danny Barker. *Bourbon Street Black: The New Orleans Black Jazzman.* New York: Oxford University Press, 1973.

Carner, Gary, ed. *The Miles Davis Companion.* New York: Schirmer Books, 1996.

Charles, Ray, and David Ritz. *Brother Ray: Ray Charles' Own Story.* New York: Warner Books, 1978.

Cohn, Lawrence, Mary Katherine Aldin, and Bruce Bastin, eds. *Nothing But the Blues: The Music and the Musicians.* New York: Abbeville Press, 1993.

Cole, Bill. *John Coltrane.* New York: Schirmer Books, 1976.

Coleridge-Taylor, Avril. *The Heritage of Samuel Coleridge-Taylor.* London: Dobson Books Ltd., 1979.

Cone, James H. *The Spirituals and the Blues: An Interpretation.* New York: Seabury Press, 1972.

Curtis, Susan. *Dancing to a Black Man's Tune : A Life of Scott Joplin.* Columbia: University of Missouri Press, 1994.

Dance, Stanley. *The World of Duke Ellington.* New York: Charles Scribner's Sons, 1970.

————. *The World of Swing.* New York: Da Capo Press, 1974.

Daniels, Douglas. "History, Racism, and Jazz: The Case of Lester Young," *Jazz Forschung* 16 (1985): 87–103.

————. "Lester Young: Master of Jive," *American Music* 3, no. 3 (1985): 313–28.

Davis, Francis. *Bebop and Nothingness: Jazz and Pop at the End of the Century.* New York: Schirmer Books, 1996.

Dickerson, James. *Goin' Back to Memphis: A Century of Blues, Rock 'n' Roll, and Glorious Soul.* New York: Schirmer Books, 1996.

Ellington, Duke. *Music Is My Mistress.* New York: Da Capo Press, 1973.

Emery, Lynne Fauley. *Black Dance: From 1619 to Today.* 2nd rev. ed. Princeton, N.J.: Princeton Book Company, 1988.

Epstein, Dena J. *Sinful Tunes and Spiritual: Black Folk Music to the Civil War.* Chicago: University of Illinois, 1977.

Erlewine, Michael, Vladimir Bogdanov, and Chris Woodstra, eds. *All Music Guide to the Blues: The Experts' Guide to the Best Blues Recordings.* San Francisco: Miller Freeman, 1996.

Feather, Leonard, and Ira Gitler. *The Encyclopedia of Jazz in the 70s.* New York: Da Capo Press, 1976.

Ferrett, Gene. *Swing Out: Great Negro Dance Bands.* New York: Da Capo Press, 1993.

Floyd, Samuel A., ed. *Black Music in the Harlem Renaissance: A Collection of Essays.* Knoxville: University of Tennessee Press, 1990.

———. *The Power of Black Music: Interpreting Its History from Africa to the United States.* New York: Oxford Univesity Press, 1995.

Garland, Phyl. *The Sound of Soul.* Chicago: Henry Regnery Company, 1969.

Garon, Paul. *Blues and the Poetic Spirit.* New York: Da Capo Press, 1975.

George, Nelson. *Where Did Our Love Go?* New York: St. Martin's Press, 1985.

———. *The Death of Rhythm and Blues.* New York: E. P. Dutton, 1989.

———. *Buppies, B-Boys, Baps, and Bohos: Notes on Post-Soul Black Culture.* New York: HarperCollins, 1992.

Gillespie, Dizzy, with Al Fraser. *To Be, or Not . . . To Bop: Memoirs.* New York: Doubleday, 1979.

Gitler, Ira. *Jazz Masters of the Forties.* New York: Collier Books, 1974.

Goldberg, Joe. *Jazz Masters of the Fifties.* New York: Da Capo Press, 1965.

Gordy, Berry. *To Be Loved: The Music, the Magic, the Memories of Motown: An Autobiography.* New York: Warner Books, 1994.

Gourse, Leslie. *Unforgettable: The Life and Mystique of Nat King Cole.* New York: Da Capo Press, 1992.

———. *Straight, No Chaser: The Life and Genius of Thelonious Monk.* New York: Schirmer Books, 1997.

Gourse, Leslie, ed. *The Billie Holiday Companion.* New York: Schirmer Books, 1997.

———, ed. *The Ella Fitzgerald Companion.* New York: Schirmer Books, 1998.

Govenar, Alan. *Living Texas Blues.* Dallas: Dallas Museum of Art, 1985.

Gridley, Mark C. *Jazz Styles: History and Analysis.* 6th ed. Englewood Cliffs, N.J.: Prentice-Hall, 1996.

Guralnick, Peter. *Sweet Soul Music: Rhythm and Blues and the Southern Dream of Freedom.* New York: Harper & Row, 1986.

Haas, Robert Bartlett, ed. *William Grant Still and the Fusion of Cultures in American Music*. Los Angeles: Black Sparrow Press, 1975.

Hadlock, Richard. *Jazz Masters of the Twenties*. New York: Collier Books, 1965.

Hagan, Chet. *Gospel Legends*. New York: Avon Books, 1995.

Hajdu, David. *Lush Life: A Biography of Billy Strayhorn*. New York: Farrar, Straus, and Giroux, 1996.

Hampton, Lionel, with James Haskins. *Hamp: An Autobiography*. New York: Warner Books, 1989.

Handy, W. C. *Father of the Blues: An Autobiography*. New York: Da Capo Press, 1969.

———, ed. *Blues: An Anthology*. New York: Da Capo Press, 1972.

Harison, Daphne Duval. *Black Pearls: Queens of the 1920s*. New Brunswick, N.J.: Rutgers University Press, 1990.

Harris, Michael W. *The Rise of Gospel Blues: The Music of Thomas Andrew Dorsey in the Urban Church*. New York: Oxford University Press, 1992.

Haskins, James. *Scott Joplin: The Man Who Made Ragtime*. New York: Stein and Day, 1978.

———, with Kathleen Benson. *Nat King Cole: A Personal and Professional Biography*. Chelsea, Mich.: Scarborough House Publishers, 1990.

Hasse, John Edward, ed. *Ragtime: Its History, Composers, and Music*. New York: Schirmer Books, 1985.

Hawes, Hampton, and Don Asher. *Raise Up off Me*. New York: Da Capo Press, 1979.

Hodeir, Andre. *Jazz: Its Evolution and Essence*. New York: Grove Press, 1956.

Holiday, Billy, with William Duffy. *Lady Sings the Blues*. Reprinted with revised discography. New York: Penguin Books, 1992.

Jones LeRoi (Amiri Baraka). *Black Music*. New York: William Morrow, 1968.

———. *Blues People: The Negro Experience in White America and the Music That Developed from It*. New York: William Morrow, 1970.

Jost, Ekkehard. *Free Jazz*. New York: Da Capo Press, 1994.

Keil, Charles. *Urban Blues*. 6th ed. Chicago: University of Chicago Press, 1970.

Kenney, William Howland. *Chicago Jazz: A Cultural History, 1904–1930*. New York: Oxford University Press, 1993.

Kofsky, Frank. *Black Nationalism and the Revolution in Music*. New York: Pathfinder Press, 1970.

Kostelanetz, Richard, ed. *The B.B. King Companion*. New York: Schirmer Books, 1997.

Krehbiel, Henry Edward. *Afro-American Folksongs: A Study in Racial and National Music*. New York Frederick Ungar, 1962; originally published: New York: G. Schirmer, 1914.

Lewis, David Levering, ed. *Harlem Renaissance Reader*. New York: Viking, 1994.

Lovell Jr., John. *Black Song: The Forge and the Flame*. New York: Macmillan, 1972.

McCarthy, Albert. *Big Band Jazz*. New York: Berkley Publishing Corporation, 1974.

Meier, August, Elliot Rudwick, and John Bracey Jr., eds. *Black Protest in the Sixties*. New York: Markus Weiner Publishing, 1991.

Mellers, Wilfrid. *Music in a New Found Land*. New York: Hillstone, 1975.

Mingus, Charles. *Beneath the Underdog*. New York: Vintage Books, 1991.

Murray, Albert. *Good Morning Blues: The Autobiography of Count Basie*. New York: Da Capo Press, 1995.

Nicholson, Stuart. *Jazz: The Modern Resurgence*. New York: Simon & Schuster, 1990.

Oliver, Paul. *Savannah Syncopators: African Retentions in the Blues*. New York: Stein and Day, 1970.

————. *The Meaning of the Blues*. New York: Collier Books, 1972.

————. *Kings of Jazz: Bessie Smith*. New York: A. S. Barnes and Company, 1991.

————. *Blues Fell This Morning*. New York: Cambridge University Press, 1994.

Oliver, Paul, Max Harrison, and William Bolcom. *The New Grove: Gospel, Blues and Jazz*. New York: Norton, 1986.

Owens, Thomas. *Bebop: The Music and Its Players*. New York: Oxford University Press, 1995.

Porter, Lewis, and Michael Ullman. *Jazz: From Its Origins to the Present*. Englewood Cliffs, N.J.: Prentice-Hall, Inc., 1993.

Porter, Lewis, ed. *Jazz: The First Century. Readings and New Essays*. New York: Schirmer Books, 1997.

Potash, Chris, ed. *The Jimi Hendrix Companion*. New York: Schirmer Books, 1996.

Radano, Ronald M. *New Musical Figurations: Anthony Braxton's Cultural Critique*. Chicago: University of Chicago Press, 1993.

Rattenbury, Ken. *Duke Ellington, Jazz Composer*. New Haven, Conn.: Yale University Press, 1990.

Roach, Hildred. *Black American Music: Past and Present.* Boston: Crescendo Publishing Company, 1976.

Roberts, John Storm. *Black Music of Two Worlds,* 2nd ed. New York: Schirmer Books, 1998.

Rose, Phyllis. *Jazz Cleopatra: Josephine Baker in Her Time.* New York: Vintage Books, 1991.

Rosenthal, David H. *Hard Bop: Jazz and Black Music, 1955–1965.* New York: Oxford University Press, 1992.

Russell, Ross. *Jazz Style in Kansas City and the Southwest.* Berkeley and Los Angeles: University of California Press, 1973.

Sargeant, Winthrop. *Jazz: Hot and Hybrid,* 3rd ed. New York: Da Capo Press, 1975.

Sayers, W. C. Berwick. *Samuel Coleridge-Taylor, Musician: His Life and Letters.* London: Cassell and Company, Ltd., 1915.

Schafer, William J., and Johannes Riedel. *The Art of Rag-Time.* New York: Da Capo Press, 1977.

Schuller, Gunther. *Early Jazz: Its Roots and Musical Development.* New York: Oxford University Press, 1968.

———. *The Swing Era: The Development of Jazz, 1930–1945.* New York: Oxford University Press, 1989.

Scott, Frank. *The Down Home Guide to the Blues.* Pennington, N.J.: A Cappella Books, 1991.

Shaw, Arnold. *Honkers and Shouters: The Golden Years of Rhythm and Blues.* New York: Macmillan, 1978.

———. *Black Popular Music in America.* New York: Schirmer Books, 1986.

Silvester, Peter J. *A Left Hand like God: A History of Boogie-Woogie Piano.* New York: Da Capo Press, 1989.

Singer, Barry. *Black and Blue: The Life and Lyrics of Andy Razaf.* New York: Schirmer Books, 1992.

Southern, Eileen. *Biographical Dictionary of Afro-American Musicians.* Westport, Conn.: Greenwood Press, 1982.

———. *The Music of Black Americans: A History.* 3rd ed. New York: Norton, 1995.

Spencer, Jon Michael. *Black Hymnody: A Hymnological History of the African-American Church.* Knoxville: University of Tennessee Press, 1992.

Stancell, Steven. *The Rap Whoz Who.* New York: Schirmer Books, 1996.

Stanley, Lawrence A., ed. *Rap, The Lyrics.* With an introduction by Jefferson Morley. New York: Penguin Books, 1992.

Stearns, Marshall W. *The Story of Jazz.* New York: Oxford University Press, 1977.

Stewart, Rex. *Jazz Masters of the Thirties.* N.Y.: Da Capo Press, 1972.

Taylor, Arthur. *Notes and Tones: Musician-to-Musician Interviews.* New York: Da Capo Press, 1993.

Thorpe, Edward. *Black Dance.* Woodstock, New York: Overlook Press, 1990.

Tirro, Frank. *Jazz: A History.* New York: Norton, 1977.

Titon, Jeff Todd. *Downhome Blues Lyrics: An Anthology from the Post-World War Two Era,* 2nd ed. Urbana, Ill.: University of Illinois Press, 1991.

Tracy, Steven C. *Langston Hughes and the Blues.* Chicago: University of Illinois Press, 1988.

Vincent, Rickey. *Funk: The Music, the People, and the Rhythm of the One.* New York, St. Martin's, 1996.

Walton, Ortiz M. *Music Black, White and Blue: A Sociological Survey of the Use and Misuse of Afro-American Music.* New York: William Morrow, 1972.

Williams, Martin. *The Jazz Tradition.* New York: New American Library, 1971.

Wilmer, Valerie. *As Serious As Your Life.* Westport, Conn.: Lawrence Hill and Company, 1980.

Wolff, Daniel. *You Send Me: The Life and Times of Sam Cooke.* New York: William Morrow, 1995.

Woll, Allen. *Black Musical Theatre: From Coontown to Dreamgirls.* Baton Rouge, La.: Louisiana State University Press, 1989.

Yurochko, Bob. *A Short History of Jazz.* Chicago: Nelson Hall Publishers, 1993.

## Part Two: Musical Scores

### Folk Songs, Spirituals, Blues, and Gospel Music

Aikens, Margaret. "He Is the Surest Way." Chicago: The First Church Of Deliverance, 1957.

————. "How God's Spirit Comes Within." Chicago: M. and M. Aikens, 1958.

————. "Jesus Is the Victory Way." Chicago: Aikens and Lafayette, 1961.

Akers, Doris. "All You Need." Los Angeles: Distributed by Simmons and Akers, 1961.

Alexander, Clarence. "Child of God Well Done." Chicago: Bowles Music House, 1949.

Anderson Jr., Robert. "All That I Ask of Thee Dear Lord." Gary, Ind.: Good Shepherd Music House, 1955.

Androzzo, Alma, and Morris, Kenneth. "Deliver Me from Evil." Chicago: Martin and Morris Studio, 1950.

Austin, Rev. D. L. "He Did It." Arranged by Kenneth Woods, Jr. Chicago: Bowles Music House, 1962.

Beal, Elliot. "Going Home." Gary, Ind.: Good Shepherd Music House, 1944.

Bradford, Alex, and La Bostrie. "Blessed Mother." Hollywood: Venice Music, 1955.

Bradford, Alex. "Do You Know Jesus?" Aranged by Roberta Martin. Chicago: The Roberta Martin Studio of Music. 1953.

Brewster, Herbert C. "I Thank You Lord." Chicago: The Martin Studio of Gospel Music, 1945.

Brewster, W. Herbert. "How Far Am I from Canaan." Chicago: Martin and Morris Studio, 1946.

———. "He Has a Way That's Mighty Sweet." Chicago: Theordore R. Frye, 1949.

———. "I'm Getting Richer." Philadelphia: Ward's House of Music, n.d.

Burgess, Carlton. "After the Rain." Washington, D.C.: Complete Praise Publishing, 1989.

Burleigh, H. T. *The Spirituals of Harry T. Burleigh*. (High Voice). Melville, N.Y.: Belwin Mills Publishing Corporation, 1984.

———. *Album of Negro Spirituals*. Melville, N.Y.: Belwin Mills, n.d.

Campbell, Lucie E. "In the Upper Room with Jesus." Nashville, Tenn.: Lucie Campbell-Williams, 1942.

———. "A Sinner like Me." Memphis, Tenn.: Lucie Campbell's Music Studio, 1952.

Carr, Wynona. "I Just Rose to Tell You What the Good Lord's Done for Me." Indianapolis, Ind.: Brown's Music House, 1947.

———. "I Know Someday God's Going to Call Me." Arranged by Kenneth Morris. Hollywood: Martin and Morris Studio, 1950.

————. "A Letter to Heaven." Hollywood: Venice Music, Inc., 1952.

Cleveland, James. "He Won't Fail." Chicago: Martin Studio of Gospel Music, 1960.

Cooke, Sam. "Be with Me Jesus." Hollywood: Venice Music, Inc., 1955.

Crenshaw, L. D. "A Consecration." Chicago: Martin and Morris Studio, 1946.

Curtis-Burlin, Natalie. *Negro Folk-Songs*. Recorded by Curtis-Burlin. New York: G. Schirmer, 1918.

Davis, Mary J. "Have You any Witness in Your Heart?" Chicago: Martin's Studio of Gospel Music, 1944.

Dett, Robert Nathaniel, ed. *Religious Folk Songs of the Negro*. Hampton, Va.: Hampton Institute Press, 1927.

Dewitty, Virgie Carrington. "I Want to Stay As Close As I Possibly Can." Austin, Tex.: Virgie C. Dewitty, 1964.

————. "I'll Never Come Back." Los Angeles: Ford's Studio of Music, n.d.

Dorsey, Thomas A. "I Am a Pilgrim, I Am a Stranger." Chicago: Thomas A. Dorsey, 1933.

————. "I Can't Forget It, Can You?" Chicago: Thomas A. Dorsey, 1933.

————. "I Just Can't Keep from Crying Some Time." Chicago: Thomas A. Dorsey, 1933.

————. "I'm Going to Walk Right In and Make Myself at Home." Jubilee Spiritual. Chicago: Thomas A. Dorsey, 1938.

————. "Does It Mean Anything to You?" Chicago: Thomas A. Dorsey, 1940.

————. "He Is Risen for He's Living in My Soul." Chicago: Thomas A. Dorsey, 1941.

————. "How About You?" Chicago: Thomas A. Dorsey, 1941.

————. "I'm Going to Live the Life I Sing about in My Song." Chicago: Thomas A. Dorsey, 1941.

————. "I Want Jesus on the Road I Travel." Chicago: Thomas A. Dorsey, 1942.

————. "Be Thou Near Me All the Way." Chicago: Thomas A. Dorsey, 1943.

————. "Come unto Me." Chicago: Thomas A. Dorsey, 1946.

————. "It's Not a Shame to Cry Holy to the Lord." Chicago: Thomas A. Dorsey, 1946.

———. "He Is the Same Today." Chicago: Thomas A. Dorsey, 1949.

———. "He Never Will Leave Me." Chicago: Thomas A. Dorsey, 1949.

———. "Give Me a Voice to Sing Thy Praise." Chicago: Thomas A. Dorsey, 1950.

———. "It's a Blessing Just to Call My Savior's Name." Chicago: Thomas A. Dorsey, Copyright 1950.

———. "Consideration." Chicago: Thomas A. Dorsey, 1953.

———. "In My Savior's Care." Chicago: Thomas A. Dorsey, 1953.

Dorsey, Thomas A., and Mason Effie. "Hide Me, Jesus, in the Solid Rock." Chicago: Thomas A. Dorsey, 1939.

Douroux, Margaret Pleasant. "The Glow of Glory Bless Me Lord." Thousand Oaks, Cal.: Rev. Earl A. Pleasant Publishing, 1988.

Eggleton, Clarence. "He Knows My Heart." Nevada City, Cal.: Epiphany Enterprises, Inc., 1994.

———. "Hold to God's Unchanging Hand." Sacramento, Cal.: Epiphany Enterprises, Inc., 1994.

———. "Praise Ye the Lord." Sacramento, Cal.: Epiphany Enterprises, Inc., 1994.

Flagler, Mae Dean, and Roberta Martin. "He's Only One Stop Away." Chicago: Roberta Martin Studio of Music, 1966.

Ford, H. J. "Breathe a Pray'r." Chicago: Martin and Morris Studio, 1948.

Franklin, Kirk. "Whatcha Lookin' 4." Inglewood, Cal.: GospoCentric, Inc., 1995.

Frazier, Thurston G., and Orange J. Dobson. "Come Holy Spirit." Los Angeles: Voices of Hope Publishing House, 1959.

Gisdon, Ezekiel, and Elmer Ruffner. "I Claim Jesus First and That's Enough for Me." Chicago: Thomas A. Dorsey, 1933.

Grissom, Mary Allen, ed. *The Negro Sings a New Heaven.* New York: Dover Publications, 1969.

Handy, William Christopher, ed. *Blues: An Anthology.* New Introduction by William Ferris. With Historical and Critical Text by Abbe Niles. New York: Da Capo Press, 1972.

Hoffman, Rev. Elisha A. "Is Thy Heart with God?" Chicago: Martin and Morris Studio, n.d.

Hutchins, Artelia, and Thomas Dorsey. "God Be with You." Chicago: Thomas A. Dorsey, 1940.

Jackson, Emma L. "Don't Forget the Family Prayer." Chicago: Jackson Studio of Music, 1945.

Johnson, I. J. "Help Us Lord Each Other's Burden to Bear." Chicago: Bowles Music House, 1948.

———. "I've Been Tried, and I'm Satisfied." N.p.

Johnson, J. Rosamond. *Album of Negro Spirituals*. New York: Edward B. Marks Music Corporation. Distributed by Belwin Mills, New York. N.d.

Johnson, James Weldon, and J. Rosamond Johnson, eds. *American Negro Spirituals, Volumes One and Two*. New York: Da Capo Press, 1969. Unabridged republication of original editions published in New York in 1925 and 1926 as two separate volumes.

Lewis, Sammy. "A Beacon Light," arranged by M. Brown. Chicago: Martin and Morris Studio, 1950.

Lillenas, Bertha Mae. "Jesus Is Always There." Chicago: Martin and Morris Studio, 1934.

———. "Beyond the Sunset." Chicago: Martin and Morris Studio, 1936.

Martin, Cora. "Heaven Sweet Heaven." Chicago: Martin and Morris Studio, 1953.

Martin, Cora, and Robert Mosely. "I Know It's Well with My Soul." Los Angeles: Los Angeles Gospel Music Mart, 1952.

Martin, Roberta. "I Want the World to See Jesus in My Life." Chicago: Roberta Martin Studio of Music, 1950.

———. "He's Merciful." Chicago: Roberta Martin Studio of Music, 1963.

Martin, Sallie. "I Tried Jesus and I Know." Chicago: Martin and Morris Music Studio, 1946.

Martin, Sallie, and Thomas A. Dorsey. "I Can Depend on Jesus, He Can Depend on Me." Chicago: Thomas A. Dorsey, 1933.

———. "Inside the Beautiful Gate." Chicago: Thomas A. Dorsey, 1950.

Martin, Sallie, and Kenneth Morris, arranger. "Any How (Negro Spiritual)." Chicago: Martin and Morris Studio, 1942.

McDonald, Louise. "I Love the Lord." Chicago: Roberta Martin Studio of Music, 1959.

Miles, C. Austin. "Good Morning to Heaven." Chicago: Martin and Morris Studio, n.d.

Morris, Kenneth. "All I Need Is Jesus." Chicago: Martin and Morris Studio, 1941.

———. "Jesus Steps Right In Just When I Need Him Most." Chicago: Martin and Morris Studio, 1945.

———, arranger. "He That Believeth." Chicago: Martin and Morris Studio, 1958.

Music Committee of the Sunday School Publishing Board, eds. *Gospel Pearls.* Nashville, Tenn.: Townsend Press of the Sunday School Publishing Board. National Baptist Convention, USA, 1994; copyrighted in 1921.

Norwood, Dorothy. "Come on Jesus." Chicago: Martin and Morris Studio, 1957.

Pace, Charles H. "Can I Ride?" Pittsburgh, Pa.: Old Ship of Zion Music Company, 1943.

Roberts, Steven. "Give Him Praise!" Hayward, Cal.: SR Music Publishing Company, 1989.

Robinson, Rev. C. "Bye and Bye." Houston, Tex.: Lion Publishing Company, 1960.

Rubin, Mary G. "His Name Is Ev'rything to Me." Los Angeles: Mary Rubin, 1950.

Sims, Robert. "He's Already Done." Chicago: Martin Studio of Gospel Music, 1958.

Smith, Harold. "Are You Able to Count Your Blessings?" Chicago: Martin and Morris Music, 1958.

Turner, C. W. "He's Sweet to Me." Los Angeles: C. W. Turner, 1958.

———. "Anchored with Jesus." Los Angeles: Ford's Studio of Music, 1961.

Vance, Augusta. "I Just Can't Keep It to Myself Alone." Chicago: Martin and Morris Studio, 1942.

Walker, Albertina, and Louis McDonald. "It's My Plan." Chicago: Martin and Morris Music, 1960.

Ward, Clara. "I Know It Was the Lord." Philadelphia: Ward's House of Music, 1953.

Waters, Henry. "Hallowed Be Thy Name." Los Angeles: Henry C. Waters, 1954.

Watts, Myrtle E. "He Knows." Philadelphia: Clara Ward Publications, 1956.

Work, John W. *American Negro Songs and Spirituals: A Comprehensive Collection of 230 Folk Songs, Religious and Secular.* New York: Bonanza Books, 1940.

## Classical, Ragtime, Third Stream, Jazz, and Musicals

Blesh, Rudi, ed. *Classic Piano Rags.* New York: Dover Publications, 1975.

*The Book of the Blues.* Milwaukee, Wis.: MCA Music Publishing, 1963.

*Count Basie Anthology.* Secaucus, N.J.: Warner Brothers Publications, n.d. ‒

Ellington, Duke. *The Great Music of Duke Ellington.* Melville, N.Y.: Belwin Mills, 1973.

Gershwin, George. *Music by Gershwin.* Secaucus, N.J.: Warner Brothers Publications, 1975.

*Immortal American Big Bands.* Secaucus, N.J.: Warner Brothers Publications, 1985.

Jasen, David A., ed. *Ragtime: 100 Authentic Rags.* New York: The Big 3 Music Corporation, 1979.

Jones, Quincy. *Roots.* Secaucus, N. J.: Warner Brothers Publications, 1977.

Lawrence, Vera Brodsky, ed. *The Collected Works of Scott Joplin*: Volume II. New York: The New York Public Library, 1972.

———. *Scott Joplin: Collected Piano Works.* New York: New York Public Library, 1972.

Milhaud, Darius. *La Création du monde.* Paris: Éditions Max Eschig, n.d.

Still, William Grant. *Afro-American Symphony.* Kent, England: Novello, n.d.

Tichenor, Trebor Jay, ed. *Ragtime Rarities: Complete Original Music for 63 Piano Rags.* New York: Dover Publications, 1975.

———. *Ragtime Rediscoveries.* New York: Dover Publications, 1979.

Tippett, Michael. *A Child of Our Time.* London: Schott & Co., n.d.

## Modern Popular Music and Jazz

(Collections of Leadsheet and Piano Arrangements)

*Flashback: Great Rhythm and Blues.* Miami, Fla.: CPP Belwin, 1992.

*I'm Gonna Make You Love Me: And the Best of the Philadelphia Sound.* Secaucus, N.J., 1991.

*The New Real Book*. Volume I. Petaluma, Cal.: Sher Music Co., 1988.

*The New Real Book*. Volume II. Petaluma, Cal.: Sher Music Co., 1991.

*The Top 100 Motown Hits*. Miami, Fla.: CPP Belwin, 1984.

Wonder, Stevie. *Stevie Wonder Complete: Volume I/Through 1975*. Miami, Fla.: CPP Belwin, 1985.

Wonder, Stevie. *Stevie Wonder Complete: Volume III/1980–1985*. Miami, Fla.: CPP Belwin, 1985.

# SELECT DISCOGRAPHY

## Jazz

### Available Titles

Armstrong, Louis. *Louis Armstrong and His Hot Five: The Louis Armstrong Story, Volume 1*. Columbia 44049.

Basie Count. *The Count at the Chatterbox*. AOJ 116.

Basie, Count. *Count Basie And His Orchestra*. LRL 15763.

Basie, Count. *Cute*. JTM 8110.

Basie, Count. *Jumpin' at The Woodside*. J2H73543.

Basie, Count, and Billy Eckstine. *Basie/Eckstine Incorporated*. CAP 28636.

Batiste, Alvin. *Centennial One, Featuring the 1980 Southern University Jazz Ensemble*. NRI 12045.

*The Best of the Jazz Pianos*. MC-8519.

*Black Bands: 1927–1934*. HLP-35.

*Blue Piano, Volume One*. B4-96580.

*Blue Piano, Volume Two*. B4-96904.

*The Blues in Modern Jazz*. Atlantic 1337.

Brown, Clifford. *Clifford Brown*. CAP 46850.

Byrd, Donald. *Street Lady*. CAP 53923.

Byrd, Donald. *Black Bird*. CAP 84466.

Dameron, Tadd. *Fountainbleu: Tadd Dameron and His Orchestra*. OJC 55.

Dameron, Tadd. *The Magic Touch*. OJC-143.

Davis, Miles. *Gold Collection*. Dejavu 5-118-4.

Davis, Miles. *Miles Davis +19*. Columbia CL 1041.

Davis, Miles. *Quiet Nights*. Columbia. TSM 36652.

Davis, Miles. *'Round Midnight*. COL40610.

Davis, Miles. *The Collection: A Retrospective*. CAT 243.

Ellington, Duke. *Duke Ellington and His Cotton*. RCA 2499.

Ellington, Duke. *Duke Ellington at the Cotton Club-1938*. V.1 AOJ 112.

Ellington, Duke. *Duke Ellington at the Cotton Club-1938*. V.2 AOJ 113.

Ellington, Duke. *The Far East Suite*. RCA 66551.

Ellington, Duke. *Jungle Nights in Harlem: 1927–1932*.

Ellington, Duke. *Latin American Suite. Duke Ellington and His Orchestra*. OJC 469.

Ellington, Duke. *Live in Paris. Duke Ellington and His Orchestra*. Magic AWE 19.

Ellington, Duke. *New Orleans Suite*. CS 1580.

Ellington, Duke. *Third Sacred Concert: The Majesty of God*. CLO 142.

Gillespie, Dizzy. *Bahiana*. PAB 2625-708.

Goodman, Benny. *The Great Benny Goodman*. COL 8643.

Hampton, Lionel. *Flyin' Home*. DRV 3536.

Hawkins, Coleman. *Hollywood Stampede. Coleman Hawkins and His Orchestra*. CAP 92596.

Hawkins, Coleman, and Lester Young. *Classic Tenors*. COL 38446.

Henderson, Fletcher. *Fletcher Henderson and the Dixie Stompers: 1925–1928*. DRG 8445.

Henderson, Fletcher. *The Fletcher Henderson Story: A Study in Frustration*. Columbia/Legacy. 57596.

Herman, Woody. *Early Autumn. Capitol Jazz Series, Volume Nine*. RCA 61062.

Hines, Earl. *Earl Hines and His Orchestra: 1934–1935*. AOJ 102/CRL 15762.

Hines, Earl. *The Essential Earl "Fatha" Hines*. Laserlite.

Holiday, Billie. *God Bless the Child*. Columbia 30782.

Holiday, Billie. *The Original Recordings by Billie Holiday*. Columbia 32080.

James, Bob. *Bob James Two*. WAR 45965.

Jones, Quincy. *Quintessence. Quincy Jones and His Orchestra*. GRP 222.

Jordan, Edward "Kidd." *New Orleans Rising*. Konnex KCD 5076.

Jordan, Edward "Kidd." *Nickelsdorf Konfrontation. The Joel Futterman–Kidd Jordan Quintet*. Silkheart. SHDC 143.

Lateef, Yusef. *The Gentle Giant*. Atlantic. ATL 1602.

Powell, Bud. *Jazz at Massey Hall*. V.2. Bud Powell Trio. OJC 111.

Powell, Bud. *The Blue Note Years*. CAP 93204.

Rollins, Sonny. *Now's the Time*. CRC 2927.

Sanders, Pharoah. *The Best of Pharoah Sanders*. Impulse. AS-9229-2.

Shorter, Wayne. *Phantom Navigator*. CBS 40373.

Shorter, Wayne. *Super Nova*. BST 84332.

Silver, Horace. *Silver 'N' Brass*. Blue Note. BN-LA406-G.

Smith, Bessie. *The Empress*. CG 30818.

Smith, Bessie. *Empty Bed Blues*. GT 30450 (MONO).

*The Smithsonian Collection of Classic Jazz*. P6 11891.

*Strictly Bebop. Capitol Jazz Classics, Volume Thirteen*. M-11059.

Tatum, Art. *The Best of Art Tatum*. Pablo Records. 52405 418.

Taylor, Billy. *A Touch of Billy Taylor*. PR 7664.

Taylor, Cecil. *In Transition*. Blue Note BN-LA458-H2.

Taylor, Cecil. *Nefertiti. The Beautiful One Has Come*. AL 1905.

Tyner, McCoy. *Fly with the Wind*. Milestone M-9067.

Tyner, McCoy. *Just Feeling*. PAC-8083-N.

Tyner, McCoy. *Song of the New World*. OJC-5618.

Vaughan, Sarah. *Sarah Vaughan*. Everest Records, Archive of Folk and Jazz Music. FS-250.

## Out of Print Titles

Note: Some recordings listed here, particularly LPs, may be currently out of print, but can still be found at university and public libraries.

Armstrong, Louis. *Ambassador Satch*. Columbia. JCL 840.

Armstrong, Louis. *The Genius of Louis Armstrong: Volume 1: 1923–1933*. Columbia. CG 30416.

Art Ensemble of Chicago. *The Third Decade*. ECM Records. 823-213-4.

Atlantic Jazz. *Piano*. Atlantic. 81707.

Basie, Count. *Corner Pocket*. Count Basie and His Orchestra. 15789.

Basie, Count. *Count Basie and His Orchestra*. BT 13312.

Basie, Count. *Count Basie, 1944–45*. Jazz Society. AA 505.

Bechet, Sidney. *Rare Recordings: 1957–1953*.

Brown, Clifford. *Blue Note*. BN-LA 267.

Brown, Clifford. *Historical Performances*. CLD 802.

Brown, Clifford. *The Quintet, Volume One*. EMS-2-403.

Brown, Clifford. *Remember Clifford*. Mercury. SR 60827.

Brown, Donald. *Sources of Inspiration*. Muse. MCD 5385.

Byrd, Donald. *Getting Down to Business*. Donald Byrd Sextet. LLP 51523.

Capers, Valerie. *Come on Home*. Columbia. CK 66670.

Carter, Benny, and Cootie Williams. *Capitol Jazz Classics, Volume Eleven*. M-11057.

*The Changing Face of Harlem*. The Savoy Sessions. Savoy. SJL 2208.

Christian, Charles. *Charlie Christian: Live 1939/1941*. Jazz Anthology. 30JA5181.

Christian, Charles. *Charlie Christian, with Dizzy Gillespie and Thelonius Monk*. Up Front. UPF-181. Stereo.

*Classic Jazz Piano*. RCA 6754-4-RB.

Coltrane, John. *Gold Collection*. Dejavu 5-119-4.

*A Decade of Jazz, Volume One: 1939–1949*, Blue Note. BN-LA 158-G2.

*A Decade of Jazz, Volume Two: 1949–1959*. Blue Note, BN-LA 159-G2.

*A Decade of Jazz, Volume Three: 1959–1969*. Blue Note. BN-La 160-G2.

Ellington, Duke. *The Afro-Eurasian Eclipse*. A Suite in Eight Parts. Fantasy. F-9498.

Ellington, Duke. *The Ellington Era: 1927–1940, Duke Ellington and His Famous Orchestra, Volume One.* Columbia. C31 27.

Ellington, Duke. *I Like Jazz.* Columbia. CT47129.

Ellington, Duke. *Jazz Collector Edition.* 79753.

Ellington, Duke. *Piano Reflections.* Capitol Jazz Classics, Volume Twelve. M-11058.

Fitzgerald, Ella. *Gold Collection.* Dejavu 5-104-4.

Gale, Eric. *Forecast.* KU-11.

Gale, Eric. *Part of You.* Columbia 35715.

Henderson, Fletcher. *Harlem in the Thirties.* Olympic Records. 7118.

Hubbard, Freddie. *Polar. AC.* CTI 6056 S1.

Human Arts Ensemble, with Oliver Lake and Lester Bowie. *Under the Sun.* AL 1022.

Johnson, Pete *Boogie Woogie Mood: 1940–1944.*

*The Jones Boys: Quincy, Thad, Jimmy, Jo, Eddie, and Elvin.* Everest Records. Archive of Folk and Jazz Music. FS 270.

Jones, Quincy. *The Birth of a Band.* TLP-5596.

Jones, Quincy. *I Heard That!!* Mercury. SP 3706.

Jones, Quincy. *Mode.* ABC Records. ABCX-782/2

Jones, Quincy. *Ndeda.* SRM 2-623.

Jones, Thad. *The Definitive Thad Jones.* The Mel Lewis Orchestra. 5046-2-C.

Jones, Thad. *Live in Munich.* Horizon SP-724.

Jones, Thad. *Thad Jones.* OJC-5625.

Jones, Thad, and Mel Lewis. *New Life. Dedicated to Max Gordon.* Horizon SP 707.

Jones, Thad, and Mel Lewis. *Potpourri.* KZ 33152.

Jones, Thad, and Mel Lewis. *Suite for Pops.* Horizon. SP-701.

Kenton, Stan. *Artistry in Blue.* Capitol Jazz Classics, Volume Two. M-11027.

*Kings and Queens of Ivory: 1935–1940.* Jazz Heritage Series Volume 30. MCA 1329.

Klugh, Earl. *Earl Klugh.* BN-LA 596-G.

Lateef, Yusef. *The Complete Yusef Lateef.* Atlantic. SD 1499.

Lunceford, Jimmie. *The Greatest Jazz Band.* Olympic Records. 7123.

Lunceford, Jimmie. *Jimmie's Legacy: 1934–1937.* MCA 1320.

Lunceford, Jimmie. *The Last Sparks: 1941–1944.* Jazz Heritage Series Volume 22. MCA1321.

Lunceford, Jimmie. *Live at Jefferson Barracks, Missouri.* HSR-221.

McRae, Carmen. *Setting Standards.* MSC 35094.

Mingus, Charles. *Epitaph.* Columbia. C2K 45428.

Mingus, Charles. *Mingus Ah Um.* Columbia 8171.

Modern Jazz Quartet. *The Last Concert.* Atlantic. SD 2-909.

Morton, Jelly Roll. *The Pearls.* Bluebird. 6588-2-RB.

Morton, Jelly Roll. *Some Rags, Some Stomps, and a Little Blues.* Columbia. M 32587.

Navarro, Fats. *Prime Source.* Blue Note. BN-LA-507-H2.

Oliver, Joseph. *The Immortal King Oliver.* Milestone. MLP 2006.

Ory, Kid, and Jimmy Noone. *New Orleans Jazz.* Olympic Records. 7109.

Parker, Charles. *Charlie Parker: The Verve Years (1950–51).* VE-2-2512.

Roach, Max, and Art Blakey. *Percussion Discussion.* Chess Jazz Masters Series. 2ACMJ-405.

Roach, Max, and Anthony Braxton. *Birth and Rebirth.* BSR 0024.

Whiteman, Paul. *The Victor Masters. Paul Whiteman and His Orchestra, Featuring Bing Crosby.* 9676-4-R.

Williams, Cootie. *Cootie Williams and His Orchestra.* OSR 2440.

Wilson, Teddy. *Teddy Wilson and His All-Stars.* Lusicraft Records. MVS 502.

## Blues, Rhythm and Blues, Gospel Music, Folk Music

*Al Green and Teddy Pendergrass.* S21-18246.

*All of My Appointed Time.* STASH Records. ST-114.

*Ben E. King and Percy Sledge.* BU6374.

Berry, Chuck. *School Day.* SSI-490.

Bignon, James, and the Deliverance Mass Choir. *Heaven Belongs to You.* AIR.

Brown, James. *Papa's Got a Brand New Bag.* PSP 847 982-4.

Brown, James. *Star Time.* 4-cassette edition. Polydor. 849 108-4.

Brown, James. *Twenty All Time Greatest Hits*. 314 511 326-2.

Charles, Ray. *The Complete Atlantic Rhythm and Blues Recordings, 1952–1959*. Atlantic. 7 82310-4.

Charles, Ray, *True to Life*. Atlantic. SD 19142.

Coasters. *Greatest Hits*. PDK-2-1306.

Cole, Nat King. *Greatest Hits, Volume One*. S41-56922.

Cole, Nat King, with the Orchestra of Gordon Jenkins. *Love Is the Thing*. SM 824.

*The Complete Stax/Volt Singles: 1959–1968*. Atlantic. 7-82218-2.

*The Complete Stax/Volt Soul Singles: 1968–1971, Volume Two*. 9SCD-4411-2.

Cooke, Sam. *Live at the Harlem Square Club, 1963*. AFK1-5181.

Cooke, Sam. *The Man and His Music*. PCD1 7127.

Delphonics. *The Best of the Delphonics*. Artista ACB 6 8333.

*Diana Ross and the Supremes*. Anthology Series 31453-0511-4.

*Doo Wop Uptempo*. Golden Archive Series. Rhino. R4-70182.

Dramatics. *Gimme Some Good Soul Music*. RSP 53318.

*The Earliest Negro Vocal Quartets (1894–1928)*. DOCD-5061.

Flack, Roberta. *Chapter Two*. Atlantic. 1569-2.

Flack, Roberta. *Feel Like Makin' Love*. SD 1813.

Four Tops. *Four Tops*. Motown. 374635314-4.

Franklin, Aretha. *Aretha Gold*. Atlantic. CS 8227.

Franklin, Aretha. *Thirty Greatest Hits*. Atlantic. 81668-4.

Gaye, Marvin, and Smokey Robinson and the Miracles. *Best of Two Super Acts*. Motown. 3063-4.

Gospel Music Workshop of America National Mass Choir. *Dawn of a New Era. Live in Chicago*. Benson. 84418-2950-4.

Gospel Music Workshop of America National Mass Choir. *Live in L.A.* Benson. 84418-4261-4.

Gospel Music Workshop National Mass Choir. *Torchbearers of Excellence*. Benson. B4418-4067-4.

Gospel Music Workshop of America. *Live from Salt Lake City Utah*. Savoy Records. SC 7105.

Gospel Music Workshop of America. *Live in St. Louis*. Savoy Records. SC 7096.

Gospel Music Workshop of America. *Rev. James Cleveland Founder and President.* Savoy Records. SC 7100.

*Great Groups of the Fifties, Volume One.* COL-5037.

*Great Groups of the Fifties, Volume Two.* COL-5038.

*Handel's Messiah: A Soulful Celebration.* Reprise Records. 9 26980-4.

Hayes, Isaac. *Black Moses.* ENS-5003.

Hayes, Isaac. *Chocolate Chip.* ABCD-874.

Hayes, Isaac. *Hot Buttered Soul.* Enterprise Records. ENS-1001.

Hayes, Isaac. *Joy.* ENS-5007.

Hayes, Isaac. *Live at the Sahara Tahoe.* ENX-2-5005.

Hip Hop from the Top. *Street Jams: Part One.* R2 70577.

Hip Hop from the Top. *Street Jams: Part Two.* R2 70578.

Hip Hop from the Top. *Street Jams: Part Three.* R2 71555.

Hip Hop from the Top. *Street Jams: Part Four.* R2 71556.

Hitsville USA. *The Motown Singles Collection: 1959–1971.* Motown. 374637312-2/4.

Hitsville USA. *The Motown Singles Collection: 1972–1992. Volume Two.* Motown. 3746363584.

*I'm the Rapper, He the DJ.* RCA 1091-4-J.

Ink Spots. *Swing High, Swing Low.* Eclipse Music Group. 64046-4.

Ink Spots. *The World of the Ink Spots.* Trace. 0400122.

Isley Brothers. *Hits, Volume One.* PZT39240.

Jones, Quincy. *Body Heat.* SP 3617.

Jordan, Louis. *Let the Good Times Roll.* 64740-4.

King. B. B. *The Best of B. B. King.* MCA HANC-20233.

Knight, Gladys. *All the Greatest Hits. Gladys Knight and the Pips.* Motown. 374635303-4.

Legendary Blues. *Blues Classics.* SSI-497.

Little Anthony and the Imperials. *Tears on My Pillow.* R4 7034.

Mayfield, Curtis. *The Anthology, 1961–1977.* MCA C2-10664.

Mills Brothers. *Sweet and Low.* 64051-4.

*On the Rap Tip.* 4XL 7940.

*Queens of Rap.* 4XL 7916.

Pickett, Wilson. *The Best of Wilson Pickett.* Atlantic. 81283-4-Y.

*Preachin' the Gospel, Holy Blues.* CK 46779.

*Rap Attack.* K-Tel 762-4.

Redding, Otis. *The Definitive Otis Redding.* 4-cassette edition. Rhino. R4-71439.

Redding, Otis. *The Very Best of Otis Redding.* Rhino. R2 71147.

*Rock, Rhythm & Blues.* Warner Brothers. 4-2517.

*Roots of Soul.* 10152.

Sam and Dave. *Soul Men.* R2 70296.

Sam and Dave. *Soul Study, Volume One.* BT 18257.

Scott-Heron, Gil. *The Revolution Will Not Be Televised.* 6994-2-RB.

Sledge, Percy. *It Tears Me Up.* R2740285.

Sly and the Family Stone. *Greatest Hits.* EK 30325.

*Sound of Philadelphia.* BT 14915.

Spinners. *Pick of the Litter.* Rhino. R2 71884.

Spinners. *Spinners.* Rhino. R2 71882.

Spinners. *The Best of the Spinners.* Atlantic. CS19179.

*The Story of the Blues.* CG30008.

Stylistics. *The Best of the Stylistics.* AMH 5743.

Stylistics. *Round Two.* AMH 747-2.

Temptations. *A Song for You.* Motown. 374635272-4.

Temptations. *Just My Imagination.* Motown. MOTC 3749.

Tex. Joe. *I Believe I'm Gonna Make It! The Best of Joe Tex.* R2 70191.

*Three Decades of Blues.* Priority. P2 53736.

Vee Jay. *Celebrating 40 Years of Classic Hits.* Vee Jay. NVS2-3-400.

Warwick, Dionne. *Friends.* Arista. AC8398.

Warwick, Dionne. *Top Hits.* BT 21711.

Winans, Ce Ce. *Alone in His Presence.* G2 7243 8 51441 2 7.

*The Wiz. Original Cast Recording.* Featuring Stephanie Mills. SD 18137.

Wonder, Stevie. *Songs in the Key of Life, Volumes One and Two.* Motown 374630340-4.

Wonder, Stevie. *Talking Book.* T319L.

## Classical, Third Stream, Diasporadic, Eclectic, Musicals

Adderley, Julian. *Big Man: The Legend of John Henry.* Fantasy. F-79006.

Coleman, Ornette. *Skies of America.* KC 31562.

Coleridge-Taylor, Samuel. *Hiawatha.* Welsh National Opera. Kenneth Alwyn, conductor. Argo. 430 356-2.

Coleridge-Taylor, Samuel. *Symphonic Variations on an African Air.* Royal Liverpool Philharmonic Orchestra. Grant Llewellyn, conductor. Argo. 436-401-2.

Coleridge-Taylor, Samuel. *Twenty-Four Negro Melodies, op. 59.* Francis Walker, pianist. ORS78305/306.

Dawson, William Levi. *Negro Folk Symphony.* Detroit Symphony Orchestra, Neeme Jarvi, conductor. Chandos. 9226.

Dawson, William Levi. *Negro Folk Symphony.* Leopold Stokowski, conductor. VC 81056.

Duke, George. *Muir Woods Suite.* Warner Brothers. 9 46132-2.

Dvořák, Antonin. *Symphony no. 9 in E minor, op. 95, "From the New World."* Czech Philharmonic Orchestra, Vaclav Neuman, conductor. PAD 157.

Ellington, Duke. *Four Symphonic Works by Duke Ellington.* Music Masters. 7011 2 C.

Fisher, William. *Circles.* Embryo. SD 529.

Gould, Morton. *Spirituals for Strings. Morton Gould and His Orchestra.* LSC-2686.

Hannibal. *African Portraits.* Chicago Symphony Orchestra. 4509-98802-2.

Jones, Quincy. *The Wiz.* Movie musical. MCA2-14000.

Lewis, John. *European Windows.* RCA APM1-1069.

Mendes Brothers. *Bandera.* MB 0012.

Mendes Brothers. *Palonkon.* Sony. 11.275-2.

Mendes, Ramiro. *Diplomadu.* MB Records, Inc. MB0011.

Price, Leontyne. *Swing Low, Sweet Chariot: Fourteen Spirituals.* RCA Victor. LSC-2600.

Roberts, Marcus. *Portraits in Blues.* Includes James P. Johnson's *Yamekraw.* Sony. SK 68488.

Still, William Grant. *Symphony no. 1 (Afro-American).* Detroit Symphony Orchestra. Neemi Jarvi, conductor. Chandos. CHAN 9154.

Tippett, Michael. *A Child of Our Time.* BBC Symphony Orchestra and Chorus, Colin Davis, conductor. Philips. 6500 985.

Williams, Mary Lou. *Zodiac Suite.* Smithsonian/Folkways. SF CD 40810.

*The Wiz. Original Cast Recording.* Featuring Stephanie Mills. SD 18137.

# INDEX OF TITLES

# GENERAL INDEX

# PERMISSIONS

The excerpt from "Car Tunes" on page 188 courtesy of Donald Brown. Used by permission.

Photograph of Valery Capers on page 194 by David Katzenstein. Courtesy of Valcap Music, Inc. Used by permission.

The excerpt from "Waltz for Miles" on page 197 courtesy of Valery Capers. Used by permission.

Musical transcriptions for the following titles courtesy of Earl Stewart. Page 232: "B-A-B-Y"; p. 232: "My Girl"; p. 233: "Get Ready"; p. 235: "These Arms of Mine"; p. 236: "Take Me to the River"; p. 237: "Baby I Need Your Loving"; p. 238: "Let's Stay Together"; p. 239: "I Got a Sure Thing"; p. 239: "Never Can Say Goodbye"; P. 240: "My Cherie Amour"; p. 240: "If I Were Your Woman"; p. 241: "My Cherie Amour."

Every effort has been made to identify the sources of all photographs, music, and lyrics and to make full acknowledgments of their use. If any error or omission has occurred, it will be rectified in future editions, provided the appropriate notification is submitted in writing to the publisher or author.